TOWARD A NEW
INTERNATIONAL
FINANCIAL ARCHITECTURE

BARRY EICHENGREEN

TOWARD A NEW INTERNATIONAL FINANCIAL ARCHITECTURE
A Practical Post-Asia Agenda

INSTITUTE FOR INTERNATIONAL ECONOMICS
Washington, DC
February 1999

Barry Eichengreen is John L. Simpson Professor of Economics and Political Science at the University of California, Berkeley; Research Associate at the National Bureau of Economic Research; and Research Fellow of the Centre for Economic Policy Research (London). He has published numerous studies of international monetary and financial affairs, including *Globalizing Capital: A History of the International Monetary System* (Princeton University Press 1996) and, with Richard Portes, *Crisis? What Crisis? Orderly Workouts for Sovereign Debtors* (CEPR 1995).

INSTITUTE FOR INTERNATIONAL ECONOMICS
11 Dupont Circle, NW
Washington, DC 20036-1207
(202) 328-9000 FAX: (202) 328-5432
http://www.iie.com

C. Fred Bergsten, *Director*
Christine F. Lowry, *Director of Publications*
Brett Kitchen, *Marketing Director*

For reprints/permission to photocopy please contact the APS customer service department at CCC Academic Permissions Service, 27 Congress Street, Salem, MA 01970.

Printed in the United States of America
01 00 99   5 4 3 2 1

Library of Congress Cataloging-in-Publication Data
Eichengreen, Barry J.
   Toward a new international financial architecture : a practical post-Asia agenda / Barry Eichengreen.
      p. cm.
   Includes bibliographical references and index.
      1. International finance.   2. Monetary policy.   3. Financial crises—Asia.   4. International Monetary Fund.   I. Title.
HG3881 .E348 1999
332'.042—ddc21   98.52724
                                          CIP

ISBN 0-88132-270-9

For Mish

Contents

Figures

Preface

The Institute has done extensive work over the years on the design of international monetary and financial arrangements, ranging from the seminal work of John Williamson on exchange rate systems to Morris Goldstein's recently adopted proposals for an international banking standard. Volumes such as *Private Capital Flows to Emerging Markets after the Mexican Crisis*, edited by Guillermo Calvo, Goldstein, and Eduard Hochreiter, have pointed to the dilemmas for policy that are posed by high capital mobility. Several years ago, on the fiftieth anniversary of the Bretton Woods conference, the Institute published *Managing the World Economy: Fifty Years after Bretton Woods*, edited by Peter B. Kenen, which anticipated many of the issues now at the center of the debate over the reform of the international financial architecture.

Barry Eichengreen's new study, which synthesizes and significantly advances that debate, is a fitting addition to this list of publications. The crisis in emerging markets, which began in Asia in the summer of 1997 and has become a global phenomenon, has created widespread dissatisfaction with the international monetary and financial system. It has moved the debate over how to improve the operation of that system from the business pages to the front of the daily press.

This new book addresses the entire array of issues in that debate. It clearly explains the problems that have been highlighted by the Asian, Mexican, and earlier crises and a variety of possible solutions to each. It includes a synopsis and evaluation of all major reforms proposed to date. Hence, it provides a cogent guide to understanding both the calls for "a new international financial architecture" and what can be done by way of response.

As a result of the current debate, ambitious proposals for reform abound. Many of them would not be helpful, however, and many are politically unrealistic at this time. Eichengreen offers a practical agenda for reform that systemically identifies and then addresses the major risks to monetary and financial stability that have arisen in the wake of the Asian crisis (and earlier disruptions). He proposes an agenda for action at the national and international levels that should have a realistic prospect of being implemented in the near future and hence offers a pragmatic guide for early improvement in the system.

The Institute for International Economics is a private nonprofit institution for the study and discussion of international economic policy. Its purpose is to analyze important issues in that area and to develop and communicate practical new approaches for dealing with them. The Institute is completely nonpartisan.

The Institute is funded largely by philanthropic foundations and private corporations. Major institutional grants are now being received from The German Marshall Fund of the United States, which created the Institute with a generous commitment of funds in 1981, and from The William M. Keck, Jr. Foundation and The Starr Foundation. A number of other foundations and companies also contribute to the highly diversified financial resources of the Institute. About 18 percent of the Institute's resources in our latest fiscal year were provided by contributors outside the United States, including about 12 percent from Japan.

The Board of Directors bears overall responsibility for the Institute and gives general guidance and approval to its research program—including identification of topics that are likely to become important to international economic policymakers over the medium run (generally, one to three years), and which thus should be addressed by the Institute. The Director, working closely with the staff and outside Advisory Committee, is responsible for the development of particular projects and makes the final decision to publish an individual study.

The Institute hopes that its studies and other activities will contribute to building a stronger foundation for international economic policy around the world. We invite readers of these publications to let us know how they think we can best accomplish this objective.

C. FRED BERGSTEN
Director
January 1999

Acknowledgments

The impetus for this book was the year I spent, from July 1997 through July 1998, as a visiting scholar at the International Monetary Fund (IMF). But writing it was possible because my year at the IMF came after a long period of research and collaboration with academic colleagues on issues related to financial crises. My longest-standing such collaboration, with Richard Portes, now stretches over nearly 15 years. It is to Richard that I owe the opportunity of coauthoring a background paper for the UK Treasury and Bank of England that helped inform the deliberations of the Group of Ten study group on sovereign liquidity crises, a project out of which many of my ideas on this subject grew. Andrew Rose and Charles Wyplosz have been my collaborators for nearly as many years. Together we have tried to reorient academic work on currency and banking crises away from purely theoretical exercises and toward the systematic analysis of actual experience. That analysis is the empirical foundation for all that follows.

For comments on a preliminary draft of the manuscript I am grateful to readers both anonymous and not so anonymous, including Charles Wyplosz, Daniel Tarullo, Nouriel Roubini, Adam Posen, David Hale, Jeffrey Frankel, Richard Cooper, and especially C. Fred Bergsten. The Institute for International Economics also convened a study group that spent nearly half a day critiquing the manuscript. This experience, while sobering for the author, was invaluable. I would be amiss not to also acknowledge ongoing discussions on these issues with Caroline Atkinson, Owen Evans, Matthew Fisher, Stanley Fischer, and Michael Mussa.

Financial support for my research was provided by the Ford Foundation, the Committee on Research of the University of California, Berkeley and the Institute for Global Conflict and Cooperation of the University of California System. Galina Borissova provided able research assistance. The help of Kira Reoutt was indispensable in keeping my office running when I disappeared.

1

Introduction

International economic policymakers are currently confronted by two urgent problems. One is to contain and resolve the macroeconomic and financial crisis threatening much of the world. The other is to reform the institutions, structures, and policies—the international financial architecture—through which crises are predicted, prevented, and dispatched. This book addresses the second of these tasks.

There is no shortage of proposals for reforming the international financial architecture. The French government has one, the German government has one, the Canadian government has one, the US government has one. The Group of 22 (G-22), an ad hoc grouping of developing and advanced industrial countries, has released three reports on the reform of international financial institutions and arrangements. Group of Seven (G-7) ministers have issued a separate declaration about how to renovate the international financial house. International Monetary Fund Managing Director Michel Camdessus has made a series of speeches with titles such as "Toward an Agenda for International Monetary and Financial Reform." Voices from academia and the markets have chimed in with yet additional schemes.

Many of these proposals are contradictory and mutually incompatible. Some recommend that policymakers renew their efforts to liberalize international capital markets, while others plump for the reimposition of capital controls. Some insist on the need for greater exchange rate flexibility, while others regard nothing as more important than the reestablishment of stable, even fixed, rates between currencies. Some suggest that the international community should respond more forcefully to crises, while others recommend that it stand back and let nature, in the form of the

1

markets, take its course. Some emphasize the need for more funding for the International Monetary Fund (IMF, or the Fund), while others call for the abolition of the institution. Some suggest that the Fund must root out corruption and compel countries to install the institutional prerequisites for stable financial markets, while others insist that it should limit its advice to monetary and fiscal policies and refrain from meddling in the internal affairs of its members.

Different observers offer such radically different recommendations because they define the problem differently and because they have different views of how the international economic and financial system works. Thus, anyone writing on this subject must lay his or her views on the table. The recommendations in this book follow from six assumptions that I make about the operation of the international financial system.

First, liberalized financial markets have compelling benefits. They encourage savings mobilization and efficient investment allocation while allowing consumption smoothing and portfolio diversification. Financial markets do not work perfectly, to be sure, but to paraphrase Winston Churchill, they are the worst way of allocating resources except for all other forms that have been tried. Compared to the earlier era, when developing countries repressed private financial transactions and governments employed policies of directed credit to dictate resource allocation, there are clear efficiency gains from relying on the market. This is especially true in an age when growth depends so heavily on product and process innovation. In other words, the days when East Asian governments could "pick winners" simply by following the Japanese example—allowing them to minimize the role of the market mechanism—are long past.

Second, international financial liberalization and growing international capital flows are largely inevitable and irreversible. Domestic and international financial liberalization go hand in hand, in the sense that it is extremely difficult to keep a lid on international financial transactions if domestic financial transactions are freed. And, as explained above, the logic for domestic financial liberalization is compelling. In addition, financial liberalization, both domestic and international, is being driven by powerful changes in information and communications technologies that make it far more difficult to restrict the financial transactions in which market participants engage. Controls on international transactions, to retain their effectiveness, must therefore become more onerous and distortionary. For all these reasons, capital mobility is the wave of the future. This does not mean that capital-account liberalization must be embraced before banks have upgraded their risk-management practices, supervisors have strengthened their oversight of financial institutions, and governments have corrected their macroeconomic policies; to the contrary, there are compelling arguments against precipitous liberalization. But greater capital mobility is coming, like it or not.[1]

Third, notwithstanding the manifest benefits of financial liberalization, capital markets are characterized by information asymmetries that can give rise to overshooting, sharp corrections, and, in the extreme, financial crises. Even in the age of the information revolution, information remains costly to obtain and evaluate. Some of the relevant "data," such as whether a government will follow through on reform and maintain its commitment to monetary and fiscal discipline, are unavoidably based on opinion and conjecture as much as hard evidence. This encourages imperfectly informed investors to draw inferences from one another's actions and to move in a herd. This behavior can precipitate sharp market moves and, in the extreme, financial crises. Distress can cascade through the financial system, because of the widespread use of leverage and because information asymmetries prevent banks and other financial intermediaries from raising liquidity in a crisis.

Fourth, this instability provides a compelling argument for erecting a financial safety net despite the moral hazard that may result. History shows the need for deposit insurance and a lender of last resort to contain systemic risks to the financial system. To be sure, provision of this safety net encourages market participants to take on additional risk, heightening the need for vigorous supervision and regulation of the recipient institutions. In a world of global financial markets, there is an argument by analogy for an international lender of last resort, although there are questions as to whether the IMF or any other candidate for this role has either the capacity to carry it out or the ability to contain the moral hazard that results. And if there are good political reasons why there will be no international lender of last resort, then countries need to take measures to protect themselves from the consequences of its absence.

Fifth, information and transactions costs can prevent decentralized markets from quickly and efficiently resolving financial problems. These costs create coordination problems that can encourage creditors to scramble for the exits and make it prohibitively difficult to restructure defaulted debts. They are why countries have insolvency and bankruptcy codes that give the courts the power to impose an automatic stay, coordinate restructuring negotiations, and, if necessary, cram down settlement terms. They are why the absence of an international bankruptcy court with

---

1. That all of today's mature, advanced industrial economies have liberalized international financial flows is evidence that most emerging markets are ultimately heading toward capital-account liberalization. This reality is similarly evident in the growing number of IMF member countries that have taken steps to liberalize their capital accounts and in the fact that reversals in this trend, whether associated with the Latin American debt crisis of the 1980s or the crisis now infecting emerging markets generally, have been limited and no more than temporary.

comparable powers is a problem. They are why international debt crises are so protracted.

Sixth and finally, economic policy is framed in a politicized environment. It cannot be assumed that regulators and other economic policymakers will carry out their tasks without allowing themselves to be influenced by political considerations. To the contrary, lobbying and pressure politics inevitably shape the policies that are pursued. Realistic policy advice requires acknowledging these pressures and not assuming, for analytical convenience, that policymaking institutions such as the IMF can be made to follow rigid apolitical rules. Moreover, national governments are jealous of their prerogatives; aside from special cases such as the European Union, they remain reluctant to cede control of domestic economic affairs to an international body. Realistic policy reform requires recognizing these uncomfortable facts.

My recommendations for reforming the international financial architecture flow from these assumptions. They are predicated on the notion that international capital mobility is now a financial fact of life and that the problem for policy is to ensure that the benefits of capital mobility exceed its costs rather than pretending that it can be made to go away. They are based on the belief that financial markets can malfunction, creating a case for a financial safety net and therefore a role for the IMF, but also posing problems of moral hazard that must be addressed. They acknowledge that crises will still occur and that there is a need to create institutional mechanisms to overcome the information asymmetries and collective-action problems that prevent them from being rapidly resolved. They acknowledge the existence of political limits on the practicable; because they lack political feasibility, I do not devote much attention to pie-in-the-sky schemes for a world currency, a world central bank, a world financial regulator, or a world bankruptcy court.[2] My recommendations may seem unambitious in comparison, but they at least have a chance of being implemented. In effect, I stake out a middle ground between the overly ambitious and politically unrealistic schemes of independent commentators and the excessively timid and ambiguous reports of international bodies and organizations. Academics should be bolder than bureaucrats, but their recommendations should take the political realities into account.

My conclusions have most in common with the three reports on preventing crises and reforming the financial architecture issued by the G-22 in October 1998 (1998a, b, c).[3] But while these reports adopt a generally sensible approach to the crisis problem, in the end they back away from the important implications. The do not go far enough.

---

2. I do, however, take a critical look at some of these ideas in chapter 6.

3. I compare the recommendations of these reports with my own conclusions in appendix A below.

Just as I am critical of these international reports for backing away from the important implications, others will criticize me for rejecting radical proposals to fundamentally alter the international financial architecture. Radical therapy is required, they insist, because international financial markets are "coming apart at the seams," creating a "crisis of global capitalism" (Soros 1998). This is not my view. To be sure, the current crisis in emerging markets has revealed serious flaws in the structure of financial markets and in the ways they are regulated that urgently require correction. The urgency of reform is evident in the severity of the crisis that has infected emerging markets in the last two years. But that crisis comes at the end of an extended period of growth and prosperity for many parts of the developing world, which has benefited enormously from the advantages of liberalized markets, including international financial markets. Those gains can now be secured by following a strategy of robust incrementalism, not by throwing the baby out with the bathwater.

Unlike other schemes, mine are not primarily proposals for reforming the IMF, although I will have something to say about the topic. A theme of this book is that the most important changes in the international financial architecture involve not changing the way that the Fund goes about its business but rather modifying the environment in which it operates. Appropriately reformed, the IMF can make the world a safer financial place, but even the most ambitious schemes to remake the Fund will, by themselves, provide only limited traction on the crisis problem. In large part, the solution lies elsewhere.

Any set of recommendations for more effectively preventing and managing financial crises should respond to the kind of crises one anticipates encountering in the future. While the assumptions laid out above provide an implicit answer to this question, it is worth being explicit.[4] Financial crises have always come in different flavors; this will be true in the future as it has been in the past. Some countries will continue to experience old-fashioned balance of payments crises as a result of pursuing excessively expansionary monetary and fiscal policies that were incompatible with their exchange rate commitments. Their currencies will grow increasingly overvalued, their current-account deficits will widen, and their international reserves will fall to the danger point where a crisis erupts. Other countries, in contrast, will experience newfangled high-tech crises driven by the interplay of domestic financial-sector weaknesses and international capital flows. In their case, a crisis will erupt when investors lose confidence in the country's banking system, stock market, or public debt management and when their scramble for the exits, facilitated by the existence of an open capital account, brings both the financial system and the

---

4. I lay out my view on the dominant sources of potential future crises at more length at the beginning of chapter 3. Readers preferring a purely theoretical treatment will find it in appendix B.

currency crashing down. Macroeconomic imbalances can play a part in this second class of financial crises, but theirs is not the leading role. My focus here is on this second class, for two related reasons. First, it is my judgment that financial factors have played an increasingly prominent role in recent crises not by happenstance but for fundamental structural reasons that will be felt even more powerfully in the future than in the past. Their role has been elevated by domestic financial deregulation and international financial liberalization, trends that are unlikely to be reversed in the future. Admittedly, some countries will continue to suffer crises purely because their governments follow reckless macroeconomic policies, but these old-fashioned balance of payments crises will become more the exception and less the rule. Second, there is relatively little confusion about how to treat crises caused by macroeconomic excesses, namely, by administering an appropriate dose of monetary and fiscal austerity, thereby eliminating the macroeconomic imbalances that created the problem in the first place. There is less agreement on how to prevent and manage their newfangled Asian-style equivalents. These are all justifications for focusing on so-called high-tech crises in which financial factors play the dominant role.

Before proceeding, it is important, as political scientists say, "to clearly define the dependent variable." The goal here is not to construct an international financial system that is immune from crises.[5] North Korea's financial system is immune from crises because it is subject to such draconian controls, but as a result its economy suffers from worse ills. My goal instead is to suggest some practical reforms that will improve the tradeoff between financial liberalization and financial stability.[6] While the benefits of a market-led financial system are compelling, that system will inevitably remain imperfect given the information environment in which it operates, and crises will still occur. My goal is thus to identify measures that promise to minimize their incidence and to help to resolve them at lower cost, therefore making it more attractive for countries to partake of the manifest advantages of liberalized financial markets.

Outline of the Book

Following this introduction, chapter 2 summarizes my policy recommendations. Chapter 3 lays out the case for international standards as a way

---

5. The dependent variable, in other words, is not simply the prevalence of financial crises.

6. Reforms that, as economists say, allow societies to maximize the social welfare (rather than simply to minimize crises). Thus, the argument in the text about the benefits of a market-led financial system does not imply that countries will necessarily want to move to fully liberalized international financial markets, but that they should be able to choose their preferred point somewhere on the best possible frontier of feasible combinations of financial liberalization and financial stability.

of upgrading national financial practices that have first-order implications for international financial stability. Inspired by Morris Goldstein's work on the idea of an international banking standard (1997), standard setting has become de rigueur as an approach to reconciling national regulation with international markets. What have been overlooked in this enthusiasm are the obstacles to IMF-led standard setting and the need to rely on the resources and expertise of the private sector as the only practical way of promulgating effective standards in the relevant areas; that is my emphasis here. Chapter 4 considers the special problems of the banks and the dangers of an open capital account when risk management is inadequate, supervision and regulation are less than effective, and there is a culture of explicit guarantees. Unlike official reports, which acknowledge the problem but back away from its implications, I am explicit about the need for Chilean-style capital-inflow taxes as the only effective solution to this problem for the vast majority of developing countries.

Chapter 5 turns to the problem of bailing in the private sector. While acknowledging the desirability of having the private sector share more of the burden of crisis management, I argue that there in fact exist very serious obstacles to achieving this when a crisis hits. Unlike official reports, which invoke the desirability of private-sector burden sharing without offering specifics, I argue that the only effective way of preventing short-term bank creditors from getting off scot-free is to not borrow from them in the first place—in other words, to use taxes, controls, and exchange rate flexibility to discourage the practice—and that the single most important way of facilitating restructuring is to add renegotiation-friendly provisions to loan agreements.

Chapter 6 dismisses more radical schemes for reforming the international financial architecture as either undesirable or unrealistic. Reform, if it is to occur at all, means reform within the confines of the existing architecture, broadly defined. Chapter 7 therefore reconsiders the role of the IMF, concluding that there will remain a role for its lending, although this will be more limited than in the past, and arguing that the Fund needs to become a more active proponent of capital-inflow taxes and flexible exchange rates.

Readers will forgive, I hope, the repetition that creeps in as I approach the same issues from several different angles. This is one way of driving home the point that you inevitably arrive at the same conclusion—and the same policy recommendations—regardless of where you start.

2

Summary of Recommendations

The current crisis is for those concerned with the operation of international financial markets what the collapse of the Eastern Bloc was to Sovietologists. It has forced old models of the international financial architecture to be abandoned and prompted some radical new thinking. The UK government proposes merging the IMF, the World Bank, and the Bank for International Settlements (BIS) to create a single superregulator of financial markets. The French propose vesting additional decision-making power in the Interim Committee of finance ministers, which oversees the operation of the IMF, with the goal of enhancing accountability, allowing the institution to respond more quickly to crises, and not incidentally giving Europe a counterweight to the disproportionate influence enjoyed by the US Treasury as a result of its physical and intellectual proximity to the Fund. The German government has mooted the idea of target zones for exchange rates to prevent currencies from misbehaving. The Canadian government proposes providing for an IMF-sanctioned pause or payments standstill to be invoked in the event of financial difficulties. George Soros proposes an international debt insurance corporation, Henry Kaufman an international credit-rating agency, Jeffrey Garten an international central bank, Jeffrey Sachs an international bankruptcy court. The one thing that these proposals have in common is their impracticality. They have not a snowball's chance in hell of being implemented. They all assume a degree of intellectual consensus and political will that simply does not exist.

My goal here is different. It is to provide a set of practical, pragmatic proposals for reforming the international financial architecture that actually have a chance of being implemented. While more ambitious schemes at least have the merit of focusing attention on the nature of the problem, they have little chance of making the world a safer place in the time frame relevant for practical policy analysis.

My conclusions and recommendations fall under three headings: crisis prevention, crisis prediction, and crisis management.

Crisis Prevention

For financial crises, as for health maintenance, prevention is the better part of cure. There is little disagreement about the steps needed to minimize the incidence of crises. Better information on the economic and financial affairs of governments, banks, and corporations will strengthen market discipline (encourage lenders to ration credit to borrowers who fail to take the steps needed to maintain their financial stability) and help policymakers to identify the need for corrective action. Upgrading the supervision and regulation of financial markets and especially banks will strengthen the weak link in the financial chain. Exchange rate flexibility will encourage banks and corporations to hedge their foreign exposure, enhancing their ability to withstand unexpectedly large exchange rate changes.

Although some progress has been made in these areas, much remains to be done. A first area requiring a major international initiative is international financial standards. In a world of integrated financial markets, international financial stability is impossible without domestic financial stability. Stabilizing the financial system consequently requires institutional reforms extending well beyond policies toward external trade and payments. That it requires rigorous disclosure requirements and effective supervision of banks and corporations borrowing on financial markets is now agreed on. Some will argue that this is as far as the international community and the IMF should go in intruding into the internal affairs of countries. I argue that they must in fact go further—that the need for domestic institutional reforms with implications for the stability of international financial markets extends beyond this point. It extends to the use of internationally recognized auditing and accounting practices so that lenders can accurately assess the financial condition of the banks and corporations to which they lend. It extends to effective creditor rights, so that claimants can monitor and control the economic and financial decisions of managers. It extends to investor protection laws to prevent insider trading, market cornering, and related practices in whose absence securities markets will not develop. It extends to fair and expeditious corporate bankruptcy procedures, without which debt problems can cascade from borrower to borrower. While these are problems for individual countries to address as they see fit, whether they arrive at an adequate solution is also of pressing concern to the international policy community, given the scope for financial problems to spill contagiously across borders.

This is an ambitious agenda for reform. The fact of the matter is that neither the IMF nor any other international organization has the resources to provide every emerging market with advice on each item on this list. The IMF in particular needs to acknowledge its limited administrative capacity. Instead of trying to solve all problems by itself, it must therefore encourage the promulgation of standards of acceptable practice by private-sector bodies with expertise in these areas (the International Accounting Standards Committee, the International Corporate Governance Network, and the like) and by international committees of national regulators (e.g., the Basle Committee). National arrangements may differ, but countries participating in international financial markets all must meet minimally acceptable standards. But while relying on private-sector expertise, the IMF also needs to take ownership of the resulting standards. It should therefore collaborate with these private-sector bodies in the design of the relevant standards, bestow official status to the standards they promulgate, monitor countries' compliance, encourage information on that compliance to be disseminated to the markets (doing so itself if and where necessary), and condition its lending on steps to comply. In other words, both IMF conditionality (for program countries) and market discipline (for other countries) should be relied upon to encourage adherence to these standards.

But there remains the question of whether these two incentive mechanisms will be enough. Only a fraction of IMF member countries are subject to a program at any point in time, and there are good reasons to question whether market discipline will be applied promptly and systematically. This creates an argument for reinforcing these other incentives to comply by having national regulators key capital requirements for foreign lending to whether the IMF rates the borrowing country as in compliance with the relevant international financial standards. The decennial review of the Basle Capital Accord currently underway is an appropriate occasion to implement this regulatory discipline.

A second area requiring a major new initiative concerns banks and capital flows. Recent experience has demonstrated too well that badly managed banks and open international capital markets are a combustible mix. The obvious way of reducing this danger is to strengthen banks' risk-management practices and supervisors' oversight and regulation of those practices. Everyone agrees on the need for banks to better manage credit and currency risk, on the dangers of connected lending, on the need to insulate supervisory authorities from political influence, and on the need to raise bank capitalization as a way of giving bank owners and managers a financial cushion and something to lose.[1] But the sad truth

---

1. See Goldstein (1997), BIS (1997), and Folkerts-Landau and Lindgren (1998).

in all too many countries is that banks have a limited capacity to manage risk and that regulators have limited capacity to supervise their actions. In a sense, this limited capacity is the very definition of a financially underdeveloped, or less-developed, or developing economy. In such countries, moreover, capital requirements in theory and capital requirements in practice are two very different things, given the inadequacy of auditing and accounting standards. The political realities in many emerging markets are such that bank capital is all too rarely written down. This means that revising the Basle Capital Standards to key capital requirements to the source of banks' funding as well as the riskiness of their investments is unlikely to prove effective. If bank capital is not written down, in other words, how can capital requirements deter excessive risk taking?

In an environment with these characteristics, free access to foreign finance, short-term finance in particular, is incompatible with financial stability. Foreign funding gives banks gambling for redemption and otherwise seeking to take on excessive risk an additional way to lever up their bets. Government guarantees for banks regarded as too big to fail encourage foreign investors to provide those funds. But a blow to confidence may prompt these foreign investors to flee at any time, and the short maturity of their loans provides ample opportunity for them to get out. Their rush for the exits can precipitate a crisis that brings down both the banking system and the currency. This creates an argument for limiting or taxing bank borrowing abroad as a third line of defense against banking-system instability in countries where the first and second lines of defense—banks' own risk-management practices and regulatory supervision, respectively—do not suffice. And where banks can circumvent these measures by having the corporations do the borrowing and pass on the proceeds to them, broader measures may be required. Financial stability may have to be buttressed by a Chilean-style tax to limit short-term foreign borrowing by all domestic entities.

The international policy community must become a stronger advocate of these measures. The IMF should make unambiguous its support for the approach. The US Treasury needs to overcome the "Wall Street complex" that renders it reluctant to embrace such policies. Doing so requires that both of them more clearly articulate the exact circumstances under which such measures are warranted. This means understanding that capital-inflow taxes are necessary as a third line of defense against financial instability in countries where the first and second lines of defense are underdeveloped. In practice, this means that they are necessary in most "underdeveloped" countries. With time, of course, underdeveloped countries will develop. Their financial markets will deepen, and their macroeconomic and regulatory institutions will grow more robust. With these institutional preconditions in place, they will graduate to the club of mature markets, at which point restrictions on international financial transactions can come off. But until then, cautious steps in the direction of capital-account liberalization, which are inevitable given the desire to liberalize domestic financial markets and given ongoing changes in information and communications technologies, should not extend to the removal of taxes on capital inflows.

Crisis Prediction

However extensive progress is in these areas, crises will still occur. Sudden reactions to new information, or new interpretations of old information, can still precipitate sharp market moves. Such is the nature of financial markets, or so suggest hundreds of years of financial history. Only placing the markets in a regulatory straitjacket can prevent this. And severe repression means forgoing the benefits of domestic financial liberalization. It is a route that virtually no country is prepared to go.

Observations such as these have encouraged the official community to invest in early-warning indicators of currency and banking crises in the hope that they will see what is coming. Unfortunately, these models will have about as much success in predicting financial crises as geologists' models have in predicting earthquakes. Earthquakes and financial crises are products of complex nonlinear systems whose parts interact in unpredictable ways. Consider the following entirely realistic example. The government will devalue the currency only if it fears that the interest rate increases required to defend it will irreparably damage a weak banking system. But the banking system will weaken to this point only if investors withdraw their deposits from the country because they anticipate a devaluation. Thus, it is equally possible that everyone will wake up in the morning to a strong currency and a strong banking system or to panicked depositors and an incipient devaluation. There is no way of predicting which of these outcomes will obtain.[2] Whether speculators attack depends not only on the weakness of a country's banking system but on how much a government cares about further aggravating this problem when deciding whether to defend the currency. And the only thing more difficult to measure than a government's resolve is investors' assessment of it.

It is not surprising, therefore, that there is typically less to these statistical models than meets the eye. The models that perform best rely on reversals in the direction of capital flows and sudden reserve losses, variables that are properly regarded as concurrent rather than leading

---

2. This is an example of a so-called second-generation model of currency crises, in which multiple equilibria may arise. This class of models is described in more detail in appendix C. As explained in chapter 6, multiple equilibria of this sort make it more difficult to predict crises with the precision relevant for practical policy analysis.

indicators of currency crises. These models are like Richter scales registering the severity of earthquakes: in other words, not reliable predictive devices.

None of this is to dispute that further work on the causes and consequences of financial crises will continue to improve our understanding of these complex phenomena, just as further research into the interaction of tectonic plates will deepen our understanding of earthquakes. But this is a far cry from saying that better economic models will allow us to reliably predict financial crises. There will always be surprises—unanticipated crises will still occur, notwithstanding forecasters' best efforts.[3]

The attractions of this intellectual game are such that it will continue to be played. But this is not where the international policy community's scarce intellectual and political capital should be expended. And there is an associated danger, namely, that early-warning exercises will produce an unwarranted sense of complacency in the official community. They may lull officials into false confidence that they know what is coming.

Crisis Management

If there will always be crises, there will always be the need to clean up after them. This is where the existing international financial architecture is most obviously deficient. The international community has two ways of responding to crises: running to the rescue of the crisis country with a purse full of funds or standing aside and letting nature run its course. For two years following the Mexican rescue and for a year following the outbreak of the Asian crisis, the IMF was subjected to a firestorm of criticism for bailing out governments and international investors. Its actions, in the view of the critics, only reduced the incentives for meaningful policy reform and, by shielding the private sector from losses, encouraged more reckless lending and set the stage for further crises. Then in the summer of 1998, Russia provided an alarming illustration of the alternative when it devalued and suspended debt service payments, with devastating impacts on the Russian economy and global financial markets. Confidence was destroyed; the country's access to international capital markets was curtailed; and financial markets were roiled in East Asia, Eastern Europe, Latin America, and even Europe and the United States. This is not an experience anyone wishes to repeat. One cannot avoid concluding that both alternatives—bailouts on the one hand, and standing back and letting events run their course on the other—are unacceptable.

---

3. In addition, there is the danger of type II error—of warning and in the worst case precipitating crises that would not otherwise occur, a problem to which I return in chapter 6.

Avoiding both routine rescues and devastating defaults will require creating a more orderly way of restructuring problem debts. Under present circumstances, restructuring is too difficult and protracted. It *should* be difficult, of course, or borrowers would find it too easy to walk away from their debts. But the point here is that the difficulties of restructuring are greater in international than domestic markets and that this problem needs to be corrected. Capitalism without bankruptcy is like Catholicism without sin, it is said, but the sovereign bankruptcy option is simply too costly to contemplate under present institutional arrangements. Radical reform of those arrangements—that is, creation of an international bankruptcy court—is unrealistic. Discussing these ideas is a waste of breath. Yet, something must be done to create an acceptable alternative to massive international rescue packages.

In fact, a number of modest steps might realistically be taken to make international debt restructuring a viable option. Majority voting and sharing clauses could be added to loan contracts. This would prevent isolated creditors from resorting to lawsuits and other means of obstructing settlements that improve the welfare of the debtor and the vast majority of creditors. Other desirable changes to loan contracts include collective-representation clauses (making provision for an indenture trustee to represent and coordinate the creditors in the case of sovereign debts) and clauses providing that a minimum percentage of bondholders must agree for legal action to be taken. The addition of such clauses to bond contracts is the only practical way of creating an environment conducive to flexible restructuring negotiations. It can be done by legislators and regulators in the United States and the United Kingdom, the principal markets in which the international bonds of emerging economies are issued and traded, without ceding any jurisdiction or authority to a supranational agency.[4] This approach is therefore infinitely more realistic than imagining the creation of some kind of supranational bankruptcy court for sovereign debts that is empowered to cram down settlement terms.

In addition, standing committees of creditors should be created to provide better communication between lenders and borrowers, jump-starting negotiations and diminishing the information asymmetries that encourage the two sides to fight a protracted war of attrition. The IMF could lend to countries in arrears on their external debts so long as the recipients are making a serious adjustment effort and are engaged in good-faith negotiations with their creditors, providing the equivalent of the debtor-in-possession finance available to US corporations under Chapter 11 of the US bankruptcy code. Not only will this help to keep running the economy that is in crisis, but it will encourage the creditors to come to the bargaining table, again working to speed restructuring negotiations.

---

4. Assuming, that is, strong leadership at the national level.

And when the problem is defaulted corporate and bank debts, the solution lies not in unrealistic designs for an international bankruptcy court but in strengthening national bankruptcy statutes, reinforcing the independence of the judicial system administering them, and harmonizing those laws across countries.

These recommendations are not new. New provisions for loan contracts and IMF lending into arrears were discussed in a Group of 10 (G-10) report issued in the aftermath of the Mexican crisis (1996). The need for creditors' committees was developed in a background paper for the G-10's deliberations commissioned by the Bank of England and UK Treasury (Eichengreen and Portes 1995). Unfortunately, those discussions were not followed by action. Officials imagined that the markets would be so impressed by their insights that they would rush to amend loan contracts, form creditors committees, and endorse IMF lending into arrears. Predictably, little happened over the subsequent two years. No country is prepared to be first to add sharing and majority voting provisions to its loan contracts for fear of sending a bad signal to the markets; this is something that can be achieved only if everyone moves together. The markets are reluctant to form standing committees of creditors for fear that deciding who will be on the other end of the line will make it too easy for the financially distressed to pick up the phone. These recommendations have now been repeated by the G-22 and the G-7, but words need to give way to deeds. Regulators, led by those in the advanced industrial countries, need to require that internationally traded securities include majority voting, sharing, nonacceleration, minimum legal threshold, and collective-representation clauses. The United States, the G-7, and the IMF need to press for the formation of creditors' committees. The IMF should test the market's reaction to lending into arrears when an occasion arises.

Even together, these measures will not create the ideal orderly workout system. But they are the only practical alternative to pie-in-the-sky schemes for creating global monetary and regulatory institutions and assuming a political and economic consensus that does not exist. If we wish to create a viable alternative to massive bailouts and devastating defaults, they are the only game in town.

Reforming the IMF

The IMF will still have a role to play following these changes in the international financial architecture. There will still be a need for it to provide financial assistance, ideally in conjunction with credit lines extended by commercial banks, to countries running fundamentally sound economic and financial policies but suffering a temporary loss of investor confidence. But it will have to become less of a fireman and more of a policeman. It will have to police countries' conformance with international standards in areas related to the operation of financial markets. This means working with private-sector bodies and international committees of regulators in establishing those standards, monitoring the compliance of its members, and informing the markets of their progress. It means conditioning its lending on their compliance.

In addition, the Fund will have to become increasingly active as the facilitator or coordinator of restructuring negotiations. As honest broker it will have to bring debtors and creditors together like the Federal Reserve Bank of New York did for Long Term Capital Management and its bank creditors in September 1998. But supplying a conference room and hinting at the need for accommodation will not be enough, given the special difficulties of restructuring international debts, sovereign debts in particular. In addition, the Fund will have to more forcefully encourage the parties to come to the bargaining table by lending into arrears. It needs to use its position at the center of the international financial stage to push for the institutional reforms needed to create a viable alternative to ever-larger bailouts. It will need to push for the creation of standing committees of creditors and, if necessary, provide incentives for their formation by making clear its willingness to meet with such committees when exceptional circumstances arise. It will need to lobby for the addition of innovative clauses in loan contracts designed to smooth the restructuring process and lend at lower interest rates to countries that adopt them.

All this presupposes that the Fund will take steps to enhance its own legitimacy. The institution has acknowledged most of the obvious needs and begun to move in the requisite direction by strengthening its surveillance of financial markets, promoting the dissemination of information, and releasing more documentation on its programs and decision-making process. But these are the uncontroversial decisions. The heavy lifting will be for staff, management, and directors to reach a consensus on what kind of macroeconomic and financial policies to recommend to its developing-country members, given the realities of today's immensely liquid and not always reliable capital markets. Countries need to do more to protect themselves against the dangers posed by those markets, and the IMF needs to do more to encourage them. As noted above, the Fund should actively encourage countries in which banks have limited ability to manage risk and regulators have limited ability to supervise their actions (in other words, the vast majority of its members) to use Chilean-style holding-period taxes to discourage excessive short-term capital inflows, and it should more forcefully press for the adoption of more flexible exchange rates by most of its developing-country members, especially by those with open capital accounts. The first measure is needed to prevent borrowers who might otherwise be regarded as too big to fail from levering up their bets, the second as an incentive for banks and corporations to hedge their foreign exposures so that they can cope with unexpected large exchange rate movements if and when these occur. These are not areas where there yet exists a consensus within the IMF or among its principal shareholders. The Fund and its members need to move swiftly to establish it.

3

Standards for Crisis Prevention

Once upon a time, long, long ago in a place far, far away, crisis prevention and crisis management were so straightforward that they could be delegated to macroeconomists. Currency crises were caused by recklessly expansionary monetary and fiscal policies that resulted in excess demand, overvalued exchange rates, and unsustainable current-account deficits. Preventing them meant restoring monetary and fiscal balance before these excesses got out of hand. For the IMF, crisis management meant providing temporary financial assistance so that macroeconomic retrenchment did not produce or aggravate recessions. It meant conditioning that assistance on the restoration of monetary and fiscal discipline. It was not necessary for those whose objectives were the maintenance of exchange rate and macroeconomic stability to concern themselves with a country's financial nuts and bolts—that is, with bank supervision and regulation, auditing and accounting, bankruptcy procedures, and corporate governance. One can question whether things were ever so simple, but there is some truth to the view that for its first half century the IMF rightly focused on countries' monetary and fiscal policies and was only tangentially concerned with their internal institutional arrangements.

In Asia (and, for that matter, in its other recent programs), the IMF has become more deeply entangled in countries' internal affairs. It has sought to encourage the authorities to improve prudential supervision, root out corruption, eliminate subsidies, break up monopolies, and strengthen competition policy. In virtually every program country, this has incited a backlash against the Fund, which is resented for its intrusiveness. Martin Feldstein (1998a) and others have questioned whether such intimate involvement in the internal affairs of sovereign states is really necessary for the restoration of currency stability. What business is it of the Fund, Feldstein asks, to demand that Indonesia scale back its national car program or break up its clove monopoly? The IMF, in this view, should focus on the monetary and fiscal imbalances that are at the root of balance of payments problems. Not only does the Fund lack a secret formula for how every country should organize its internal affairs, but its advice is more likely to receive domestic backing and to be sustainable politically if it avoids infringing unnecessarily on the sovereignty of its members.

This view sits uneasily with the fact, widely acknowledged, not least by Feldstein himself, that monetary and fiscal profligacy was not endemic in Asia in the period leading up to its crisis. Since monetary and fiscal excesses were not at the root of the crisis, how then can it make sense to recommend focusing on monetary and fiscal variables when devising a response? The problem and the solution must lie elsewhere.

A hint to its location follows from the observation that high international capital mobility has all but erased the line between the domestic and international financial systems. This makes it impossible to "fix" the *international* balance of payments without also "fixing" the *domestic* financial system. So long as the domestic and international financial systems were strongly segmented by capital controls, balance of payments deficits arose out of current-account deficits that were financed with international reserves. Restoring balance of payments equilibrium meant restoring balance to the current account, which implied the need to restrict monetary and fiscal policies. But now that capital is so mobile internationally, stabilizing the balance of payments means stabilizing the capital account, which requires restoring investor confidence. And restoring investor confidence means restoring confidence in the stability of the domestic financial system.[1]

Inevitably, this draws those seeking to prevent and limit the severity of crises into involvement in the supervision and regulation of banks and corporations issuing publicly traded securities. It directs attention to auditing and accounting, the disclosure of financial information, and corporate governance. Recent models point to banking system weaknesses, the opacity of balance sheets, and moral hazard from government guarantees as the causes of currency and financial crises (e.g., Dooley 1997; Krugman 1998a).[2] Guarantees encourage excessive foreign short-

---

1. In the language of appendices B and C, the balance of payments disequilibrium does not reflect a flow problem (that the flow of government expenditures and the flow supply of new domestic credit emissions exceed the current period's additions to demand), as in first-generation crisis models. Rather, it is a stock problem, in which investors skeptical of the liquidity or solvency of the banking system have to be induced to hold the outstanding stock of bank liabilities rather than shift into foreign exchange.

2. The point applies not just to the Asian crisis. Thus, postmortems on the 1992 European and 1995 Mexican crises, while focusing on other factors as the proximate source of financial

term funding of the banking system, while directed lending leads banks to invest in low-return projects that ultimately damage their balance sheets. The fragility of the financial system then prevents the authorities from mounting a concerted defense of the currency. Inadequate auditing and accounting prevent investors from distinguishing good banks from bad and set the stage for economywide banking crises, while poorly designed or enforced insolvency procedures precipitate creditor grab races and cascading debt defaults. The undeniable implication is that far-reaching institutional reforms are needed to root out the causes of financial crises.

The problem is that neither the IMF nor other international financial institutions have sufficient staff and expertise to proffer advice in all these areas. The Fund cannot realistically master the regulatory particulars of banking systems in all 182 member countries. Hiring or borrowing bank supervisors from its members would simply remove them from where they are needed most urgently. The problem grows more severe when one turns from bank regulation to auditing and accounting, insolvency codes, and corporate governance—issues in which macroeconomists have little formal training or experience.

At the same time, problems in these areas are too pressing to do nothing about. The response to those who say that financial supervision, auditing and accounting, insolvency and reorganization procedures, and corporate governance are mere window dressing is that institutional arrangements in these areas are key to financial stability in our modern world. If the Asian crisis has taught us one thing, it is that countries cannot restore exchange rate and balance of payments stability without rectifying deficiencies in their domestic financial systems.

The Standard Solution

The only feasible approach to this problem is for national governments and international financial institutions to encourage the public and private sectors to identify and adopt international standards for minimally acceptable practice. National practices may differ, but all national arrangements must meet minimal standards if greater financial stability is to be achieved. All countries must have adequate bank supervision and regulation. All must require financial-market participants to use adequate accounting and auditing practices. All must have transparent and efficient insolvency codes. The particulars of these arrangements can differ—countries can reach these goals by different routes—but any country active on international financial markets must meet internationally accepted standards.

difficulties, point to the weakness of banking systems as one important reason why governments were unable or unwilling to defend their currencies when these came under attack (see, inter alia, Eichengreen and Wyplosz 1993).

An advantage of this approach, along with its ability to accommodate variations in national traditions and economic cultures, is that the burden of setting these standards need not fall primarily on the IMF, multilateral institutions in general, or even national governments. In most cases, the relevant standards can be identified or defined by private-sector bodies. Although those entities can be aided in their work by officials, the role for international institutions should be limited mainly to recognizing those standards, urging adoption by their members, monitoring compliance, and—in the case of the IMF—conditioning its assistance on a country's commitment to meeting them.

This approach is very different from that of the G-7, the G-22, and the IMF, which emphasize the role of official bodies in the process of standard setting and enforcement. It is different from that of commentators such as Richard Dale (1998), who suggests that responsibility for standard setting and enforcement should be lodged in a single international agency. It differs from Henry Kaufman's proposal to create a new international institution to establish uniform capital standards and trading, reporting, and disclosure standards and to monitor the performance of financial institutions and markets (Kaufman 1998a, b).[3] It will be obvious that the problem is not just one of limited expertise. In addition, there would be strong resistance, and not only in the United States, to the idea of vesting such formidable powers in the hands of an international institution.

Fortunately, the relevant private-sector bodies already exist. In accounting there is the International Accounting Standards Committee (IASC), consisting of representatives of the accounting profession from 103 countries at last count, which promulgates international accounting standards.[4] There is the International Federation of Accountants, with parallel membership, which has gone some way toward formulating international auditing standards.[5] The International Organization of Supreme Audit Institutions (INTOSAI) similarly issues auditing guidelines and standards. Committee J of the International Bar Association is developing a model insolvency code to guide countries seeking to reform and update their bankruptcy laws. For corporate governance there is the International Corporate Governance Network (ICGN), which seeks to improve standards of business management and accountability worldwide.

---

3. I return to these ideas in chapter 6.

4. The objectives of the IASC as stated in the committee's constitution (see http:// www.iasc.org.uk) include formulating and publishing "accounting *standards* to be observed in the presentation of financial statements and to promote their worldwide acceptance and observance ..." (emphasis added). Thirty-eight standards have been issued at the time of writing.

5. In addition, the federation, in its discussions, has paid special attention to the role that sound accounting practices can play in the development of capital markets in emerging economies.

In other areas, responsibility for setting standards has been taken on by international committees of regulators. In securities-market regulation there is the International Organization of Securities Commissions (IOSCO), which serves as a forum for securities regulators and has established working groups to set standards and coordinate regulatory initiatives. For bank regulation there is the Basle Committee on Banking Supervision, made up of supervisors from the leading industrial countries, whose Core Principles for Effective Banking Supervision codify Morris Goldstein's 1997 seminal argument for an international banking standard.[6] But even in these areas where regulators have taken the lead, there is a role for the private sector—for example, the world's largest financial institutions would develop standards for monitoring and managing financial risks, and the Basle Committee would utilize these when setting international standards for risk-management practices (G-30 1997).

Multilaterals are already active in a number of these areas, helping to identify standards or coordinating the process through which others agree to them. Thus, the Organization for Economic Cooperation and Development (OECD) issued a report in 1998 on global principles of corporate governance, focusing on the accountability of management, disclosure and transparency, and communication with shareholders (OECD 1998). The United Nations Commission on International Trade Law (UNCITRAL) has adopted a model law on the treatment of cross-border insolvencies. The IMF has established a Special Data Dissemination Standard for the provision of economic and financial information by countries seeking to access international capital markets. It has promulgated a code of fiscal transparency to be adopted as a standard of good fiscal practice by its member countries and anticipates developing an accompanying code for monetary and financial practices. In all these cases the multilaterals have solicited guidance and advice from national officials and private-sector experts.

The role of the IMF and other multilaterals would be more than simply to encourage the activities of these self-organizing groups. Rather, they should actively consult with these groups (as the Fund already does with IOSCO and the Basle Committee), seek status as ex officio members, and certify the standards that they identify as measures of best practice. Active involvement in the standard-setting process, by the IMF in particular, is necessary if the Fund is to assume "ownership" of the standards it helps to set. To give teeth to its advice, the Fund should condition the disbursal of assistance on program countries meeting those standards. It will need to encourage countries to apprise the markets of their compliance, which

---

6. There is a sense, then, in which the proposals of this chapter are essentially a generalization of Goldstein's approach to the bank instability problem.

it would monitor in conjunction with its Article IV surveillance. Finally, the Fund should make public its assessment of compliance as a way of strengthening market discipline.

A more active role for the IMF and the other international financial institutions in the promulgation of standards would be a departure from past practice. But there is no alternative once one acknowledges that the Bretton Woods institutions do not possess the resources to develop standards in all these areas themselves. The process will be complicated, but the alternative—inaction—is no longer viable. There is no alternative to proceeding by way of collaboration between the public and private sectors.

Some Examples

Examples of this process include existing standards for bank supervision, securities-market regulation, data dissemination, and corporate bankruptcy reform.

Bank Regulation

The BIS already provides a venue for national bank supervisors and regulators to pool their expertise and develop international standards for bank regulation. Since 1975, prompted by the failure of the Herstatt Bank, the Basle Committee (consisting of representatives from the bank supervisory authorities of the major industrial countries) has met three or four times a year and convened a number of technical subgroups. The Basle Committee periodically consults with and attempts to gain the support of other supervisory groups such as IOSCO.

The high-water mark in the Basle process remains the 1988 Basle Capital Accord. Signatories agree to hold their banks to minimal capital requirements of 8 percent of risk-weighted assets.[7] The 1995 Market Risk Amendment permits banks to use their proprietary models to calculate correlations among and within broad risk categories (such as interest rate risk, exchange rate risk, and equity price risk) in order to come up with more economically sophisticated risk weights, and the 1997 Core Principles for surveillance of banking and financial systems identifies five categories of standards for sound supervision and regulation.[8] The Core Principles

---

7. Assets are divided into four or more risk categories (e.g., commercial loans, mortgage loan, interbank debt, and government debt), and a risk weighting is established for each.

8. Significantly, the Core Principles were negotiated by the Basle Committee in cooperation with representatives from emerging-market countries. They were endorsed by G-10 central bank governors in April 1997 and by G-7 finance ministers in June. The 25 basic principles fall under five headings: preconditions for effective banking supervision (such as granting supervisors political independence and legal protection), licensing and structure (giving supervisors the authority to see that applicants for bank licenses have a proper operating

have been embraced by the IMF, which is helping to disseminate them to its members (see Folkerts-Landau and Lindgren 1998).

The Basle Capital Accord and the Core Principles demonstrate the feasibility of standard setting in the financial realm. At the same time, this case is revealing of the difficulty of the approach. The Committee on Banking Supervision has no enforcement power.[9] Most of its recommendations are undemanding minima; countries attaching a higher value to domestic financial stability have seen fit to opt for significantly more demanding standards.[10]

Notwithstanding the limited scope of these standards, agreement has been difficult to reach. The committee makes decisions by consensus, which allows dissidents to hold up progress. Representation on the Basle Committee is limited to high-income, financially developed economies. The Basle Capital Standards are designed to apply only to international banks. These limitations are all indicative of the difficulty of negotiating standards in all the relevant areas.

Securities-Market Regulation

A second example of standards-related work already under way is in the area of securities-market regulation. The most important organization in this area is the International Organization of Securities Commissions, a forum for cooperation among national securities regulators headquartered in Montreal. Its regular membership consists of government regulators of securities and futures markets such as the US Securities and Exchange Commission (those of nearly 150 member agencies from 94 countries at

---

plan, internal controls, and capital base), methods of ongoing bank supervision (including on-site and off-site inspections), information requirements (giving supervisors responsibility for seeing that each bank maintains adequate records and uses consistent accounting policies), and cross-border banking (that supervisors practice global consolidated supervision of home-country institutions and exchange information with other national supervisory authorities) (see BIS 1997). I return to these points in chapter 4.

9. The Basle Capital Standards are merely recommendations; nothing requires countries to accept them.

10. In addition, the Basle Standards as currently constituted say nothing about minimum capital requirements for nonbank financial institutions, notably hedge funds. And given the footloose nature of these funds (that is, their option of legally domiciling themselves in offshore tax havens), the Basle approach could not be used to address their behavior short of expanding the BIS to the point where country membership was universal and compliance with its standards was obligatory, neither of which is realistic. The only effective way of dealing with the hedge fund problem is, on the creditor-country side, to strengthen regulation of the commercial banks providing them credit and, on the debtor-country side, to use Chilean-style capital-inflow taxes to make it more difficult for hedge funds to get in and out of emerging markets (see chapter 4).

last count).[11] Essentially all countries with stock exchanges are represented, giving IOSCO a more broadly based membership than the Basle Committee. IOSCO consults extensively with international organizations, including the IMF.

IOSCO initially concentrated on coordinating efforts to curb and punish securities fraud, encouraging its member commissions to adopt bilateral and multilateral agreements to initiate proceedings against those suspected of committing such fraud in jurisdictions other than their own. Following the failure of Barings PLC, it turned its attention to a wider range of regulatory issues with implications for systemic risk.[12] Its Technical Committee has made recommendations regarding trigger levels for identifying large exposures on futures exchanges, for developing information-sharing agreements among regulators, for developing standards for transparency in the case of default procedures, for the disclosure of customer positions, and for best practice in the treatment of positions, funds, and assets in the event of default. Its working group on multinational disclosure and accounting has identified accounting issues that should be included in a core international accounting standard to be recognized by members. In 1995 it reached an agreement with the IASC on a schedule for establishing an international accounting standard to be used for quotations on all stock exchanges. In 1997 it circulated for consultation a draft setting out core principles for securities regulation. In 1998 it issued for public comment a set of international disclosure standards for cross-border offerings and initial listings by foreign issuers. It is working with the Basle Committee and the IASC to develop standards for the consolidated supervision of industrial groups and conglomerates.

IOSCO's broad membership, encompassing emerging as well as advanced industrial countries, positions it to address issues relevant to emerging markets. It operates an Emerging Markets Committee that "endeavours to promote the development and improvement of emerging securities markets by establishing principles and minimum *standards* . . ." (see http://www.iosco.org, emphasis added). Much of the discussion at its annual meetings is concerned with issues related to securities regulation in emerging markets. Thus, IOSCO illustrates the feasibility of extending standards-related work to financial issues relevant to emerging economies.

That said, international agreement has been elusive. Agreeing on accounting standards for research and development, discontinued busi-

---

11. It does not include self-regulating organizations like the Board of the New York Stock Exchange or the National Association of Securities Dealers. The self-regulating organizations are, however, represented on a consultative committee.

12. Its work program is expressly designed "to develop high-quality *standards* and promote market integrity through a process of member consensus and cooperation" (Folkerts-Landau and Lindgren 1998, 72, emphasis added).

ness, lease contracts, and retirement provisions has been especially problematic. IOSCO recommendations are advisory and nonbinding on members. The organization has no enforcement powers.

Data Dissemination

Another precedent is the IMF's initiatives on the data dissemination front. Its General Data Dissemination System (GDDS) and the Special Data Dissemination Standard are clear international standards (a fact evident in the latter's name). The SDDS, targeted at countries possessing or seeking access to international capital markets, is intended to provide them a standard for the provision of economic and financial data to the public.[13] Countries subscribe voluntarily, but in doing so they commit to providing information to the IMF about their practices in disseminating and publishing 17 categories of economic and financial data.[14] They agree to take specific steps to improve data integrity, data quality, and access to data and to emphasize transparency in the compilation and dissemination of statistics. They are encouraged to announce publication calendars in advance, to make data available simultaneously to all interested parties, and to describe the terms and conditions under which official statistics are produced. They are urged to document their statistical methodology and frameworks to assist users in assessing data quality. The IMF operates an electronic bulletin board where information on countries' subscription status can be found, with electronic hyperlinks to national sources of the data.[15]

---

13. Whereas the SDDS focuses on data dissemination by countries that generally already meet high-quality data standards, the GDDS concentrates on improvement in data quality generally, including in those countries that have not secured access to international capital markets.

14. Subscription was opened in April 1996 by a letter from the IMF's managing director to all IMF members and governors. As of September 1998, 46 members subscribed to the SDDS. There is a transitional period through the end of 1998, after which subscribers have committed to be in full observance of the standard. Information about the SDDS bulletin board is available at http://dsbb.imf.org.

15. One can distinguish several rationales for this initiative. First, better information strengthens the ability of regulators and other national officials to recognize problems in their banking and financial systems, enabling them to take prompt corrective action. In the same way, countries' compliance with these provisions can aid the IMF's surveillance activities. Second, subscription status provides an objective indicator of countries' creditworthiness, providing an alternative to the judgments of commercial credit agencies. Investors might become reluctant to lend to countries that fail to subscribe to the standard or might use interest rate spreads to ration credit to them. The hope is that better information will enable capital markets to draw back more smoothly, curtailing their lending more gradually in advance of the buildup of unsustainable pressures. Third, to the extent that bank runs, financial panics, and international contagion are driven by the inability of market participants to distinguish between good and bad credit risks, better information provision by governments and other financial-market participants may help to moderate herd behavior and

The SDDS as currently constituted is far from a complete solution to data-related problems, however. The IMF bulletin board provides only "metadata"—that is, descriptions of how various statistics are compiled and a road map of where they are found. It does not vouch for or assess the accuracy of countries' economic and financial statistics or even of the metadata, much less analyze the implications of data quality for country risk.

Corporate Bankruptcy Reform

Many emerging markets lack adequate bankruptcy procedures. Where the bankruptcy code is opaque or enforcement is arbitrary, creditors may be reluctant to lend for fear of being unable to collect in adverse states of the world. Moreover, the lack of an efficient bankruptcy procedure can compound the effects of other problems. When business conditions deteriorate, creditors anticipating that the firms to which they have lent will experience financial distress, and lacking confidence that they will be treated fairly, will scramble to liquidate their claims. Thus, the effects of the initial shock can be aggravated by the desire of investors to scramble for the exits. And if borrowers default, the inability of lenders to repossess collateral may produce a cascade effect where the debtor's nonperformance forces its creditors into default. When the creditors include banks, the worst-case scenario is a financial panic.

Many Asian countries entered their crises with archaic bankruptcy codes. Some of these made provision for the liquidation of insolvent enterprises, for example, but not for their reorganization and continued operation. Some made no provision for debtor-in-possession financing— that is, for giving seniority to creditors injecting new money. Their judiciaries lacked the independence and ability to move quickly, frustrating creditors' attempts to take effective legal recourse. This uncertainty about how the legal process would play itself out removed the incentive for the parties to negotiate voluntary workouts in the shadow of the court.[16]

---

violent market reactions. Chapter 6 critiques these justifications, emphasizing their limitations.

16. Thailand in 1997 is illustrative. When the crisis erupted, it had an archaic bankruptcy law whose sole purpose was to provide an orderly way of winding down the affairs of insolvent companies; it made no provision for corporate restructurings. It relied on the appointment of a receiver whose powers were limited to preparing a schedule of how the proceeds from liquidation would be distributed among the creditors. It barred creditors who advanced funds with knowledge of the debtor's insolvency from filing claims in bankruptcy proceedings, effectively precluding the provision of debtor-in-possession financing. Information provided to auditors and creditors was incomplete. The courts were lenient in granting adjournments and postponements; most liquidation proceedings took years. Where debt adjustments and restructurings did take place, they proceeded as out-of-court workouts negotiated by the company and its creditors, typically Thai and international commercial banks. Workouts became more difficult when there were numerous bondholders

Repairing this situation is conceptually straightforward. Archaic bankruptcy procedures should be updated. The development of a model bankruptcy code by the International Bar Association and international standards for insolvency and reorganization procedures can give governments the guidance they require. The key steps are strengthening the independence, integrity, and capacity of the judiciary, giving it the power to impose its decisions, and specifying firm deadlines for rendering judgments. While this is easier said than done, Thailand and Indonesia have made progress in the requisite direction even under duress.

For countries experiencing a full-blown economic and financial crisis, bankruptcy reform will have to extend beyond this. Collapse of the exchange rate can complicate restructurings by creating uncertainty about the future price of foreign exchange and hence about the fundamental value of firms. A temporarily weak exchange rate may leave creditors reluctant to settle because they continue to hope that the exchange rate will recover subsequently, enhancing the value of their claims. But the exchange rate is unlikely to recover so long as creditors hesitate to settle and the country's international financial relations are not normalized. To help debtors and creditors break out of this trap, governments have assumed the exchange risk. The Mexican FICORCA and Indonesian INDRA programs provide companies restructuring their debts a limited exchange rate guarantee, with the goal of eliminating some of the risks and costs that would otherwise stand in the way of the successful conclusion of negotiations. Unfortunately, such programs are not always effective, owing to design flaws. The design of such arrangements has not been addressed by the International Bar Association. The international policy community needs to press it or, more likely, another standards-related body to take on this task.[17]

---

involved and when bank workout groups were overstretched, as in 1997. By the end of the year, "loan workouts in Thailand [had become] . . . characterized by a highly disorderly process . . ." in the words of one set of experts (Darrow, Chandler, and Campbell 1997, 9). One could tell similar tales about other countries.

17. In addition, when many private borrowers find themselves simultaneously unable to service their debts because of the collapse of the exchange rate, it may be necessary to appoint an ombudsman or "workout czar" to coordinate their interlocking negotiations. This individual—supported by a small cadre of accountants, lawyers, and economists— would organize meetings of borrowers and lenders, encourage the provision of accurate information on the debtor's financial condition, and act as an honest broker. This approach was tried with some success by the Mexican government following the Tequila crisis when it established a Restructuring Commission (UCABE) to consult behind the scenes with key constituencies and coordinate negotiations. The Thai variant has been for the government to issue a nonbinding 19-point plan to be used as the framework for all corporate workouts involving multiple creditors, backed up by the threat that the government would step in and enforce its timetable for implementing those guidelines if creditors and debtors made insufficient progress. The 19-point plan specified that debt restructuring should involve corporate reorganization as well as new repayment terms, agreement by creditors to a debt

Finally, there is the need to harmonize bankruptcy procedures across countries. Even the most basic feature of a national bankruptcy procedure, the stay on payments, can be vitiated if the debtor has assets in more than one country and if the conditions under which a stay can be imposed differ across them. Not much progress has been made in the last three decades despite a series of international conferences and draft conventions. But as the integration of capital markets proceeds, it becomes more urgent for policymakers to redouble their efforts on this front.

Problems

In several important areas, no consensus exists on what an international standard should entail. Insolvency procedures, for example, differ across OECD countries in the rights they assign creditors and the powers they allot the courts. Even within the European Union, a relatively homogeneous group of nations, efforts to harmonize insolvency laws have come to naught.[18] The debate in the Congress on reform of the US bankruptcy code is indicative that there is not even agreement on these issues within individual countries.

Nor are disagreements limited to economists; they infect other disciplines, notably the law. Corporate governance, to take an obvious example, entails questions of contract enforcement, shareholders' rights, private property rights, and mechanisms for the fair resolution of conflicts among stakeholders, all of which raise sticky legal issues. Little agreement exists on internationally accepted standards for these areas because countries have very different legal traditions and systems. It is optimistic to think that the elements of all of these traditions can be brought under a single international standard.[19]

These are difficult problems. But given that countries coming from all these different traditions will be increasingly active participants on international capital markets, there is no alternative to attempting to define international standards that are general enough to accommodate their different legal traditions but at the same time rigorous enough to

---

standstill, and a pledge by creditors to provide timely and accurate financial information (see Bardacke 1998).

18. After many years of preparatory negotiations, a limited convention on insolvency procedures, concerned mainly with establishing common rules of law to adjudicate difficult creditor relationships, was issued in 1995; but it has not been ratified, owing mainly to opposition by the United Kingdom (see Fletcher 1997 for background).

19. Indeed, the efforts of the International Corporate Governance Network to agree on a statement of global corporate governance principles at its third plenary meeting in 1998 revealed deep disagreements among delegates over even the most basic questions (see Taylor 1998).

provide the effective corporate governance and market discipline required for efficient market outcomes.

Enforcement

In some cases, the threat to financial stability arises not from the letter of the law but from how the law is (or is not) enforced. The problem with Indonesia's bankruptcy law, with Indonesia's and South Korea's regulations on connected lending, and with Malaysia's and Indonesia's accounting standards was not so much that they were poorly designed (although this can be argued in some cases) as that they were badly or arbitrarily enforced. Failure to implement or enforce laws can occur for a number of reasons: conflicts of interest, political pressures, corruption, limited administrative capacity, and the absence of an independent judiciary.[20] However much national governments and the international community strive to bring domestic laws into conformance with international standards, their efforts will be of little consequence if enforcement is not fair and vigorous.

The controversy over Indonesian bankruptcy reform is illustrative. Indonesia amended its bankruptcy law at the end of August 1998 to impose a deadline of 30 days for court decisions, set up a new commercial court with specially trained judges, and introduced a 270-day suspension of payments as an alternative to liquidation. It introduced independent receivers for liquidation and administrators for the 270-day stay as alternatives to the state receivership agency. However, there remains a shortage of trained accountants and lawyers, weakening the operation of the receivership and administration system. This has allowed debtors to use the 270-day stay as an opportunity to strip assets and transfer them to the distressed subsidiaries' parent companies. In addition, the courts remain unpredictable. The first case filed under the new law was dismissed on technical grounds (namely that a similar case was already pending against an affiliate). By the end of November, only five cases had been evaluated by the commercial court (of 17 filed under the provisions of the new law), and three of those, including a case against Pacific International Finance, owned by associates of former president of Indonesia Suharto, had been rejected on technical grounds.

---

20. The problem of limited administrative capacity is illustrated by South Korean bankruptcy procedures, while that of lack of judicial independence is evident in the case of their Indonesian counterparts. In South Korea, the Seoul district court had only four bankruptcy judges at the beginning of 1998 to handle cases numbering in the hundreds. In Indonesia, "People wish to avoid courts because they are considered expensive, notoriously unpredictable and unreliable. In addition there is a pervasive culture of corruption at all levels. High-profile persons are perceived as exempt from the process. The government may also step in at any point to rearrange the process to suit what it considers its interest" (Gamble 1998, 3).

Enforcement has also been a sticking point in international efforts to strengthen bank supervision and regulation, the area where international standards are most advanced. The Basle Committee's early efforts to strengthen the supervision and regulation of cross-border banking (starting with the Basle Concordat in 1975) focused on the letter of the law. More recently, the IMF, building on the Basle Core Principles, has emphasized the need to establish a legal and political setting in which the relevant regulations will be enforced (see Folkerts-Landau and Lindgren 1998, chapter 7). It has stressed the need to vest responsibility for the function in an independent agency, to ensure that the supervisory authority receives adequate operating income from a source other than the regular budget, and to appoint the head of the supervisory authority to a fixed term in office so that he is protected from the threat of termination. It has recommended that supervisory authorities not be held personally liable for damages caused by any actions legitimately performed in the course of their duties and that they be required to publish periodic reports so that the basis for decisions can be assessed and conflicts of interest can be ferreted out. It has taken steps, in other words, to establish international standards not just for what kinds of bank regulations should be adopted but also for what kind of institutional arrangements should be put in place to ensure that they are enforced.

Thus, the fact that the enforcement of statutes is problematic only reinforces the argument for standards in whose context those enforcement problems can be addressed.

The Role of the International Financial Institutions

While some would say that these are matters best left to the private sector, there are compelling arguments for the multilaterals to be involved. Actively contributing to the process on behalf of their members would put the international financial institutions in a stronger position to insist on compliance by those members. And since the IMF will need to use those standards in its surveillance activities, it will have proprietary information about suitable designs and an interest in seeing that they are appropriately tailored for this use. For all these reasons, it is important for the Fund to take "ownership" of these standards (to apply to it the same terminology it is fond of applying to its members), and this will require it to be actively involved in the standard-setting and dissemination process.

There is no question that the IMF should condition its assistance on implementation of the resulting standards. Countries that borrow from the Fund and whose national practices are judged deficient should be required to take specific steps to bring domestic arrangements into line with international standards as a condition for the disbursal of funds. The

IMF already conditions its assistance, where appropriate, on governments agreeing to close problem banks; from there it is a small step to ask them to reform the ways in which they supervise and regulate the banking system. Similarly, the Fund has already made agreement to reform national bankruptcy procedures a precondition for the disbursal of funds to Indonesia and South Korea; there is no reason that such reforms should be asked only of program countries. To be sure, more work in this area will stretch the expertise and resources of IMF staff to their limit; but the advantage of relying on private-sector bodies to identify standards is precisely that the those standards provide a manual or guidebook of measures to which policymakers and Fund staff can refer.

Finally, the IMF should inform the markets of its members' compliance. The Fund already publishes such information in areas where its Articles of Agreement give it a mandate. Thus, it reports annually on whether each member complies with Article VIII of the IMF Articles of Agreement requiring it to make its currency convertible for purposes of current account transactions. It publishes a table of "bullet points" indicating the presence or absence of various categories of exchange and capital controls in its *Annual Report on Exchange Controls and Exchange Restrictions*. In theory, there is no reason why it could not do the same for the IASC's 38 accounting standards, IOSCO's 10 principles for use by securities and futures regulatory authorities, and the International Bar Association's guidelines for a model bankruptcy law. It could issue an annual report that rated countries' compliance in each of these areas.[21]

In some cases this exercise would be straightforward; in auditing, for example, the question could boil down to whether banks and companies were required to hire reputable international accounting firms to examine their books.[22] In other areas, evaluating compliance will unavoidably require a considerable element of judgment, exposing the Fund to complaints of political bias. The difficulty is heightened by the fact that the Fund possesses no explicit mandate for work in this area. And it may find it hard to blow the whistle on countries that fail to comply for fear of compounding their financial difficulties.

These are arguments for relying on the relevant self-organizing private-sector body to carry out the compliance exercise itself wherever possible.

---

21. The G-22 and G-7 have suggested something along these lines—an IMF "Transparency Report"—albeit without providing specifics. The way this exercise is described suggests a relatively limited assessment of transparency. Rather than an annual report akin to *Exchange Controls and Exchange Restrictions* or the European Bank of Reconstruction and Development *Transition Report*, the G-22's and G-7's language suggests a qualitative report on each country in conjunction with its Article IV consultations, limited primarily to fiscal transparency, monetary transparency, and the like.

22. Although the criticism that the World Bank and others have levied on the big five accounting firms raises questions about whether this would be a desirable way to go.

Each committee should be encouraged to establish an electronic bulletin board where such information could be centralized. Hyperlinks could be provided to the Fund's own electronic bulletin board, as they already are for financial-market data. Where the self-organizing committee is composed of national regulators, the rating function could be privatized; it could be spun off to commercial auditing and accounting firms or commercial concerns such as Fitch-IBCA with expertise in the relevant areas.[23] Their assessments might well be subject to the same kind of criticism presently levied at commercial credit-rating agencies, namely, that changes in their evaluations tended to lag changes in actual market conditions. If private-sector assessments are deficient, then the Fund itself should take on responsibility for compliance evaluation. The best way of doing so would be by publishing an annual report, in which it rated each of its member's compliance in each of the relevant subareas.

Incentives for Compliance

One can all too readily imagine an outcome in which countries agree to adhere to an international standard but where actual practice is another matter. What then would be the incentives to comply?

For program countries the answer is clear: the IMF should condition the disbursal of funds on countries taking steps to comply.[24] For the others, having the Fund release its assessment of countries' compliance will encourage the operation of market discipline. But only a subset of IMF member countries is under a program at any point in time, and one can imagine backsliding after a country exits from its program. Market discipline, for its part, is notoriously erratic, as recent events have underscored. There is an argument, consequently, for regulators to reinforce these other mechanisms. Most obviously, the Basle Capital Accord could be revised to allow the decennial review currently under way to be an occasion for making capital requirements on lending to a country a function of IMF assessments of that country's compliance with the relevant international standards. The United States has effectively made adherence to its guidelines for comprehensive consolidated bank supervision by

---

23. Recall that the US Commerce Department has successfully spun off the Index of Leading Economic Indicators to the Conference Board. There is no reason why the Fund should not start with a similar strategy with respect to rating countries' compliance with standards and see whether it works.

24. While there are likely to be serious limitations, as emphasized in chapter 7, on the scope for preapproved (contingent) credit lines for countries with strong policies, to the extent that credit lines for such countries can in fact be preapproved, compliance with the relevant international financial standards is an obvious criterion for the Fund to use when deciding who qualifies.

home-country supervisors a condition for approving a foreign bank's application to establish a US office.[25] This precedent can be extended to other standards (besides comprehensive consolidated bank supervision) and adopted by other countries (indeed, coordinated across them).

Implications

Promoting the development of and compliance with standards for financial regulation, auditing and accounting, corporate governance, and insolvency law might seem like a radical departure for international financial institutions such as the IMF. In reality, the official community has already moved in this direction, notably in the activities of the Basle Committee but also in the efforts of the OECD to negotiate principles for corporate governance and of the United Nations to sketch a model bankruptcy code. The IMF is involved, having established a data dissemination standard for countries intending to access international capital markets and a code of fiscal (and, soon, monetary and financial) transparency. That governments and international organizations are being pushed into involvement in this area over their own protests is evidence that financial regulation, auditing and accounting, corporate governance, and insolvency law are too important to financial stability to ignore. It is evidence that the development and promulgation of international standards are the only practical way of addressing these problems.

Differences in economic, social, and legal traditions complicate the process of reaching agreement on standards, much less effectively enforcing them. Solutions to these problems will not be reached quickly. The danger is that they will never be reached if the IMF, the Basle Committee, and the rest of the international financial community do not rely more heavily on the private sector. The thousand-some economists of the IMF, even together with their colleagues at the World Bank and the BIS, lack the time and expertise to negotiate and implement international standards in the all the relevant areas in all 182 IMF member countries. They need rely on the IASC, IOSCO, Committee J of the International Bar Association, and their counterparts with expertise in other issue areas to develop the relevant standards. They then need to publish information on adoption and enforcement so that the markets can sanction countries that fail to comply. The G-7's and G-22's acknowledgment of the desirability of taking advantage of the expertise of IASC and IOSCO are small steps in the right direction. They now need to be followed up by more systematic and extensive collaboration between the public and private sectors.

---

25. Under the provisions of the Foreign Bank Supervision Act of 1992, as described in G-22 (1998b, 41). The G-22 concludes that this has at least marginally encouraged other countries to improve their supervisory systems.

4

Banks and Capital Flows

As Asia's experience so graphically illustrates and a flurry of scholarly studies have sought to explain, banks are a special problem in emerging markets. They are far and away the most important providers of financial intermediation services. This is evident in the ratio of stock- and bond-market capitalization to credit provided by deposit-taking banks, which is significantly below that in the advanced industrial economies.[1]

This predominance of banks in emerging markets reflects their relatively early stages of economic and institutional development.[2] A deep and liquid securities market presupposes a well-developed information environment and reliable contract enforcement, the legal and institutional prerequisites for which are demanding. In particular, in the absence of mandatory disclosure requirements, insider-trading prohibitions, and effective laws protecting credit rights, the scope for cornering or manipulating markets and expropriating minority creditors tends to inhibit participation in over-the-counter markets and centralized exchanges. In turn, the absence of these institutional prerequisites limits the role of such markets in mobilizing savings, financing investment, and providing corporate governance. Banks, in contrast, can use long-term relationships

---

1. Similarly, the share of banks in the assets of bank and nonbank financial institutions is unusually large in developing countries (Goldstein and Turner 1996).

2. Banks similarly dominated financial markets in the early stages of development of all of today's advanced industrial economies. This is true even of the United Kingdom and the United States, where the development of securities markets was most precocious (see Goldsmith 1985).

with their customers to obtain favorable access to information about their financial condition and can defend their rights as creditors by virtue of their economic size. It follows that in less-developed countries, where legal and regulatory infrastructure is relatively weak, banks are relied upon disproportionately for the provision of intermediation services.[3]

An economy that relies disproportionately on banks for the provision of financial services is vulnerable to problems of financial and macroeconomic instability. Sharp changes in stock and bond prices are not without their adverse consequences, but such consequences are mild compared to those caused by shocks to the banking system. This creates an argument for seeking to buttress financial stability by diversifying the financial sector to include a significant role for both banks and securities markets.

Observers such as Donald Tsang, the financial secretary of Hong Kong, therefore argue that emerging economies need to develop securities markets to supplement their banking systems (see Tsang 1998). In this they will be aided by ongoing changes in financial technology such as computerized trading and the computer-based pricing of derivative financial instruments, which are making the development of well-functioning securities markets easier and more attractive. But the special information and contracting problems characteristic of emerging economies will continue to slow the development of securities markets until rules for financial disclosure, auditing and accounting, insolvency procedures, and corporate governance, as described in chapter 3, are promulgated and rigorously enforced. This is a lot to ask of governments that have limited administrative capacity. It makes it naive to think that the forward march of technology will soon diminish the special importance and therefore the special problem of the banks.

Causes and Consequences of Bank Fragility

Hence, financial systems in emerging markets will remain centered on banks for the foreseeable future. And bank-based systems are intrinsically fragile. These facts have several important consequences.

---

3. A mature financial system in which information and contracting problems have been ameliorated will have a place for both financial institutions and financial markets. Banks are the cost-effective way of providing external finance for industries whose technology is stable and for which there is a consensus about managerial competence and expected returns. Where there is widespread agreement on these matters, it will pay to exploit the economies of scale in monitoring that banks can provide. But when technology is changing rapidly and management is faced with unusually complex decisions, no consensus will generally exist about managerial competence and prospective returns. It will then pay to use stock and bond markets to pool diverse assessments, the balance of which will be reflected in the prices of securities.

Macroeconomic Instability

My work with Andrew Rose on banking crises in emerging markets shows that an economywide banking panic typically depresses output by 1 percent of GDP in the year it occurs, by fully 3 percent of GDP in the next year, and by somewhat less in the year following (Eichengreen and Rose 1997).[4] An emerging-market banking crisis, in other words, costs upwards of a year's worth of normal economic growth. These macroeconomic effects are larger in emerging markets than in advanced industrial economies, because banks dominate the financial system in the former to such an extent and there are few other channels for obtaining credit.[5]

These macroeconomic costs are distinct from the resolution costs of banking crises—the costs of taking over bad loans and recapitalizing insolvent banks—which tend to be borne by the public sector and, ultimately, the taxpayer. Bank losses and public-sector resolution costs have exceeded 10 percent of GDP in more than a dozen episodes since the late 1970s, sometimes approaching twice that level. Resolution costs are typically larger in emerging markets than in advanced industrial economies, again reflecting the disproportionate importance of the banking system.

Finally, there is the damage that banking crises do to the credibility of a government's economic-policy strategy. High resolution costs wreak havoc with fiscal control. The government's inability to rein in its budget deficit, together with its inability to raise interest rates when the banking system is weak, can in turn destroy its capacity to mount a credible defense of the currency.

Understanding the Fragility of the Banking System

One reason banks pose a threat to the stability of the financial system is that they are linked together by the interbank market—because they manage fluctuations in their liquidity by borrowing from and lending to one another. It follows that the sudden inability of one bank to meet its obligations can cascade through the banking system, threatening the financial sector as a whole. Moreover, banks have only limited ability to protect themselves against these dangers. Their liabilities are more liquid than their assets because of the information environment in which they

---

4. This study analyzed the experience of 105 developing countries, many of which, though not all, experienced banking crises sometime in the last 30 years.

5. Other studies surveyed by Goldstein (1997) reach similar conclusions. The grave impact of the Japanese banking crisis on the Japanese economy provides proof by counterexample. The ratio of market- to bank-intermediated finance is unusually low in Japan, and hence the macroeconomic effects of its banking crisis have been disproportionate.

operate.[6] Information asymmetries are intrinsic to financial markets—there is no avoiding the fact that borrowers know more than lenders about the borrowers' intentions and investment projects. Savers use banks as "delegated monitors" of borrowers in response to this fact (see Diamond 1984). But precisely because they invest in information on the creditworthiness of their borrowers and thereby acquire more knowledge of this than the market as a whole, banks are able to sell off their assets and raise liquidity in a crisis only at a loss. Other creditors will be willing to purchase those assets, about which there is relatively poor public information, only at fire-sale prices. Consequently, a loss of depositor confidence, even when unjustified, can bring down a bank, because the latter can raise liquidity only by doing further damage to its balance sheet.

The illiquidity of bank assets reflects the fact, already noted, that banks operate in an environment of incomplete and asymmetric information. This information environment also creates the danger that initially isolated runs can spread contagiously to other banks and threaten the system as a whole. Because information about bank customers is incomplete, it will be hard for outsiders to know whether problems affecting a particular institution are bank specific or also pervade the balance sheets of other intermediaries. Hence, a run on a bank can spread contagiously and threaten the stability of the entire system.

In response, governments and central banks provide deposit insurance and lender-of-last-resort services to the banking system. A century and more of experience points to the need for these backstopping functions to prevent financial markets from seizing up. But provision of this financial safety net encourages bank management to take on additional risk, because while their losses are limited to their capital, their potential income, enhanced by the use of leverage, is unbounded. If supervision and regulation are not strengthened to limit the scope for banks to respond in this way, the moral hazard associated with the provision of deposit insurance and lender-of-last-resort services may in the end produce more bank failures and banking crises, not fewer.

Triggers

In many emerging markets, the stage has been set for banking crises by financial liberalization that creates opportunities for banks to expand their risky activities without concurrent upgrading of supervision and regulation to ensure that those risks are appropriately managed and to

---

6. This is what we mean when we say that banks are in the business of providing "liquidity-transformation services."

limit them where they are not.[7] Asli Demirguc-Kunt and Enrica Detragiache (1997) show that banking crises have typically occurred in the wake of financial liberalization that ignites a credit boom in which the banks significantly expand their lending activities.[8] The lending boom then leads to a construction and a real estate boom. The real exchange rate appreciates in response to the increased demand for home goods, creating competitiveness problems for domestic exporters and widening the current-account deficit.

External events can then trigger a crisis by raising doubts about the creditworthiness of bank borrowers. The single most powerful trigger, historically, has been a rise in world interest rates (Eichengreen and Rose 1997). Higher foreign interest rates mean higher domestic interest rates when financial markets are integrated internationally. As domestic banks pass the higher cost of funds along to their customers, the real estate bubble begins to deflate. Investment declines and growth slows. Borrowers find it more difficult to repay their loans. Rising defaults can then throw the entire banking system into crisis.

Capital Mobility and Crises

These dangers can be greatly heightened by the liberalization of international capital flows. The more integrated are domestic and foreign financial markets, the greater will be the sensitivity of the domestic economy and financial system to foreign interest rates. If foreign interest rates are the immediate trigger for banking crises, that trigger can now operate more powerfully.

Moreover, the higher is capital mobility, the greater is the scope for banks seeking to expand their risky activities to do so by funding themselves abroad. When the capital account is open, there will be more scope for banks gambling for redemption to lever up their bets.[9] Critically, foreign investors will be inclined to let them do so. Foreigners will more freely fund the risky activities of emerging-market banks if they are confi-

---

7. Similarly, in countries where deposit insurance coverage is universal, market discipline will be less, because depositors bear no risk of losses from reckless bank behavior; the expansion of risky bank activities will be correspondingly greater.

8. The tendency for a domestic credit boom to precede a banking crisis is also a theme of Gavin and Hausmann (1996).

9. The World Bank (1998, 144) illustrates the problem by referring to South Korea. "In the Republic of Korea, excessive domestic financial risk taking—including low equity and heavy bank borrowing—was a long-standing practice. What may have tipped the balance in the 1997 crisis, however, was capital flows; when in the context of its entry into the OECD, Korea liberalized the ability of its banks to borrow (short term) abroad (instead of tightening safeguards), there was a massive surge in such inflows; their reversal subsequently precipitated the crisis."

dent that governments regard those banks as too big to fail. In the presence of government guarantees, they will be attracted by the high interest rates characteristic of capital-scarce emerging markets without being deterred by the risk. They know that governments in emerging-market economies are loath to let their banks fail because the latter so dominate their financial systems, rendering them politically powerful and critical to economic stability, and because guarantees are the quid pro quo extended to the banks in return for their being used as instruments of industrial policy. The other side of what Ronald McKinnon and Huw Pill refer to as the "overborrowing syndrome" is thus overlending by foreigners lured by government guarantees (see McKinnon and Pill 1997). And this overlending and overborrowing mean that when banks fail and recapitalization is required, the resolution costs will be that much greater.

It is fashionable to assert that foreign bank creditors should be made to "take a hit" when an emerging market experiences a currency and banking crisis. If the banks' short-term foreign deposits are running off, then the government, it is said, should refuse to use its scarce foreign-exchange reserves to replace them. Not only will replenishing bank liabilities endanger the stability of the currency, but allowing foreign depositors to get out whole will only encourage more overlending and overborrowing in the future, and even greater crises.

Unfortunately, the alternatives to rescuing the banks are less than palatable. For the government or central bank to refuse to act as a lender of last resort, causing the entire banking system to come crashing down, would be one way of "teaching a lesson" to foreign creditors, but at very great cost to the economy. Alan Greenspan has put the dilemma succinctly. "Cross-border interbank funding . . . [is] the Achilles' heel of the international financial system. Creditor banks expect claims on banks, especially banks in emerging economies, to be protected by a safety net and, consequently, consider them to be essentially sovereign claims. Unless those expectations are substantially altered—as when banks actually incur significant losses—governments can be faced with the choice either of validating those expectations or risking serious disruption to payments systems and to financial markets in general" (Greenspan 1998b, 7).[10]

Preventing Banking Crises

In principle, the solution to this problem is straightforward: strengthen supervision and regulation of the banking system. This means identifying banks that are incapable of managing market risks, including the risks associated with the new activities made available by financial liberalization, and preventing them from taking on additional risk in response to

---

10. I return to the problem and discuss some recent proposals for solving it in chapter 5.

provision of the financial safety net. Properly supervised and regulated banks will be compelled to follow sound practice with respect to management of their assets and liabilities, and there will be no reason to regard short-term liabilities denominated in foreign currency as posing special dangers or to regulate the capital-account transactions of the banking system in a special way.

The Elements of Prudential Supervision

The elements of sound prudential supervision and regulation are well known.[11] Supervisors should monitor the adequacy of banks' internal controls, external audits, loan and investment policies, and risk-management techniques to identify banks incapable of managing the risks to which they are exposed. They should verify that banks have management information systems in place that enable them to identify risky loan and investment concentrations. They should verify that banks are adequately managing liquidity and foreign-exchange risks. Banks should lend on an arm's-length basis and attach realistic values to the assets on their balance sheets. They should be required to provide adequate and accurate information to their supervisors, who should be empowered to impose remedial and punitive measures, including revocation of the license to operate, in the event of noncompliance. Supervisory oversight should be strengthened by giving bank supervisors political independence, financial autonomy, legal immunity, and the power to conduct on-site inspections. Other desirable elements include limiting deposit insurance to small deposits, establishing a credible exit policy for unprofitable banks, and eliminating government guarantees where possible. They include the adoption of regulations requiring public disclosure of intermediaries' financial condition as a way of strengthening market discipline and helping depositors to distinguish good and bad banks, thereby limiting the tendency for runs to spread contagiously throughout the system.

Finally, banks should be required to meet internationally recognized capital-adequacy standards so that they have the financial cushion needed to cope with volatility and so that their owner/managers have something to lose. Capital requirements should be keyed to the riskiness of bank assets and corrected for discrepancies between the private and social costs of banks taking on additional risk (where the latter include the costs of threats to systemic stability). In the mature markets, prudential regulation has tended to evolve away from regulations that mechanically attach different weights to different types of assets in favor of more complex

---

11. The particulars that follow are drawn from the Core Principles for Effective Banking Supervision (Basle Core Principles), which in turn build on Goldstein (1997) (see also Folkerts-Landau and Lindgren 1998 and G-22 1998b).

models, including the banks' own proprietary (value at risk) models, that take into account correlations in the returns on different classes of assets when calculating risk weights.

Political and Developmental Constraints on Regulation

The length of this list is one clear indication that all this is easier said than done. Considerable administrative capacity is required, for one thing. Moreover, meaningful reform that subjects banks to serious regulatory and market constraints will be opposed by vested interests that benefit from access to subsidized credit. Political pressure for regulatory forbearance will be intense in emerging markets where banks so dominate the financial system. And the expertise required to evaluate bank balance sheets is in short supply, nowhere more than in emerging markets (see Gould and Amaro-Reyes 1983). This problem deepens as banks branch into new lines of business and with the proliferation of exotic, thinly traded derivative financial instruments. The use of proprietary models to calculate risk weights pushes the envelope of competence of bank regulators and managers even in countries with the most advanced financial markets (witness US and European bank exposure to the hedge fund Long Term Capital Management). In emerging markets it is likely to create more problems than it solves.

One suggestion is that in less mature markets, where supervisory capacity is least and the pressure for regulatory forbearance is greatest, banks should be held to higher than conventional capital standards. George Benston and George Kaufman argue that regulators in such countries should rely even more heavily on regulations requiring banks to hold capital and issue subordinated debt (Benston and Kaufman 1988).[12] Where the government's capacity to supervise banks is least, there is a particularly compelling argument for strengthening the incentive for owners and creditors to manage balance sheet risks prudently because their own capital and credits are at stake.

Raising capital requirements will not hurt.[13] But relying on capital requirements higher than the Basle Standards to deter excessive risk taking

---

12. The advantage of subordinated debt is that debtholders are exposed only to downside risk (in contrast to those who contribute to bank capital, they do not also share in exceptional profits), so they have a particularly strong incentive to encourage management to avoid taking on excessive risk. In addition, the interest rate on subordinated debt provides a particularly transparent indicator of the adequacy of a bank's risk-management practices, which should serve to focus the attention of regulators on potential problems and make it more difficult for them to forebear (see also Calomiris 1998b).

13. Except in countries already suffering from severe financial distress, where forcing banks to raise additional capital would only aggravate the existing credit crunch and is therefore best delayed. That said, this is an approach that has been successfully implemented by a number of emerging markets, notably Argentina and Singapore.

will work only if there is a realistic prospect of bank capital being written down. If there is political pressure for the authorities to recapitalize an otherwise insolvent bank on concessionary terms or to establish a special public facility that takes nonperforming loans off the banks' books in return for government bonds in excess of those loans' marked-to-market value, as is the case in many emerging markets, bank owners may be let off the financial hook.[14] Higher capital requirements will then have little effect. They will be similarly ineffectual when accounting standards are inadequate, since there can then be considerable slippage between actual and putative capital (Reisen 1998, 25).

Another approach, inspired in part by these problems, relies instead on rules limiting portfolio concentrations, illiquid investments, and foreign-currency exposures. Thus, where capital-account liberalization allows banks to borrow offshore in foreign currency, the obvious rule is to require them to match the currency composition of their assets and liabilities. Simple rules can have complex consequences, however, and unintended ones. As Thailand's experience illustrates, restricting open foreign-exchange positions may simply cause banks to pass on those exposures to their domestic customers, who are even less able to handle it. In the Thai case, banks made foreign-currency denominated loans, transforming the currency mismatch into a maturity mismatch.

These dilemmas have motivated a search for additional options for buttressing the stability of the banking sector. I consider four.

Narrow Banking

Under narrow banking, insured banks may invest their liquid liabilities only in liquid assets.[15] Eligible assets are limited to deposits with other banks and to interest-bearing assets such as short-term government securities, the market for which is deep and broad. The liquidity and transparency of their assets will allow narrow banks to raise funds in a crisis, eliminating the danger that fundamentally solvent banks can be brought down by a depositor run. Because narrow banks are still exposed to interest rate risk and depositors will still have some difficulty in evaluating institutional portfolios, there remains a case for deposit insurance. But narrow banks would have little scope for taking on additional risk in response to any consequent weakening of market discipline.[16] This option

---

14. This problem has been prominent in recent discussions of how to recapitalize the Mexican banking system, where political opposition has been fanned by the failure of prior owner/managers to take significant losses.

15. See Litan (1987) and Burnham (1990) for details on narrow banking.

16. They would be competitive with other financial institutions in the same sense as are money-market mutual funds. And were there any doubt about this, giving them exclusive access to the payments system operated by the central bank would give them a special advantage in terms of convenience in carrying out transactions for their customers.

is particularly appealing for countries with rigidly pegged exchange rates (e.g., under the provisions of a currency board), on the grounds that their central banks possess relatively little capacity to act as lenders of last resort.

But the demand for other banking services would not disappear. Firms in a position to do so would supply increasing amounts of commercial paper and junk bonds, the demand for which would be provided by mutual funds, pension funds, hedge funds, and insurance companies. In practice, of course, only relatively creditworthy borrowers are able to issue the liquid securities attractive to these investment vehicles. The demand for commercial, industrial, real estate, and consumer loans by less creditworthy borrowers would therefore tend to shift to uninsured finance companies and finance-company-like entities that are not offered deposit insurance. These nonbank intermediaries would then undertake the delegated monitoring that had traditionally been the province of banks and have an incentive to offer liquid, deposit-like liabilities to fund their investments. Many of the activities and risks traditionally associated with the banking system would thus shift to these bank-like organizations.

The question is then whether the authorities' commitment not to apply too-big-to-fail arguments to these nonbank financial intermediaries would be politically sustainable. Insofar as distress in the finance-company sector gave rise to bank-like externalities, there would be pressure for the government to intervene. And the hope that these nonbank financial intermediaries would be subject to stronger market discipline by creditors who do not enjoy deposit-insurance protection would be frustrated by the expectation that the government would ultimately be forced to leap into the breach. Some proponents of narrow banking insist that by dividing intermediaries into insured narrow banks and uninsured finance companies that can offer higher returns but assume additional risks, the authorities can make credible their commitment not to intervene. In a sense they are simply assuming a convenient answer to the question: were it so simple for governments to limit their support operations in this way, they could equally well limit their extension to existing financial institutions, obviating the need to create narrow banks.

A clear illustration of the problem is the decision of the Federal Reserve Bank of New York to coordinate a rescue of Long Term Capital Management. Long Term Capital Management presumably is the kind of nonbank entity whose risk-taking activities should have been contained by creditor discipline; it is now painfully clear that this was not the case. And the Fed was clearly very concerned about the effects of its possible failure both on Long Term Capital Management's counterparties and on the systemic stability of the markets into which it would have to sell its remaining assets. It is hard to imagine a more devastating critique of the narrow-banking proposal.

Internationalizing the Banking System

A second option is internationalizing the banking system, allowing foreign banks to set up shop domestically by either opening new branches or acquiring existing financial institutions. A banking system with an internationally diversified asset base is less likely be destabilized by a downturn in domestic economic activity and to worsen that recession in turn.[17] Domestic branches of foreign banks possess their own private lenders of last resort in the form of the foreign head office. An international bank should also be able to count on last-resort lending by the central bank of the country in which the home office resides.[18] And where competent management is in short supply, foreign banks can be a channel for importing expertise, because parent banks with reputations for financial probity have an incentive to apply to their foreign branches state-of-the-art internal controls and accounting standards.

Notwithstanding these advantages, governments are reluctant to allow entry by foreign financial institutions. Seen from the perspective of an emerging market, foreign banks are large—the entire Polish banking system is smaller than one medium-sized Western European bank—raising fears that foreigners will quickly come to dominate the local market. These are issues of high political sensitivity: the domestic banking industry is a valued symbol of national economic sovereignty behind only the national currency and the national airline.

That said, it is not clear why policies that have been discredited in other contexts should still be regarded as valid when applied to banking. Rather than relying on import substitution to promote industrialization, countries now seek to facilitate technology transfer by attracting foreign direct investment (FDI). In financial services, FDI means entry into the domestic market by branches of foreign banks. Moreover, the reluctance of governments to permit foreign banks to enter the domestic market has often been based on their desire to use banks as instruments of industrial policy. Insofar as this creates more problems than it solves—as in Asia, where it encouraged connected lending and the extension of implicit guarantees— entry by foreign banks, which are less vulnerable to having their arms twisted by the government, is a way of defusing the problem.

To be sure, eliminating statutory barriers to the establishment of foreign branches and subsidiaries will not produce a seamlessly integrated global banking system overnight. Domestic banks will have developed long-standing customer relations and proprietary sources of information with which they can defend their market share. And however invigorating are

---

17. As Alan Meltzer has observed, the entire South Korean economy is barely the size of the economy of greater Los Angeles, and US regulators would hardly regard it as prudent to prevent banks based in Los Angeles from diversifying their activities into other parts of California and the United States.

18. A counterargument is that international banks have disproportionate political influence. By lobbying and enlisting the help of their home-country government, they may actually raise rather than reduce the pressure for the host-country government or central bank to provide a bailout.

the chill winds of international competition, abruptly opening domestic banking to foreign entry can be a sharp shock to previously sheltered financial institutions. In the absence of rapid regulatory action and an orderly exit policy, this sudden intensification of competition may encourage gambling for redemption and other perverse short-run responses, undermining rather than buttressing financial stability. This is an argument for phasing in the internationalization of the banking market, which in turn suggests that this solution will take time to implement.

Limiting Banks' Foreign Funding

A third option is placing taxes (implicit or explicit) or quantitative limits on banks' short-term foreign-currency borrowing. That banks are a special source of financial vulnerability is beyond dispute. Aware that the need to maintain confidence will ultimately induce the government to make good on the banks' liabilities, international investors attracted by high interest rates will be inclined to provide short-term foreign-currency funding in the expectation of being able to get their money out. At the same time, allowing banks to borrow freely short term, in foreign currency, heightens the risk of crisis, because the domestic authorities cannot print the foreign exchange needed by a lender of last resort seeking to make good on these liabilities and can pay off banks' creditors, absent unlimited reserves, only by putting the economy through a wrenching recessionary wringer.

These are rationales for limiting banks' short-term foreign-currency borrowing.[19] Emerging markets should put in place price-based incentives by keying capital requirements to the riskiness of banks' funding as well as to the riskiness of their assets. The advanced industrial countries, for their part, should agree to raise the Basle risk weights on short-term claims on banks from their excessively low 20 percent and to differentiate lending to banks in countries that merit internationally recognized accounting, regulation, and disclosure standards from lending to countries that do not. The Basle Committee's decision this past September to undertake a decennial review of the Basle Capital Accord should be used as an opportunity to implement these changes.

This approach, or at least elements of it, has already been embraced by influential members of the official community (see, e.g., Greenspan 1998b). But while relying on differential capital standards cannot hurt, it will not by itself provide much traction on the problem. On the side of the advanced industrial countries, higher capital requirements on lending

---

19. The policy implication follows directly from the so-called theory of domestic distortions. Insofar as there exist other distortions that encourage excessive offshore bank borrowing (in the form of implicit or explicit government guarantees that relieve foreign investors of default risk), welfare can be enhanced by an intervention that works in the opposite direction to reduce excessive reliance on foreign funding.

to banks, emerging-market banks in particular, will simply encourage financial institutions to channel their lending through nonbanks. They will provide credit to hedge funds or nonfinancial firms, which will then turn around and lend to emerging markets. More comprehensive revisions of the Basle Standards to attach higher weights to bank lending to hedge-fund-like entities would then be necessary. While this will help, there is reason to worry that the markets will stay one step ahead of the regulators. And on the emerging-market side, higher capital requirements will only bite if there is the prospect of bank capital actually being written down, which, as already noted, is a dubious assumption. Where there is doubt about this, more direct measures should be contemplated. Each bank could be restricted to borrowing no more than a certain percentage of its liabilities. Alternatively, the banks' total short-term foreign-currency borrowing could be limited to a certain percentage of their liabilities, and they could trade entitlements to borrow among themselves.

Again, however, discouraging offshore operations (in this case, offshore borrowing) by banks would simply encourage nonbanks to do those operations for them. Corporations could borrow offshore in foreign currency and deposit the proceeds with domestic banks, which, with their access to external funding restricted, would offer relatively attractive deposit rates; the banks could then onlend the proceeds to their domestic customers. If corporations hedged their exposure by making foreign-currency denominated deposits, the banks would end up with the same short-term foreign-currency exposure as when there were no limits on their ability to fund themselves abroad. Assuming no change in the pressure on the authorities to provide the banks with guarantees, foreigners would have the same incentive to freely supply short-term foreign-currency funding, because there would still be little question about their ability to get their money back. The vulnerabilities to which the financial system was subject would remain unchanged.[20]

Taxing Capital Inflows

The logical consequence of starting down this road is therefore a tax on all short-term foreign capital inflows (not just on inflows into the banking system) designed to offset distortions that result in excessive reliance on short-term foreign borrowing. Given the difficulty of distinguishing the term of the investment by the type of instrument, a holding-period tax that falls disproportionately on short-term investments would work better

---

20. If, on the other hand, corporations made deposits in the domestic currency, they would assume the foreign-exchange exposure and be subject to similar insolvency risk from exchange rate changes as the banks in the no-restriction scenario. It seems likely that the authorities that had previously felt impelled to extend guarantees to the banks would now extend similar support to nonbanks, having induced the latter to take on financial-intermediation responsibilities.

than a tax on specific instruments.[21] Several countries (e.g., Chile, Colombia, and Brazil) have demonstrated the feasibility of this approach. Chile, as is well known, long required all nonequity foreign capital inflows to be accompanied by a one-year, noninterest-bearing deposit, whose tax equivalent therefore declines with the duration of the investment.[22]

Chilean-style inflow taxes should be adopted by all economies with the following characteristics. First, the capacity of bank owners and managers to manage risk is underdeveloped, and the narrowness of domestic financial markets means that their mistakes can have devastating systemic repercussions. Second, supervision and regulation of the banking system is weak—in particular, regulatory forbearance is a problem. Third, inadequate auditing and accounting standards and political pressure prevent bank capital from being written down. Fourth (and, obviously, related to the previous points), there exists a culture of implicit guarantees. Under these circumstances, banks gambling for redemption or otherwise unable to manage the riskiness of their portfolios will tend to fund themselves excessively abroad, and foreigners will tend to accommodate them. Holding-period taxes on all capital inflows are the only effective way of containing this problem.

Viewing the issue this way makes clear why emerging- and mature-market economies should adopt different policies toward the capital account. The definition of an emerging market is one where a substantial subset of the preceding conditions apply. As economic and financial development proceeds, these conditions are removed, and the emerging market emerges: it graduates to the club of countries with mature financial systems. At that point, the capital-inflow tax can be safely abolished. Thus, the fact that none of today's advanced industrial economies impose Chilean-style inflow taxes, preferring to partake of the advantages of an open capital account, hardly challenges the preceding argument. There is no double standard in arguing that emerging markets, where conditions are fundamentally different, need to follow fundamentally different policies.[23]

---

21. The difficulty of discerning a correlation between the type of investment (e.g., equity investment, bond investment, direct foreign investment) and its term and maturity is a theme of Dooley (1996) and Chinn and Dooley (1998).

22. Between May 1992 and May 1998, the required deposit was 30 percent of the capital inflow. In June 1998, in response to declining copper prices and the country's growing current-account deficit, the authorities sought to attract additional foreign financing by reducing the reserve requirement from 30 to 10 percent, and in September it reduced the rate to zero. The perspective developed below suggests that this was a very risky way of attempting to finance the current account. In addition, the Chilean government applies a number of direct controls, notably by requiring foreign bond issues by local companies to have an average maturity of at least four years.

23. This approach also points to the only effective way of dealing with the problem for emerging markets posed by hedge funds, an issue that has lately been much in the news. An effective solution requires tackling the problem on both the lending- and borrowing-

Several reservations have been voiced about the advisability and effectiveness of Chilean-style taxes. One is the compatibility of the policy with financial liberalization in general and capital-account liberalization in particular. But there is a crucial distinction between controls that seek to prevent international financial transactions from taking place at any price and taxes that merely seek to correct the price for discrepancies between private and social cost.[24] Taxes are not prohibitions.[25]

The idea of taxing capital inflows is also criticized on the grounds that it will raise the cost of short-term borrowing for emerging markets. The criticism is mistaken because this is precisely what the measure is designed to do. Raising that cost will be welfare improving (so long as the tax is not excessive) when there exist other distortions like implicit guarantees that encourage excessive foreign lending.[26]

The Evidence on Chilean Capital-Inflow Taxes

A large literature has considered these issues by referring to Chile's experience.[27] Some contributors minimize the importance of the country's policy

---

country sides. On the lending-country side, supervisors need to tighten up capital requirements and other regulatory requirements on bank lending to hedge funds to prevent the those funds from acquiring excessive leverage. On the borrowing-country side, the authorities need to use Chilean-style capital-inflow taxes to make it more costly for hedge funds to get in and out of their markets.

24. Note that the same distinction applies in discussions of current account convertibility. While current-account convertibility is defined under Article VIII of the IMF's Articles of Agreement as freedom from restrictions on the making of payments and transfers for current international transactions, it does not proscribe restrictions, such as import tariffs and taxes, on the underlying transactions. Correspondingly, capital-account convertibility means the removal of exchange and other controls but does not necessarily preclude the application of tax-like instruments imposed on the underlying transaction, which agents retain the option of undertaking.

25. Theorists point out that short-term lending and borrowing is particularly valuable where information, contracting, and agency problems are most severe. In these circumstances, creditors will prefer to lend short term because the threat that they might not roll over their maturing credits can help to discipline borrowers who might otherwise be inclined to act opportunistically. It follows that short-term foreign borrowing can be especially important for poorer developing countries whose creditworthiness is impaired. Prohibiting it may mean prohibiting essentially all borrowing, which would be an unacceptable price to pay. Again, this is an argument for avoiding controls and prohibitions and instead taxing short-term foreign borrowing where government guarantees and other distortions result in excessive reliance on short-term loans.

26. Alternatively, borrowing will be excessive insofar as banks do not fully internalize the negative implications for systemic stability of their foreign borrowing, either because their own risk-management techniques are inadequate or because bank-specific funding problems have negative repercussions external to the individual bank experiencing them.

27. Two reviews and assessments of this literature are Edwards (1998a, b).

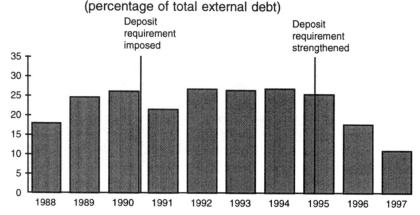

Figure 4.1 Chile's short-term external debt, 1988-97
(percentage of total external debt)

Source: Eichengreen and Mussa (1998).

of nonremunerated deposits on the grounds that it is only one of a set of initiatives adopted by the government that have helped to insulate the economy from the potentially destabilizing effects of international financial volatility. Equally important, they argue, have been measures to strengthen the supervision and regulation of the Chilean banking system and the country's relatively flexible exchange rate.

The critics are right that taxes on capital inflows alone will not solve emerging markets' financial problems. They are likely to be effective only when supplemented by other policies to encourage hedging by banks and corporations and to strengthen the domestic financial system. But upgrading financial supervision is a laborious process; it has taken Chile more than a decade to strengthen its banking system to the present point.[28] So long as banks' own risk-management techniques are underdeveloped, supervisory capacity is limited, and government guarantees are prevalent, there is an argument for capital-import taxes not as a substitute for progress in these other areas but to provide the kind of stable environment that encourages reform.

Others observe that Chile's deposit requirement has had a larger effect on the composition of inflows—shifting foreign lending toward the longer end of the maturity spectrum—than on their overall level (see figure 4.1).[29] Controlling for other determinants of capital flows and measuring

28. Calomiris (1998a) estimates that—even under the best circumstances and with the best technical assistance—upgrading risk-measurement and risk-management practices, adopting new regulations, and putting in place new supervisory procedures can take no less than five years and cites the relatively successful examples of Argentina and Chile as cases in point.

29. Cardenas and Barrera (1997) come to essentially the same conclusion in their analysis of the Colombian tax on short-term foreign capital.

the level of the tax as the ratio of tax revenues to capital inflows, Salvador Valdes-Prieto and Marcelo Soto (1997) find no impact on the level of total capital inflows but an impact on maturities, especially after 1994. That this lengthening of the maturity structure of the foreign debt is plausibly attributable to the holding-period tax is buttressed by the fact that the share of short-term debt fell significantly in a period when that same share was trending upward sharply in other countries.[30] Measuring the tax rate an entirely different way (computing it from the provisions of the statute and interest earnings on foreign funds forgone), Jose De Gregorio, Sebastian Edwards, and Rodrigo Valdes (1998) obtain the same result, namely, a significant impact on the composition of inflows but not on the level. Soto confirms the result in a multiequation model, in addition finding a small impact on the level of total inflows (1997).

That the main effect is on composition rather than the level of total capital inflows is of course hardly a devastating criticism of the tax. In fact, this is a perfectly happy result—precisely what is intended—for those who regard short-term inflows as a special problem and who see the holding-period tax as a way of offsetting other distortions encouraging excessive *short-term* borrowing abroad (see Le Fort and Budnevich 1996).

If the measure has such wonderful effects, how then are we to understand the decision of the Chilean authorities to set the unremunerated reserve requirement to zero in 1998? In fact, the Chilean authorities were actually elaborating rather than moving away from the policy: they were adjusting tax rates to the cycle. Having raised them in 1995 when large amounts of capital were flowing in and excessive short-term foreign borrowing was a problem, they now reduced them because excessive inflows to emerging markets were suddenly no longer a problem—when there was no willingness in the summer of 1998 to lend to emerging markets, short term or long.[31] As one author characterized the authorities' position, "Our tax on capital inflows is like an umbrella: you use it when it rains and close it when the rain stops" (Valdes-Prieto 1998).

In addition, supervision and regulation of the Chilean banking system has been strengthened sufficiently that it could be argued that it is no longer necessary to supplement prudential supervision with disincentives for foreign funding. But this is entirely consistent with the view that emerging markets should impose capital-import taxes as a third line of defense against financial instability until banks have upgraded their own risk-management practices and prudential supervision and regulation

---

30. De Gregorio, Edwards, and Valdes (1998) compare trends in the share of short-term debt in Chile and other emerging markets, pointing up the contrast.

31. Effective rates were raised in 1995 by requiring deposits to be made in US dollars. Previously, many investors had fulfilled the deposit requirement by depositing yen, whose interest cost was lower.

have been enhanced, at which point the measure can be removed. Chile could reduce its holding-period tax because it had made significant progress in the requisite direction.

Other critics warn that the investors will grow more adept at evading the tax over time. In Chile's case, various types of foreign borrowing were initially exempt, to which the markets responded by relabeling other investments as exempt instruments. Inflows of less than $10,000 were exempt, for example, to facilitate transfers to family members and modest trade credits; this encouraged investors to avoid the tax by breaking up larger transactions. In response, the authorities extended the coverage of the deposit requirement to virtually all forms of foreign financing other than FDI (De Gregorio, Edwards, and Valdes 1998).[32] Foreign banks then created domestic investment firms to exploit the FDI loophole; the government responded by not authorizing "financial" FDI after mid-1995.

In fact, this is precisely when the effect on maturities showed up: after the tax had been made relatively comprehensive.[33] This suggests that the measure can deliver the desired result if it is not riddled with exemptions. In any case, the Chilean tax does not have to be watertight to deliver the desired result. So long as avoidance is costly, the deposit requirement will still reduce the economy's dependence on short-term foreign borrowing.

That said, the critics have a point when they observe that financial-market participants will sooner or later devise additional ways of avoiding taxes on capital inflows, requiring the authorities to monitor private-sector behavior in increasingly invasive ways in order to maintain a given level of effectiveness.[34] To the extent that taxes on short-term inflows will not be effective forever and ultimately need to be seen as transitional measures, this makes it all the more urgent to accelerate other reforms. The authorities should use the breathing space provided by these transitional measures to eliminate the distortion that gave rise to the excessive depen-

---

32. New issues of American Depository Receipts (ADRs) remained exempt on the grounds that these, like FDI, increase the domestic stock of productive capital, although qualifying ADR issues must satisfy certain minimum rating requirements granted by internationally recognized credit-rating agencies.

33. Again, this is the finding of Valdes-Prieto and Soto (1997).

34. The obvious technique for evading the measure is for the foreign investors to purchase Chilean exports at an inflated prices and to have the exporting firm give them a share of its equity along with a put option that enables that investor to sell back that equity at a preset price. That there are costs associated with evading the tax in this way should be evident in the fact that the technique is available only to foreign importers who are also investors or to investors with close connections to them and in the fact that the courts cannot be resorted to in order to enforce such surreptitious contracts.

dence on short-term borrowing in the first place and to strengthen other forms of prudential supervision.

Conversely, Chilean-style measures toward capital inflows will be counterproductive if the authorities use the breathing space created by the tax not as an opportunity to correct imperfections in the information and contracting environment and to strengthen regulatory supervision of the banking system but as an excuse to delay in implementing reforms. It need not be this way; Chile itself is an example of a country that succeeded in wedding inflow taxes with banking-sector reform. While not all governments will be as reform minded, outside pressure can reinforce their commitment, including pressure by the IMF for its members to meet international standards for disclosure, auditing and accounting, and prudential regulation. But IMF pressure for countries using inflow taxes to complement these with accelerated reform will be effective only if the Fund acknowledges the validity of those taxes themselves.

The Importance of Not Confusing Inflow and Outflow Controls

While there is a compelling argument for taxes on short-term capital inflows as a third line of defense against excessive risk taking by domestic financial institutions (where the first and second lines of defense are banks' own risk-management practices and regulatory oversight, respectively), the case for controls on capital outflows is weaker. Given Malaysia's experiment with outflow controls and the attention it has attracted, it is important not to confuse the two arguments.

Outflow controls are less well-suited as a deterrent to excessive risk taking by bank owners and managers. They attempt to contain instability in the banking system not by preventing bank owners and managers from levering up their bets but by preventing depositors fearful of the consequences from taking flight and bringing down the banking system. They treat the symptoms, in other words, rather than the cause.

In addition, outflow controls are unlikely to be effective against pressure for devaluation except when they are aggressively enforced. A 10 percent devaluation with a 90 percent probability in the next 10 days implies an annualized return of more than 700 percent. Returns of this magnitude create powerful incentives for evasion. The government will therefore have to develop a burdensome administrative bureaucracy with the right to inspect and approve essentially all financial transactions and search travelers at the airport. This in turn creates an environment conducive to official favoritism and corruption. Chilean-style inflow taxes do not create these problems, at least not to the same extent, because inflows will not typically take place when there are expectations of a large, discrete change in the value of the currency and because they apply across the board to all financial transactions. Compared to controls and licensing require-ments, they are relatively transparent.

A different argument for outflow controls, and the one emphasized in the Malaysian context, is as a way for crisis countries to regain command of their monetary and fiscal instruments and jump-start their economic recoveries. While this book is about longer-term architectural reform, not about policy toward the crisis, it is important to be clear about these arguments so that they will not confused with those appearing elsewhere. That high capital mobility can hamstring policy in a crisis is clear. Indeed, one country after another, from Thailand, to Indonesia, to South Korea, and now to Brazil, has been forced to raise interest rates and cut govern-ment spending in the crisis—this despite suffering very serious recessions. The single greatest discovery of the Keynesian revolution, namely the importance of fiscal stabilizers, has thus been thrown out the window. Some would say this simply reflects bad advice by the IMF, which required budget cuts of the Asian crisis countries as a condition for the disbursal of official funds and which is now demanding the same of Brazil despite forecasts of recession there. But in fact, were a country, say Brazil, to respond to a slowdown in economic growth by cutting taxes and increas-ing public spending, investors would flee, the currency would crash, and the resulting investment collapse and financial distress would only make the recession worse. It seems as if market discipline is perverse. As Paul Krugman (1998c, 2) puts it, "Brazil, we are informed, must suffer a reces-sion because of its unresolved budget deficit. Huh? Since when does a budget deficit require a recession (which itself will, of course, make the deficit that much harder to bring down)."[35]

This is at least part of the rationale for the capital controls imposed by Malaysian Prime Minister Mahathir—to provide the leeway to implement a more expansionary fiscal policy and offset a potentially serious recession. Outflow controls may require the creation of a burdensome administrative bureaucracy and interrupt access to foreign sources of investment finance, but their benefits may still dominate their costs if they allow automatic fiscal stabilizers to be used in response to a serious economic downturn.

Whether this is a sensible argument hinges on which of two models of market discipline one believes. If the problem is that irrational investors panic whenever the government activates its stabilizers, then it can be sensible for countries to protect themselves from this irrationality by using controls. If, on the other hand, investors respond negatively because they

---

35. In fact, this observation that fiscal policy in developing countries tends to be perversely procyclical is not as novel as recent authors let on. Well before the current crisis, Gavin and Perotti (1997) documented that fiscal policy tends to be much more sharply procyclical in Latin America than in the OECD countries. They offered international credit constraints, which might bind more tightly in recessions than in normal periods, as one explanation for the phenomenon.

correctly anticipate that the government is about to lose all monetary and fiscal discipline, then the solution is not to use controls to relax market discipline but for the authorities to take the steps necessary to reassure investors that such fears are unwarranted. It is understandable that investors should take fright when governments with a history of fiscal laxity respond to a crisis by increasing the budget deficit; they will naturally worry that the government is about to relapse to its prior habit of living beyond its means. If they expect budget deficits to be monetized, deficits today imply inflation tomorrow and a return to the bad old days of runaway inflation. The rational investor will then respond by taking the first opportunity to get his money out of the country.

This explains the supposedly paradoxical fact that deficit spending in the United States strengthens the currency while deficit spending in Brazil weakens it. In the US case, no one expects the Fed to monetize the deficit; hence, additional government spending pushes up demand, pushes up the real interest rate, and strengthens the real exchange rate. In the Brazilian case, however, monetization is still perceived as a real and present danger, implying more inflation and ultimately the need to devalue the currency. This is also why the other textbook advice for responding to a recession, to devalue the currency and switch spending toward domestic goods, can have such catastrophic effects (particularly when devaluation is accompanied by the adoption of a more expansionary monetary policy). Many countries trying to wean themselves from inflation do so by pegging the exchange rate, which is designed to tie the hands of the central bank and to signal the government that the inflation tax will no longer be available. Countries that devalue are thus seen as returning to the bad old days of inflationary excess, which causes panicked investors to flee.

The first-best solution in this case is not to impose capital controls but to eliminate the distortions conducive to excessively expansionary monetary and fiscal policies. The most convincing way of signaling that not just current policies but also future policies will be sound and stable is to reform the economic and political arrangements by which they are made. For monetary policy this means making the central bank politically and economically independent and thereby insulating it from pressure to monetize government deficits. For fiscal policy, there are parallel arguments for creating an independent national fiscal council constitutionally empowered to set a ceiling for each year's budget deficit, along with automatic procedures specifying what will be done if deficit spending threatens to broach that limit (as proposed in Eichengreen, Hausmann, and von Hagen 1996). More modestly, fiscal reforms that vest more agenda-setting power in the hands of the prime minister or finance minister, thereby reining in the common-pool problem that arises in the presence of autonomous spending ministries (none of which has an incentive to fully internalize the impact of its additional spending on the deficit of the government as a whole), have been shown to be associated with smaller deficits and debts (see von Hagen and Harden 1994; Alesina and Perotti 1994). Similarly, measures that enhance the transparency of budgeting will make it easier for voters to detect politicians who place self-serving goals above the national interest. With these fundamental institutional reforms in place, markets will not conclude that deficits today mean deficits tomorrow or that monetary expansion today means monetary expansion tomorrow. The freedom to use fiscal and monetary instrument in countercyclical ways will be regained, and capital mobility will no longer be a constraint.

Recommending that governments should reform their monetary and fiscal institutions, strengthen their banking systems as a way of minimizing the pressure for inflationary bank bailouts, and complete other far-reaching structural reforms in order to regain control of the levers of monetary and fiscal policy is easy; actually doing so in the midst an economic and social crisis is much harder. Reform takes time, especially reform sufficient to build credibility. That said, concerted reform can restore freedom of action relatively quickly. That there are viable alternatives to draconian controls that infringe significantly on the liberty of citizens and jeopardize a country's access to international capital markets is evident in the speed with which reforms have enabled Thailand and South Korea to substantially regain their policy autonomy. Both succeeded in bringing down interest rates and in loosening their fiscal policies once it became clear that reform was under way. This is the first-best way of relaxing the external constraint on domestic policies. To say that an economic emergency such as the current crisis in emerging markets justifies the use of emergency controls on outflows such as Malaysia's is an admission that the political will to follow through with more fundamental reforms is not there.

5

Bailing in the Private Sector

A particular concern of many critics of the existing international financial architecture is that official support has been used to bail out investors. In Mexico in 1995, South Korea in 1997, and Russia in 1998, official funds were used to repurchase and retire short-term debts. Having benefited from high interest rates while their money was in place, creditors were protected from losses when it came time to sell. The moral hazard thereby created provided an obvious incentive to engage in even less prudent lending, setting the stage for still larger crises and still larger bailouts. It would be better from a public-policy standpoint were international investors and banks in particular forced to "take a hit."

The Mexican crisis illustrates the problem. The Mexican government entered its crisis at the end of 1994 with some $28 billion of short-term government obligations indexed to foreign currency (*tesobonos*) about to mature but only $6 billion of international reserves. Once confidence was lost, no investor had an incentive to make available additional foreign exchange. Had international assistance not been provided, Mexico would have been forced to suspend redemption of these debts, risking significant damage to its creditworthiness. Instead, the government used its US and IMF loans to retire its *tesobonos* at full value as they matured.

In South Korea the mechanism was more complex but the result was the same. Foreign creditors who had extended short-term loans to South Korean banks attempted to withdraw their balances all at once. Those short-term credits far exceeded the government's international reserves. The Bank of Korea's reserves fell from $31 billion at end October 1997 to $21 billion at the end of December, with more than half of this latter amount immobilized as deposits with foreign branches of domestic banks (see IMF 1998a, box II.5). Figures vary for the short-term foreign-currency obligations of the South Korean financial sector, but one seemingly reliable estimate puts them at about $26 billion in December (Shin and Hahm 1998, table 1.7).[1] Had no official assistance arrived, the South Korean authorities would have been forced to declare a moratorium. Instead, the US- and IMF-led loan enabled the government to inject more credit into the banking system, deposit more reserves at overseas branches of South Korean banks, and keep interest rates lower than would have been possible otherwise, while maturing foreign credits were paid back in full. The result was to replace a significant share of those credits with official funds.[2]

The rationale for the South Korean package, in security circles at least, was that the Korean Peninsula is too important geopolitically for the South's economy to be left unaided. Similar arguments were made about Indonesia, which sits astride some of the world's most important ocean shipping lines. Russia being "Indonesia with nukes," the South Korean and Indonesian precedents gave investors confidence that Russia would receive similar assistance. This rhetoric may seem exaggerated, but the fact of the matter is that in the wake of the IMF's Asian support programs the international investors who poured money into Russia referred to positions in Russian GKOs (treasury bills) as the "moral-hazard play." There were sizable inflows into Russia in the months following the Asian rescue packages, followed by financial difficulties, a crisis, and a new IMF disbursement in the summer of 1998. As events transpired, the Russian government devalued and suspended service on most of its debts. But these actions came as a surprise to many investors, which is the point in the present context.

In practice, not all investors have been shielded from losses. In Mexico, *tesobono* prices tumbled before it became clear that the Mexican government would be able to retire them, and many investors who scrambled out of the market did so at a loss. In neither Mexico nor Asia did official support avert major declines in equity and real estate prices, and investors in these markets incurred extensive losses. None of this is to deny that existing arrangements for handling crises are deficient but to caution that

---

1. South Korean financial institutions had foreign-currency denominated assets as well, because they were required to limit their open foreign-exchange positions. But because their loans were of longer maturity than their liabilities, there was still a liquidity problem that the central bank was in no position to address.

2. At that point, the number and exposure of the foreign bank creditors was reduced to the point where the South Korean authorities were able to negotiate a restructuring with their bank creditors, in which the latter agreed to a temporary delay in payments and then to the conversion of their short-term assets into longer-term instruments.

one should not exaggerate the extent to which investors have been shielded.

The real dilemma is that presented by bank creditors. Foreign funding of domestic banks in the form of deposits and deposit-like instruments is highly liquid. Deposits have a fixed face value. Banks being key to the stability of a country's payments and credit system, governments are reluctant to contemplate treatment of these claims that might threaten their provision. These facts make it extremely difficult to write down foreign claims on domestic banks. It would be nice if foreign bank creditors would agree to reschedule and write down their claims. But so long as they have the option of fleeing and bringing down the banking system in their wake, governments will contemplate this option only in extremes.[3]

The Need for Architectural Reform

If the tendency for official support to shield creditors from losses and to encourage imprudent investor behavior were not sufficient grounds for concern, there is also the question of whether international assistance as currently constituted can protect the recipients from serious damage. All too often, IMF-led rescues are ineffective in containing a panic because the Fund's resources are limited and doled out a drop at a time.[4] Because official support tends to be even less than meets the eye, countries receiving international assistance and trying to avoid a debt moratorium have to hike interest rates to both lure back foreign investors and satisfy the Fund.[5]

This raises the question of why governments are so willing to put their economies through the wringer. Why, in other words, do they hesitate to suspend payments and then negotiate with the creditors to restructure the debt? Doing so would certainly discourage imprudent lending. More important, governments could avoid putting their economies through

---

3. Thus, the South Korean negotiations at the end of 1997 are often cited as examples of how international banks should be bailed in during crisis negotiations. Again, however, the fact of the matter is that so long as the South Korean government was reluctant to halt service on these and other external debts, the banks still had the option of exiting. The IMF, for its part, may have been reluctant to insist on haircuts for the banks for fear of inciting a rush out of other assets and other countries. In the end, the agreement reached with the government of South Korea did not impose significant capital losses on the banks, which only agreed to a delay of service payments and, eventually, to the conversion of their short-term claims into longer-term obligations.

4. In chapter 7, I argue that this is inevitably the case and that schemes to change the international financial architecture by creating a "true international lender of last resort" are not feasible.

5. The international community committed $57 billion to Korea, for example, but released only $13.2 billion by the time the crisis there reached its height. Radelet and Sachs (1998b, 66-67).

the wrenching deflationary consequences of the adjustment required for the maintenance of external debt service.

The option is shunned because governments, and the international policy community as well, regard the collateral damage as too severe. Countries that suspend payments and attempt to restructure find it difficult and costly to reach an agreement with their creditors. Their reputations are damaged. They find it harder to borrow subsequently. In addition, there is the fear, well-founded or not, that a standstill or moratorium will unleash contagion to other countries and threaten the stability of the international system. However expedient the short-run policy, most governments and the IMF regard the long-term consequences as unsupportable.[6]

Thus, bailing in the private sector—ensuring that private investors take a hit—presupposes changes in institutional and contractual arrangements that make it palatable for governments to declare a moratorium and restructure their debts. It requires changes in the international financial architecture.

It is important to emphasize that there is unlikely to be a simple solution to this problem. A moratorium on repayment *should* be unattractive; otherwise, the sanctity of loan contracts would be jeopardized. Contracts and institutional arrangements are structured to make the suspension of debt service painful precisely in order to keep borrowers from walking away from their debts.[7] And there are good reasons why the IMF cannot be transformed into an international bankruptcy court with the power to cram down settlement terms.

Moreover, getting the banks to contribute new money to packages for crisis countries, or even to roll over maturing credits, is easier said than

---

6. There are exceptions to the rule—in other words, governments that have overcome this reluctance to suspend payments and restructure: Mexico in 1982, South Africa in 1985, Brazil in 1987, Venezuela in 1988, and Russia in 1998. Several distinctive aspects of the Russian situation help to explain why it is the most recent addition to this list of exceptions. For one, the fact that Russia, unlike say Mexico and South Korea, did not show the resolve necessary to rein in its budget deficit suggested that providing official funds to retire the existing short-term debt would not solve the problem, because additional debt would soon have to be issued; thus, international support was halted. For another, the Russian government's failure to make headway on its fiscal problems suggested that capital-market access was in any case unlikely to be maintained, which eliminated the most important incentive to continue payments. Be that as it may, the aftermath of the Russian government's action, including a full-fledged depositor panic, capital flight, and the suspension of foreign-exchange trading, hardly reassures those worried that a government's unilateral suspension of payments could damage its creditworthiness and demoralize the markets.

7. By strengthening the "bonding" role of debt, this then reduces the cost of borrowing and encourages financial transactions. Without penalties for default, in other words, the credit market will not function. Lenders will not lend, and borrowers will not be able to borrow. This point is powerfully made in the international context by Bulow and Rogoff (1989).

done. There has been much glib talk about how the banks should somehow be compelled or required to contribute, without corresponding hard thought about how exactly this might be done. Banks extend short-maturity loans for good reasons, namely because they value the security and liquidity that short-term lending entails. While one can ask them to extend longer-term, less-liquid loans, absent other changes in policy and market conditions, they are unlikely to provide a compliant answer. One can ask them to contribute additional credit lines to supplement official resources, but, as in Brazil at the end of 1998, they will have an irresistible incentive to hold off and see how things develop. One can ask them to roll over their maturing loans, as in South Korea at the end of 1997, but even this is likely to succeed only when conditions are right—that is, when only a handful of creditors are involved, when there is essentially only one debtor with whom to negotiate (in South Korea, the government, which had already moved to guarantee the banks' foreign debts), and when there is a newly elected president with a reformist mandate. All these are reasons for questioning whether what was successfully done in South Korea can be done again.

Notwithstanding the difficulty of the problem, limited steps can be taken to more effectively bail in the private sector—to see that private investors do not get off scot-free. These fall under two headings: ex ante measures to be taken before the crisis, and ex post measures to influence how it plays out.

Ex Ante Measures

Two classes of measures can be considered under this heading: measures to discourage bank-to-bank lending and the extension of standby lines of credit. The first is likely to be more effective than the second.

Discouraging Short-Term Borrowing

The most direct way to avoid letting foreign creditors off scot-free is to not borrow from them in the first place. This is not meant sarcastically. Short-term inflows, and the short-term inflows into the banking system in particular, pose a special problem because they are so liquid, allowing those extending them to scramble for the exits. They pose a special problem because the institutions dependent on them are central to financial stability. The need to preserve the stability of the banking system thus makes it hard to impose on its creditors a share of the adjustment burden. This provides an argument for discouraging excessive reliance on short-term foreign credits to the banking system in the first place. It is an argument for raising the Basle risk weights for foreign bank lending and for keying those weights to the source of banks' funding as well as the riskiness of their investments. In markets where political pressure prevents capital from being written down, it is an argument for taxes or quantitative ceilings on short-term foreign funding. Where nonfinancial firms can do the borrowing and pass the proceeds on to financial intermediaries, it is an argument for using measures such as those employed by Chile, whose government, while applying a tax to all capital inflows, structured it so that it falls most heavily on short-term inflows. If administered successfully, such measures would increase foreign portfolio investors' reliance on stocks, bonds, and other long-term instruments, on which they would automatically suffer losses in the event of a financial crisis.[8]

Negotiating Standby Lines of Credit

A second approach would be for governments to negotiate standby lines of credit with commercial banks. Foreign banks would agree to make these credit lines available in return for a commitment fee. Because foreign bank creditors would no longer be able to eliminate their exposure to the country in question, proponents of this approach argue, they would be predisposed to negotiate a restructuring plan. In addition, from the standpoint of the borrowing countries, these credit lines would provide additional resources to insure against shocks to investor confidence. Both Argentina and Mexico have negotiated facilities with international banks that omit the no-adverse-material-change clause that typically permits commercial banks to back out of an agreement in the event of a crisis.[9] They have succeeded in doing so despite the fact that neither country enjoys an investment-grade sovereign credit rating. Their success in doing so suggests that at least some other countries could do the same.

The main weakness of these arrangements is that the banks will be able to hedge their exposures. At the same time they provide additional credits, they can draw down their other exposure to the country or sell short government bills and bonds. Taken to an extreme, this "dynamic-hedging" argument suggests the country will have no additional financial resources for propping up its banking system and coping with the other consequences of a crisis.

---

8. The first three words of this last sentence are an important caveat, one that is addressed in the final part of chapter 4.

9. The Argentine facility is illustrative. Its contingent repurchase facility with 13 commercial banks provides for $7 billion in standby credits (the equivalent of about 10 percent of bank deposits), while Mexico's arrangement with 31 banks provides for $2.5 billion. Under the provisions of the former, the Argentine Central Bank can swap Argentine government securities for US dollars up to the specified ceiling, at an effective interest rate of LIBOR plus 205 basis points. The commitment fee is 33 basis points. Loan length is two to five years, depending on the commercial bank involved.

Recent evidence casts at least some doubt on the extreme version of the story. Mexico drew on its contingent credit line in September 1998 when it was about to expire and it became evident that the banks were reluctant to renew it. One is led to ask why, if dynamic hedging is so easy and efficient, the banks were so reluctant to renew their credit lines. The answer must be that there are costs of dynamic hedging, in response to which the banks anticipated being able to hedge their exposures less than fully. But the other side of the same coin is that the banks, finding it difficult or costly to hedge their exposure, will be reluctant to extend standby lines of credit to countries with a serious prospect of drawing on them.

Thus, while commercial credit lines are not a bad idea, they are likely to be available only to a select few countries with relatively strong policies, and the amount of money they actually make available may be less than meets the eye. For both reasons, then, the burden will necessarily fall on ex post measures.

Ex Post Measures

The most important changes that can be made to bail in the private sector after the fact are the incorporation of new clauses into loan contracts. This section considers the cases of bonds and bank loans in turn. It then discusses IMF lending into arrears and the establishment of standing committees of creditors.

New Provisions in Loan Contracts

International banks account for so much lending to emerging markets because they have well-developed capacities to gather information about foreign borrowers and have developed long-term relationships with their clients, which provide leverage when it comes time to collect on loans.[10] That said, changes in technology and market organization suggest that securitized instruments (bonds and derivative instruments based upon them) will account for a growing fraction of international lending over time. Improvements in information and communications technologies tend to undermine the informational advantage of banks. Advances in financial technology enable individual investors to unbundle and hedge credit and currency risks. Securitization has made considerable strides in the advanced industrial countries, where observers regularly speak of the

---

10. Some observers would add that because banks are critical to financial stability, they can count on the support of the United States and other creditor-country governments in the event of debt-servicing difficulties.

shrinking market for banking services. Even if they have not already, one can uncontroversially predict that bonds will account for a growing share of portfolio investments in emerging markets in years to come.

This technological revolution encouraging international lending to flow through bond markets rather than banks is surely a good thing on balance. Insofar as it reflects improvements in the information environment that render the market less dependent on banks as vehicles for surmounting informational obstacles, it implies a more efficient allocation of resources. And insofar as emerging-market debt becomes less concentrated in the hands of the major money-center banks, it leaves the latter less crisis prone.

But like many good things, the securitization of emerging-market debt does not come without costs. Securitization means a significant increase in the number of creditors, small creditors in particular, aggravating collective-action problems.[11] Restructuring a sovereign bond issued in the United States (or under the legal provisions that govern bonds issued in that country) typically requires the unanimous consent of the bondholders, which can be a formidable hurdle. No bondholder can be forced to agree to new terms by other bondholders, and each bondholder can sue the issuer. A successful lawsuit could trigger cross-default clauses in the country's other external instruments, in turn activating acceleration clauses requiring that debt to be immediately repaid. Unlike syndicated bank loans, bonds lack sharing clauses that require individual creditors to share any amounts recovered with other bondholders and thereby discouraging recourse to lawsuits. There are no counterparts to the central banks and regulators that used their powers of moral suasion to encourage cooperative behavior by the members of commercial bank syndicates in the 1980s.[12] Neither do sovereign issuers have recourse to a bankruptcy filing, under which they would be protected from the threat of lawsuits and in the context of which terms could be imposed on minority creditors.

Agreement being difficult to reach, issuers are understandably reluctant to contemplate restructuring. And in the event they do, "vultures" (offshore hedge funds or large individual investors) then have an incentive to purchase bonds from less patient investors and to threaten lawsuits against the debtor. Wishing to avoid expensive and embarrassing litiga-

---

11. Stein's (1989) finding that bank creditors are more likely than bondholders to support corporate debt workouts negotiated in the shadow of the court is consistent with this implication. Miller and Zhang (1997) provide some theoretical and numerical evidence designed to show that this is precisely the consequence of the switch from bank to bond finance.

12. To be sure, a nonnegligible fraction of foreign bonds are held by commercial banks. And pension funds, mutual funds, and insurance companies are also subject to regulatory oversight, if not always with the same intensity as banks. But institutional investors as a group hold only a fraction of the bonds outstanding, in contrast to the earlier situation with syndicated bank loans, rendering moral suasion less effective.

tion, the debtor may then feel compelled to buy them out at full price. Taken to the extreme, this suggests that maverick creditors will buy up all the defaulted debt and litigate to prevent sovereign issuers from settling for less than 100 cents on the dollar. Restructuring that involves writing down principal and interest will then be impossible.

One need not subscribe to this extreme version of the argument to see that the provisions governing the issuance of sovereign bonds greatly complicate renegotiation and restructuring.[13] It is hardly a mystery that under present arrangements, governments are reluctant to go this route.

Fortunately, a solution is at hand, having been suggested in 1996 by the G-10 in its report, *Resolving Sovereign Liquidity Crises*, and having been echoed in recent G-22 and G-7 declarations.[14] Nearly three years ago, G-10 deputies recommended making it easier to undertake negotiations by altering the provisions of loan contracts to include majority-voting, sharing, and nonacceleration clauses.[15] This would discourage maverick investors from resorting to lawsuits and other ways of obstructing settlements beneficial to the debtor and the vast majority of creditors. To their recommendations one might add the idea of minimum thresholds for creditor lawsuits, requiring that a certain minimum percentage of creditors, say 10 or 25 percent, would be required for legal action to be taken against the creditor.[16] The addition of such clauses to bond contracts is the only practical way of creating an environment conducive to flexible restructuring negotiations. It is infinitely more realistic than advocating some kind of supranational bankruptcy court empowered to cram down settlement terms.

---

13. Evidence against the extreme view can be drawn from four recent cases where countries succeeded in restructuring their sovereign bonds through unilateral exchange offers: Costa Rica in 1985, Nigeria in 1988, Guatemala in 1989, and Panama in 1993. In all these cases, the vast majority of bondholders, typically more than 90 percent, exchanged their old debt obligations for new ones rather than selling out to vultures (Pinon-Farah 1996). It can be questioned whether these cases are representative, however, since the terms of the exchange implied little reduction of interest or principal, only a grace period, longer maturities, and unbunching of payments.

14. These documents are G-10 (1996), G-22 (1998c), and G-7 (1998), respectively.

15. In the case of most international bonds, 10 to 25 percent of the bondholders (more precisely, those holding 10 to 25 percent of the principal) can vote to require immediate repayment of all principal and interest due in the event of default. In contrast, syndicated bank loans typically require 50 percent of creditors to vote for acceleration. This therefore raises the danger that even when a majority of bondholders prefer an orderly workout that will maximize the value of their claims, an impatient minority can trigger the clause requiring immediate repayment. The debtor would then have to reschedule not only interest payments and amounts due to be paid into a sinking fund but all principal as well.

16. Note the parallel with the minimum percentages that already exist for activating acceleration clauses.

A further advantage of these changes is that they would make it easier for governments to obtain forbearance from their creditors before the fact—to get them to roll over maturing loans instead of forcing a disruptive default. Under present circumstances, if a government seeks to induce foreign bondholders to convert their maturing securities into longer-term bonds by halting (or modifying) repayment of the old obligations, it runs the risk of investor lawsuits. This is the problem with the strategy attempted by the IMF to bail in private investors in Ukraine, where it told the government that it would violate a condition of its Fund program if it repaid investors in a maturing bond issue. Although some three-quarters of bondholders reportedly agreed to convert their maturing bonds into longer-term eurobonds, a minority threatened lawsuits capable of triggering cross-default and acceleration clauses. New contractual provisions would ameliorate this problem.

Some object that such provisions, by making it easier for developing countries to wriggle out of debt contracts, would increase borrowing costs (Institute of International Finance 1996). For those who believe that moral hazard and other market imperfections cause governments to rely excessively on foreign borrowing, this is not undesirable. In practice, however, there are grounds to question whether borrowing costs will in fact rise.[17] Majority voting, sharing, and nonacceleration may make it easier to renegotiate defaulted debts, but if this permits a long deadlock to be avoided and renders the majority of investors better off, there is no reason why they should shun bonds with these features. Small bondholders, who lack the resources to sue, would be rendered better off if such clauses averted a long period when interest was not paid and bond prices were depressed while the government and maverick creditors fought their war of attrition. Institutional investors might be better off if in the absence of this market-based solution they came under pressure from their governments to cut a deal.

It is important to understand that the normal presumption that "if we see it, it must be optimal" is questionable in the present context. Those who argue that the prohibition on majority voting to restructure the terms of a loan is the market's way of strengthening the bonding role of debt are ignorant of the measure's history. The law was introduced not by a market-driven process but by individuals deeply suspicious of the market. William O. Douglas championed it in the wake of the debt defaults of the early 1930s as one of a number of laws to protect small investors from

_____

17. At this point, there is little evidence of whether or not this is the case. While the Hong Kong Airport Authority is frequently invoked as an example of a borrower that has issued bonds with these provisions without obviously elevating its borrowing costs, it is not a fully sovereign entity, rendering it a special case. A more systematic analysis of the pricing of bonds issued under the UK and US models (with and without the relevant provisions) is clearly called for.

victimization by securities houses. This peculiar history underscores that there is no necessary reason to retain these archaic measures. So does the fact that bonds issued under the provisions of the laws of the United Kingdom, a country lacking this one's populist tradition, have provisions more friendly to renegotiation. There, bondholders are represented by a trustee and cannot sue individually.[18] British bonds also provide for the binding of all bondholders by a majority vote at a bondholders meeting.

According to the G-10's 1996 report, new provisions can be introduced into debt instruments through a "market-led process." Governments are to trumpet the virtues of new clauses but to otherwise take no action. They are to hope that the markets would see the light.

But if changes in contracts were so easily adopted, the markets would have done so already. That no progress has in fact occurred suggests that there are significant obstacles to market-driven reform. One is the adverse signaling effect. If only some issuers include qualified-majority-voting clauses in their loan agreements, creditors may suspect that those debtors anticipate having to restructure in the not-too-distant future. The clause will be regarded as a negative signal that the borrower is less than fully committed to servicing the loan, much like a bridegroom's request for a prenuptial agreement. As Mark Roe emphasizes, this can allow inefficient arrangements, put in place for historical reasons long past, to become locked in.[19]

The G-10 report, perhaps in a desire to look market friendly, said little about this dilemma. At one point it acknowledged the first-mover problem and suggested that official support for contractual innovation should be provided "as appropriate," but it failed to elaborate. The G-22 and G-7 reports reluctantly acknowledge this fact but again fail to commit to specific action. The G-22 recommends that unnamed governments, but presumably those of the United States and the other major creditor countries, "examine" the use of such clauses in their own sovereign bond issues. The G-7 recommends that its members "consider" them. They need to do more than examine and consider. Without the introduction of actual legislation and regulations in the creditor countries, progress on this front is unlikely.

One way of pushing it ahead would be for the IMF to urge its members to add majority-voting, sharing, nonacceleration, minimum-legal-threshold, and collective-representation clauses (where these last provisions make provision for an indenture trustee to represent and coordinate the bondholders) to all international bonds as a condition for their being admitted to domestic markets. It should provide an incentive for countries

---

18. Although a specified minority holding a fifth to a quarter of principal can require the trustee to do so on their behalf.

19. This path-dependence argument is a theme of Roe (1987).

to do so by indicating that it is prepared to lend at more attractive interest rates to countries that issue debt securities featuring these provisions. US and UK regulators, for their part, could make the admission of international bonds to their markets a function of whether those bonds contain the relevant sharing, majority-voting, minimum-legal-threshold, and collective-representation provisions.

To be sure, this is no panacea. Private placements would not be affected. New provisions could be added to existing loans only through a voluntary exchange of old bonds for new ones. Not only might some bondholders resist, but any one country that attempted to be the first to carry out the exchange might be seen as signaling that it was contemplating imminent default and precipitate a crisis.

All this means the incorporation of sharing, majority-voting, nonacceleration, and minimum-legal-threshold provisions into bond covenants will be slow. But slow progress is better than no progress.

New Provisions for Bank Credits

Short-term credits extended by one bank to another are a more difficult case. Because interbank loans are not governed by formal contracts, renegotiation cannot be eased by altering contractual provisions. Some commentators have suggested that this can be gotten around if countries adopt laws limiting the terms and conditions under which short-term loans to their banks can be repatriated. Robert Litan and his coauthors urge countries to enact legislation imposing an automatic reduction of the principal of all foreign-currency loans extended to banks in their countries that are not rolled over in the event of a crisis (see Litan et al. 1998). Foreign creditors could get still out, but only at a loss. The prospect of that loss would strengthen their incentive to stick around, to address their collective-action problem, and to restructure the debt.

If this legislation is only passed when the crisis strikes, such initiatives have no advantage vis-à-vis current arrangements. Nothing now prevents countries from freezing or writing down foreign loans to their banks, as Russia did. In any case, governments' own behavior suggests that they fear that freezing bank claims would provoke flight out of other assets by foreign and domestic investors, forcing the imposition of across-the-board exchange controls.[20] They regard this as too damaging to their reputations for financial probity and to their countries' ability to borrow.

If the idea is that such legislation should be adopted in advance of a crisis, then the measure is likely to be much more demoralizing to lenders

---

20. Indeed, the Russian action freezing foreign credits on 17 August 1998 dried up all credit to the Russian financial system, provoked widespread capital flight, and forced the government to halt all foreign-exchange trading several times in the final week of August.

than the addition of majority-voting clauses to bond covenants. If new clauses are added to bond covenants, the decision to halt interest payments will still be in the hands of the individual corporate, financial, or governmental borrower. The write-down of principal will be determined on a case-by-case basis in negotiations between the debtor and its creditors. In contrast, the obligatory haircut for foreign bank creditors would apply across the board. Foreign creditors would be especially alarmed if, as is likely, the circumstances under which the new law was triggered were left to the government's discretion. If the trigger were the announcement of an IMF program, on the other hand, the merest hint that a government was exploring the possibility of obtaining help from the Fund would provoke flight by its foreign bank creditors, precisely the outcome that the measure was intended to avert. More generally, foreign bank creditors worried about a mandatory haircut will be tempted to flee at the first sign of trouble. Once the provision is triggered, of course, they will have an incentive to stay in, but imagine their incentive to get out before the trigger is pulled. This perverse effect has the potential to transform small crises into big ones. Then there is the familiar "after you, Alphonse" problem: no country will want to be first to pass such legislation for fear of signaling that it is worried about an impending crisis. Finally, foreign banks are likely to respond to the measure by channeling their lending through the offshore branches of the debtor's banks. Creditors would then dispute the applicability of the developing-country law and appeal to their own courts in the effort to attach the assets of those offshore branches.

For all these reasons, the best way of dealing with the special problem created by short-term bank-to-bank lending is to discourage excessive reliance on this form of funding in the first place.

IMF Lending into Arrears

IMF policy through most of the 1980s was to lend to countries that had fallen into arrears on their external debts only after they had reached an agreement in principle with their creditors. The notion was that the Fund should provide assistance only if the banks contributed to burden sharing by at least clearing away the country's arrears.[21] Eventually, however, experience with the debt crisis raised doubts about this approach. The banks, their balance sheets strengthening as they drew down their Latin American exposure, hardened their positions. Rather than the policy providing the IMF with a lever to encourage burden sharing by the banks, the banks realized that they could use it as a club in their battle with governments. If countries refused to settle on favorable terms, the banks

---

21. The traditional IMF position on lending into arrears was stated in an Executive Board decision in 1970 (see Cline 1996).

could veto new IMF money in addition to denying their own, a fact that the banks learned to use to their advantage.

In the late 1980s, in a departure from past practice, the IMF therefore contributed to the pool of money used to retire nonperforming bank debts and replace them with Brady bonds. Since 1989 the Fund has had a de facto policy of providing support for a member's adjustment effort after the emergence of arrears but before an agreement had been reached between the debtor and its creditors, so long as the country in question was engaged in good-faith negotiations and making a serious effort to adjust. In more than three dozen instances the IMF has lent in support of adjustment programs before a member has cleared away its arrears to commercial banks. Lending into arrears can provide working capital for an economy that is making an adjustment effort and—analogous to the debtor-in-possession financing provided under US corporate bankruptcy procedures—avert unnecessary damage to its economy. Insofar as collective-action problems, exacerbated by rules requiring the unanimous assent of creditors to the terms of any restructuring plan, render negotiations between governments and their creditors excessively protracted, IMF support to a country in arrears can help to bring creditors to the bargaining table.[22] Insofar as sovereign debtors and the international community generally see the temporary suspension of payments, followed by negotiations to restructure, as too difficult and costly to pursue, it may then be desirable for the IMF to tip the balance in this way, opening up debtor-creditor negotiations as a viable alternative to regular IMF rescues.

The G-10's 1996 report acknowledged that lending into arrears was a way for the IMF to expedite restructuring and asked the Fund to consider extending the policy from commercial bank loans to bonded debts (G-10 1996).[23] The IMF's Executive Board subsequently agreed that it will consider doing so "under carefully designed conditions and on a case-by-case basis," so long as that lending was essential to the member's adjustment program and it was making a good-faith effort to negotiate a settlement

---

22. Goldstein (1996) argues that the Fund's lending into arrears was critical for driving commercial bank creditors to the negotiating table in the late 1980s and finally clearing away the Latin American debt crisis.

23. Spokesmen for the creditors responded that lending into arrears may have been appropriate in the 1980s, when the existence of a generalized debt crisis justified the provision of public-sector enhancements to support debt reduction arrangements, but that it is not warranted in "normalized" capital-market conditions (Institute of International Finance 1996). Recent experience casts doubt on this contention on two grounds: first, even normalized conditions can quickly become abnormal; and second, even if debt problems are limited in geographical scope, the provision of the equivalent of debtor-in-possession financing by the IMF may be important for preventing the kind of complete economic breakdown that can set the stage for the contagious spread of the crisis and can help to expedite a negotiated agreement to restructure.

(Camdessus 1998a).[24] And the G-7 now has urged the Fund "to move ahead, under carefully designed conditions and on a case by case basis" (notice the pattern), in implementing the policy (G-7 1998, 4).

Its feasibility has yet to be established. In particular, there is the risk that creditors might sue in an effort to attach the proceeds of the loan. While private debtors can seek shelter from a lawsuit in the bankruptcy court, sovereign debtors have no such recourse. If the creditors are commercial banks, they will be subject to moral suasion by their central banks and regulators and are unlikely to seek to attach IMF assets in this way.[25] But if they are bondholders, as will increasingly become the case as securitization proceeds, the danger is greater. The fear if not yet the reality of lawsuits is real.

Perhaps IMF balances could be transferred from the Fund's accounts to the central bank in question and the courts would recognize the central bank as a legally separate entity from the government and therefore not deem it responsible for the latter's debts.[26] Perhaps attempts to attach loan proceeds before the Fund has disbursed them would be rejected by the courts on the grounds that Article IX.8(I) of its Articles of Agreement makes the IMF immune from legal process.[27] Perhaps the courts could be swayed by a brief filed by a creditor-country government arguing against attaching IMF resources. Perhaps the creditors, knowing that they would have to do battle with the US government and the IMF, would be reluctant to throw down the gauntlet.[28]

That said, what will happen is uncertain. This has prompted discussions of whether Article VIII.2(b) of the Fund's Articles of Agreement should be amended to give official status to a country's standstill of payments and to shelter its government and any IMF resources lent into arrears from legal action. Article VIII.2(b) allows countries to apply exchange controls in response to balance of payments problems without violating

---

24. See also the comments of IMF Managing Director Michel Camdessus at his joint press conference with Philippe Maystadt, chairman of the Interim Committee, at IMF Headquarters, 16 April 1998, http://www.imf.org/external/np/tr/1998/TR980416.htm.

25. During the debt crisis of the 1980s, when the principal creditors were international banks, lawsuits were consequently rare (except for precautionary suits filed to protect against expiration of the statute of limitations). However, when Argentina defaulted on some of its bonds in 1986, three bondholders sued successfully in US courts. And when Panama defaulted in 1987, at least one bondholder pressed a lawsuit.

26. When it is not waived, central bank reserves enjoy sovereign immunity in the major financial centers, notably the United States and the United Kingdom.

27. In addition, the Fund's articles require it to deal with members only through their treasuries, central banks, and fiscal authorities. Thus, it could argue that it cannot deal directly with a court-appointed receiver or with the creditors' fiscal agent.

28. That there have been no attempts to date to attach Fund disbursements is consistent with this view.

their obligations to the IMF. That article would have to be given an authoritative reinterpretation by the Fund's executive directors or more likely be amended with the consent of countries commanding 80 percent of the Fund's voting power for it to give sanction to a standstill on external debt as opposed to the imposition of exchange controls.

It is unlikely that the requisite majority would agree to vest such powers in the hands of an international organization. Not only would market participants oppose empowering the Fund to interfere so extensively with private debt contracts, but the Fund would not be seen as possessing the impartiality and detachment of a bankruptcy judge. Among other things, it might have made loans to the country itself. Clearly, any proposal to amend Article VIII.2(b) to empower the Fund to declare a standstill would be rejected as soon as it was considered on Capitol Hill.

Fortunately, there exist alternatives. One is a limited amendment to the Fund's Articles of Agreement in which its members agree to give immunity in their national courts to the Fund's own disbursements and transactions. This could be done by each IMF member country in a manner consistent with national legal traditions and precedents without requiring domestic prerogatives to be ceded to an international entity. Another would be for countries to amend their own sovereign immunities laws to allow their courts to stay attempts to attach sovereign assets (Hurlock 1995). In the United States and United Kingdom, creditors are already prevented from attaching certain sovereign assets even when the sovereign has waived its immunity, as is commonly the practice when governments float international bonds. It would be desirable for these countries to clarify these provisions and for other countries to emulate them.

Standing Committees of Creditors

A final change in the international architecture to bail in the private sector would be to create standing committees of creditors. Restructuring negotiations are most difficult and protracted when information is least complete. Where the preferences and capacities of all parties are common information, agreement should be immediate.[29] The more asymmetric the information environment, the more likely are debtors and creditors to fight a lengthy war of attrition. Establishing a standing committee of representatives of the various classes of creditors—bondholders, banks, hedge funds, and the like—would open lines of communication and help to overcome information problems.

---

29. This is a basic premise of bankruptcy theory: in a world of complete information and absent transactions costs, there is no need for a bankruptcy code or bankruptcy court, because debtors and creditors will be able to instantaneously adjust their contracts to any unanticipated contingencies.

A standing creditors' committee would thus reduce transactions costs in times of crisis. When a crisis erupts and debt service is halted, negotiations cannot proceed until the creditors have been identified, which is time-consuming when the process starts from scratch. The existence of a representative committee in continuous contact with its constituents would ease this difficulty. Next, the debtor must decide with whom to negotiate—that is, who speaks for the creditors? The existence of a standing committee would provide the answer to this question in advance. Finally, there is the need to gain the assent of a majority of creditors to the restructuring plan and to buy out those who refuse. The existence of a standing committee on which various classes of creditors interact would create peer pressure for agreement and facilitate the extension of any required side payments. This last point is important: these committees would offer only nonbinding recommendations to the bondholders, who would then have the right to accept them or reject them. They would play much the same role as bank advisory committees in the syndicated-bank debt crisis of the 1980s.

The difficulties created by the absence of these committees are apparent in recent experience. In South Korea, for example, the problem in the last week of 1997 was to get the banks to roll over their maturing short-term loans, to accept a delay in interest payments, and to agree to the principle of converting those short-term credits into long-term loans. The South Korean government and the banks reached that agreement by the skin of their teeth. With the help of Bill Rhodes's Rolodex, the relevant bankers were located, pulled from their Christmas dinners, and thrust into negotiations.[30] The existence of a committee infrastructure would have considerably eased the process. Russia's experience in August 1998 following its suspension of payments similarly illustrates the confusion that can arise when there exists no committee of creditors (Reuters 1998). First, the Russian authorities met with a small group of Russian and foreign banks to discuss the formation of a creditors' committee. Next, it was decided that the committee would be formed only after the authorities had somehow managed to draw up a full list of creditors. Finally, there were disagreements over the composition of the creditors' club, with hedge funds complaining that they had been denied a seat at the bargaining table.

To be sure, these arrangements will grow more complex with the shift from bank to bond finance. That shift will increase the number of interested parties and vest additional power in the hands of a class of creditors less susceptible to moral suasion by their central banks. But it will erode the effectiveness of Rhodes's Rolodex even more dramatically. Standing committees will become essential.

---

30. Or so the situation is described by Lee (1998). Rhodes is the vice chairman of Citibank and a veteran of the debt crisis of the 1980s.

One sometimes hears the objection that experience with corporate debt workouts suggests that committees of creditors can be quickly constituted when the time comes. The Institute of International Finance cites the case of AeroMexico as an example of how negotiations can be concluded swiftly in the absence of a bondholders' committee (Institute of International Finance 1996). In fact, the situation for corporate bonds is different from that affecting sovereign debts. Most corporate bonds are issued in the United States through an indenture trustee. The indenture trustee is responsible for acting as a communications center to coordinate the bondholders. It must communicate with the bondholders and follow the instructions given by a majority. The trustee is the bondholders' representative in negotiations with the debtor and the court. However, the Trust Indenture Act of 1939 exempts securities issued by foreign governments, their subdivisions, and municipalities. Sovereign bonds are typically issued through a fiscal agent rather than an indenture trustee. The fiscal agent has a much more limited role, and its obligations are mainly to the issuer, not the bondholders. Its responsibilities do not extend to acting as a communications center or attempting to coordinate the bondholders (Macmillan 1997, 9-10).

History supports the argument: standing committees were precisely the channel for disseminating information and organizing negotiations when bond finance was last important, from the late nineteenth century through World War II (Eichengreen and Portes 1989). At first, ad hoc bondholders' committees were formed in response to each interruption in debt service payments. Predictably, these committees had trouble establishing contact with the bondholders and opening lines of communication with foreign debtors. In Great Britain, the leading national creditor of the era, the situation was regularized in 1868 by the creation of the Corporation of Foreign Bondholders. Composed initially of representatives of banking firms and brokerage houses, its governing body, the Council, was expanded in 1898 to include several individual bondholders and a representative of the London Chamber of Commerce. The Council became the recognized spokesman for the bondholders and their representative in negotiations, working closely with the underwriting banks and the London Stock Exchange. The same evolution occurred elsewhere with the establishment of standing bondholders committees in Paris, Amsterdam, and Berlin before World War I and in the United States in the 1930s. These committees fell into disuse after World War II because the international capital market was slow to recover from the debt crisis of the 1930s and then because bond finance was superseded by syndicated bank loans. Now, however, bonds are back, and the creditors are more numerous and heterogeneous than when international lending was the domain of bank syndicates.

The idea of creditors' committees was resuscitated in the wake of the Mexican crisis by Rory Macmillan and by Richard Portes and myself

(Macmillan 1995; Eichengreen and Portes 1995). Macmillan suggests the creation of two such committees, a resurrected Foreign Bondholders Protective Council to represent and coordinate the holders of government bonds issued under New York law and submitting to New York courts and a resurrected Corporation of Foreign Bondholders to represent and coordinate holders of government bonds issued under English law. Because the vast majority of bonds are subject to either New York or English courts and law, two councils would go a long way toward solving the problem. When problems arose with the debts of a particular country and negotiations had to be commenced, these committees, working separately or jointly, would be in a position to appoint a subcommittee to undertake the task.

To date, however, the investor community has been reluctant to act. It fears that standing committees would make it too easy for debtors to initiate restructuring negotiations, making it too tempting for them to suspend debt payments. It is better, in the self-interested view of the creditors, for there to be no one at the other end of the line to pick up the phone.

The interests of the international policy community are different. For those seeking to create a viable alternative to large-scale bailouts of crisis countries and for whom the difficulties of debtor-creditor negotiations render moratoriums and restructuring unacceptably difficult and painful, standing committees are desirable precisely because they make it easier for debtors to initiate negotiations. Their formation is important for creating a viable alternative to ever-more-costly bailouts and disastrous Russian-style defaults, neither of which is acceptable.

The creation of such committees would require moral suasion and lobbying by G-7 governments, central banks, and the IMF to overcome the markets' reluctance. There would be nothing unprecedented about their involvement. The Corporation of Foreign Bondholders received a parliamentary charter and other forms of official support. Its US equivalent, the Foreign Bondholders Protective Council, was formed with the encouragement and support of the US State Department (Eichengreen and Portes 1989). These are precedents that should be followed.

Some have suggested that such a committee, possibly with rotating membership, could also interface with the IMF and other official bodies. In practice, this would create more problems than it solved. For one thing, because membership on the committee would be selective, some in the markets might feel that other participants were getting preferential treatment from the IMF. And insofar as the problem of information asymmetries arises in negotiations between the lenders and the borrowers, it is with the debtor that the creditors' representatives most urgently need to interact. If the IMF were negotiating the extension of financial assistance while the debtors and creditors were at the same time attempting to restructure outstanding debts, there might be occasion for exceptional discussions among the three parties, but it is not obvious why regular meetings between the creditors' committee and the official sector would be essential. And to the extent that there is a need for the Fund and the financial community to exchange information in a time of crisis, this can be done more simply, by asking the central bank or national treasury in each of the creditor countries to identify a representative of their financial community.

It is important to be clear on what these committees can and cannot achieve. By creating a vehicle for exchanging information and a venue for negotiations, they can ease the process of restructuring defaulted debts, which is essential to create a viable alternative to ever-bigger bailouts. That process will remain difficult—as it must to prevent borrowers from walking away from their debts—but not as difficult as now. What the creation of committees cannot do, except under unusual circumstances, is to get the creditors to exercise collective forbearance and roll over their short-term credits as a way of averting default. It would be nice, as Jeffrey Sachs and Steven Radelet advocate, if a "committee of large-bank creditors [could] be set up . . . and proceed to negotiate directly" with governments with pressing debt service problems (Sachs and Radelet 1998). But the unfortunate fact is that collective forbearance will be difficult to arrange. The main role of creditors' committees will be to facilitate restructuring after the fact.

This means that the most important measures to bail in the private sector are, first, policies to prevent governments, banks, and firms from relying on short-term foreign credits in the first place, and, second, new provisions in loan contracts to ease the restructuring negotiations in which creditors' committees will engage.

6

What Won't Work

Reforming the international financial architecture is a game that any number can play. Predictably, there already exists an abundance of proposals. This chapter considers a number of alternative schemes that are deemed politically unrealistic, technically infeasible, or unlikely to yield significant improvements in the way crises are prevented, anticipated, and managed.[1]

Ruling out alternatives is a critical step in my strategy for crafting a practical agenda for reform; otherwise, one would remain bogged down in a morass of conflicting proposals. Because I argue partly by process of elimination, it is important to be clear about the criteria by which alternative schemes are eliminated. The first is that certain proposals will not, by themselves, significantly improve the way that crises are prevented, anticipated, and managed. Efforts to improve transparency and information provision and to construct leading indicators of crises fall under this heading. While they are useful, there are good economic reasons why they cannot be relied upon to predict or prevent crises.

A second ground for elimination is that certain proposals, however appealing in theory, are not technically feasible. A Tobin tax and George Soros's proposal for an international bond insurance agency, for example, can be eliminated on these grounds. A Tobin tax would be too easily evaded by market migration (booking foreign-exchange transactions in offshore tax havens) and asset substitution (relabeling the relevant transac-

---

1. Proposals that concentrate on reforming the IMF are left for chapter 7, which is devoted to the role of that institution.

tions), while an attempt to establish an international bond insurance agency would have to confront a host of essentially insurmountable technical and administrative obstacles, as explained below.

A third basis on which to eliminate competing proposals is that of political feasibility. There may be sound analytical grounds for arguing that effective regulation of international markets requires an international government, but there is every reason to believe that national governments remain unwilling to cede significant additional prerogatives to international bodies. Europe is a limited counterexample where national governments have moved a significant distance toward ceding control over their national economic policies, notably their monetary policies, to a transnational entity, but it is sui generis; its case reflects a unique history and integrationist tradition not present in other parts of the world.[2] However compelling in the abstract the argument for a global financial regulator, a global bankruptcy court, or a global money to complement global financial markets, realism requires acknowledging that national governments have no appetite for initiatives that imply serious compromises of national political, legal, and economic autonomy. Such initiatives should be regarded as fodder for futurists, not for practical policymakers.

Disclosure and Discipline as Solutions to All Problems

Market discipline cannot work without information. Official reports (that is, G-10 1996 and G-22 1998a) appropriately emphasize the need for borrowers to provide full information on their economic and financial condition so that lenders can identify problems, curtail their lending, and avoid problems for their own balance sheets. Bank supervisors should require prompt disclosure of financial information by intermediaries. Regulators should require issuers placing their securities publicly to follow internationally recognized auditing and accounting practices and report regularly on their financial condition. Governments should provide timely and accurate information on their own financial condition.

Without question, improving the information environment will strengthen market discipline, and promulgating international standards is the obvious way of advancing this agenda. But it is unrealistic to expect too much of these initiatives. At the deepest level, those who invoke them as a solution to financial crises underestimate the extent to which information asymmetries are intrinsic to financial markets. Even the most efficient financial markets are characterized by asymmetric information. It is unavoidable that borrowers should know more than lenders about

---

2. As I elaborate later.

how they plan to use borrowed funds, not to mention about their own innate talents. This reality is a key reason why banks exist in market economies. Banks invest in the capacity to monitor borrowers, hiring loan officers and investment analysts experienced in the task and creating a specialized capacity that allows them to exploit economies of scale and scope in assembling information about potential borrowers. In a sense, without asymmetric information to create a need for delegated monitoring there would be no banks.[3] And the fact that banks are certain not to disappear soon is indicative of the extent to which asymmetric information is a fundamental fact of financial life.

These observations have profound implications for how one thinks about the operation of financial markets. They imply that the price mechanism cannot always be relied upon to restore equilibrium.[4] They imply that banks are intrinsically fragile. As banks are in the business of building a capacity to gather and analyze information about their customers, they will find it hard to raise liquidity by selling assets in times of crisis, given the difficulty this information asymmetry poses for third-party evaluation of loans.[5] Combine this with the fact that banks provide liquidity-transformation services (they borrow short from depositors with idiosyncratic needs for liquidity and demands for less liquid, more remunerative investments), and it is clear that banks are susceptible to self-fulfilling runs in which investors, uncertain of their access to deposits, scramble to get their money out. To be sure, this problem is most severe when, as in Asia, banks fail to use recognized accounting standards or to rely on reputable international accounting firms to audit their books, leaving their creditors unable to distinguish good banks from bad ones and permitting isolated runs to become systemic banking panics. This is why better information, secured by adherence to internationally recognized auditing and account-

---

3. Banks provide other services, as acknowledged below, but the fact that bank intermediation is particularly important in emerging markets where the information environment is particularly impacted suggests that the delegated monitoring role of banks remains a major factor.

4. If information were complete, the borrowers whose risk of defaulting is greatest would be asked to pay the highest interest rates. (A default premium would be built into their borrowing costs.) But if outside investors found it difficult to determine whether borrowers are of the high- or low-risk type, they would charge them all an interest rate that is an average of those that, in a full-information world, would apply to the high- and low-risk types. Low-risk borrowers would be overcharged for their loans, high-risk borrowers undercharged. The only debtors that would wish to borrow would be the low-quality, high-risk ones. And a further rise in interest rates, rather than discouraging them from borrowing, would only cause more relatively low-risk, high-quality borrowers to drop out of the market. (This adverse-selection problem is analyzed in the emerging-market context by Mishkin 1996.) Better information can attenuate this adverse-selection problem, but it is unrealistic to assume that it can be made to disappear.

5. This point was developed in chapter 5.

ing standards and strengthened prudential supervision, can help to ameliorate the panic problem. But if asymmetric information is why most economies continue to rely on banks for intermediation services, bank fragility is unavoidable. The advocates of information-related initiatives mislead when they assume the problem away.

Analogous problems exist in securities markets, where incompletely informed investors infer information from the actions of others. It is clear how market volatility can be amplified by investors' tendency to infer that a security is of lower or higher quality than previously thought from the decisions of other investors. Delegating asset management to a specialized money manager will not help to the extent that it is hard for investors to ascertain the quality of those managers. Poor-quality managers will then have an incentive to engage in lemming-like behavior, emulating the actions of other, possibly more adept money managers in an effort to disguise their true type. Again, it is clear how this can amplify market volatility (see Devenow and Welch 1996).

If theory does not convince, then history should, for it shows that markets do not smoothly adjust the price and quantity of credit in response to new circumstances. This was apparent in 1997, when there was little tendency for the spreads on syndicated bank loans and bond issues on primary and secondary markets to move in advance of the Asian crisis (as noted in appendix C). It was apparent in the lead-up to the 1992 crisis in Europe, when the forward premium on foreign exchange failed to rise significantly before the pressures spilled over in the currency market.[6] Clearly, sudden investor reactions, volatility, and, in extreme circumstances, crises are financial facts of life even in countries with relatively sophisticated securities markets and highly developed information systems.

Then there is the practical question of whether governments can reliably promise to gather the relevant data. Consider for example the current preoccupation with the offshore borrowings of banks and corporations. Assembling data on their borrowing was straightforward when all foreign financial transactions were government controlled, but now that corporations and others are free to borrow from offshore banks and nonbank financial institutions, it is far from clear how to gather this information short of an invasive survey of all private-sector entities. It is questionable whether the US government, for example, could accurately estimate the short-term foreign liabilities of US banks and corporations.

---

6. The exception was Italy, which was in the same position in 1992 that Thailand found itself in 1997. There, investors perceived a serious problem of overvaluation, and forward rates moved outside the country's ERM band several months before the crisis (Eichengreen and Wyplosz 1993). But the same was not true of other countries whose currencies were then attacked.

More generally, the success of these initiatives will hinge on the cooperation of governments, banks, and corporations—which should not be assumed. Banks gambling for redemption have a strong incentive to disguise their true financial condition, understating nonperforming loans in an effort to delay the day of reckoning. Governments in financial straits but hoping that conditions will improve have an incentive to disguise their financial condition and to conspire with banks and corporations doing the same.[7] Central banks asked to provide data on currency forwards and futures may respond by moving into the use of more exotic derivative instruments. Data that once were useful for predicting crises may be rendered irrelevant by the international community's very commitment to provide them.

Peer pressure can help to limit such subterfuge. The IMF can blow the whistle on countries that delay or fabricate data, although the collegiality characteristic of the institution raises questions about the credibility of the threat.[8] Appointing a panel of independent experts to adjust national statistics to international standards would help. In addition, this is a place where regional surveillance has a useful role; the European Union, for example, has a committee of independent statisticians that scrutinizes EU governments' fiscal accounts and standardizes their reported deficits. This precedent might be emulated in other parts of the world.[9] Realistically, however, it has taken EU members four decades of progressively deeper political and economic integration to reach the point where they are prepared to accept such invasive and potentially embarrassing mutual surveillance. Similarly, the IMF's code for fiscal transparency and recent extensions of the SDDS to encompass the off-balance-sheet transactions of governments and central banks will make it more difficult for governments to disguise their true financial condition.[10] In practice, however, for each additional disclosure requirement adopted by the Fund, there are other steps available to governments and banks.[11]

---

7. One need only recall how the Mexican government responded to increased scrutiny of its financial position in 1994 by hiding its deficits in the accounts of the development banks. The Thai central bank's forward commitments and the South Korean central bank's transfer of international assets to overseas branches of domestic banks in 1997 further illustrate the point.

8. Note, for example, the language describing the procedures that will be used to delist a country from the SDDS: this will be done only in the event of "serious and persistent nonobservance."

9. Indeed, the need to strengthen regional surveillance in other parts of the world is the strongest argument for creating new bodies such as an Asia or Asia-Pacific Monetary Fund. This is the argument elaborated in Bergsten (1998b).

10. Before the Asian crisis, subscription to the SDDS did not entail a commitment to provide data on central banks' off-balance-sheet liabilities or the short-term foreign-currency liabilities of the corporate sector, two key indicators of problems in Thailand and Indonesia.

11. The severity of the problem—and the extent to which it pervades advanced industrial as well as emerging-market economies—is evident in the unexpected magnitude of the major money-center banks' losses on derivatives exposures in the second half of 1998.

None of these arguments vitiates the case for improving the information environment. But too much should not be expected of these initiatives. Unavoidably, information asymmetries will remain. And there will always be unexpected events. Crises will still occur, and it will still be necessary to create mechanisms for coping with them.

Leading Indicators

If investors, with so much at stake, cannot reliably forecast crises, then it is hard to see why bureaucrats should do better. This has not prevented the official community and policy entrepreneurs scenting the existence of a market from attempting to develop leading indicators of currency and banking crises.[12] Their track record is not good. Models built to explain the 1992-93 ERM crisis did not predict the 1994-95 Mexican crisis. Models built to explain the Mexican crisis did not predict the Asian crisis. These failures reflect the fact that the underlying vulnerabilities were different in each case. ERM currencies were attacked because high European unemployment sapped governments' ability to uphold their financial commitments, while the Mexican government was rendered reluctant to raise interest rates by the weakness of the banking system. Whereas the immediate problem in Mexico was high levels of short-term public debt, in South Korea it was the level of short-term bank debt, and in Indonesia it was the level of corporate debt. In other words, the existence of 31 flavors of crisis greatly complicates prediction.

Nor do the variables on which leading-indicator exercises depend offer much guidance about when the attack will come. Whether speculators pounce will depend not just on the weakness of the banking system or the level of unemployment but on how much governments are perceived to care about aggravating these problems. The only thing more difficult to measure than a government's resolve is investors' assessment of it. And even if observers conclude that the currency peg is vulnerable, no one market participant is likely to be sufficiently large to build up the short position needed to exhaust the authorities' reserves.[13] For that to occur, different investors will have to coordinate their actions.[14] And what

---

12. See, for example, IMF (1998c), Kaminsky and Reinhart (1998), Kaminsky, Lizondo, and Reinhart (1997), Hardy and Pazarbasioglu (1998), Sachs, Tornell and Velasco (1996), Tornell (1998), Radelet and Sachs (1998b), and Goldstein and Reinhart (1999). In addition, there are a number of academic studies that have sought to deepen understanding about past currency crises without making predictive claims: Eichengreen, Rose, and Wyplosz (1995, 1997), Eichengreen and Rose (1997), and Frankel and Rose (1996).

13. Or to liquidate a sufficient quantity of bank deposits to bring down an entire banking system.

14. A point given theoretical substance by Obstfeld (1996).

serves as the coordinating device will vary from case to case and generally elude prediction.[15]

Existing early-warning systems exemplify these problems.[16] The relationship between macroeconomic and financial indicators and the probability of large changes in exchange rates and reserves tends to be sensitive to the sample of countries and the period for which estimation is carried out, belying the notion that there exists a single set of variables and a stable set of relationships on which to base crisis forecasting.[17] The models that perform best rely on reversals in the direction of capital flows and sudden reserve losses, variables that are really concurrent rather than leading indicators. Once this information is available, in other words, the horse has left the barn (see Minton-Beddoes 1998).

The same criticisms apply to models that rely for their predictive power on crises in other countries in the current or preceding periods. Insofar as crises elsewhere are simply picking up common unobservables responsible for financial turbulence in all the affected countries, it will be too late for policymakers to eliminate the problem by the time evidence of those unobservables is detected. Even if measures of crises in neighboring countries are picking up not just common omitted factors but pure contagion—that is, the tendency for instability in one country to infect another, independent of macroeconomic and financial conditions in the latter—this is of little practical value for policy. The only thing that is known with certainty about contagion is that its spread is uncertain. While some crises have powerful repercussions abroad, others do not. The contagion associated with the Thai devaluation was a surprise, for example, and its spread to Indonesia was particularly unexpected. Far more work will be needed on contagion before we will possess reliable early-warning indicators of whether it is loose upon the land.

Even if all these problems were solved, there would still be reason to doubt that crises could be predicted with high reliability, because of the market's reaction to the provision of leading indicators. If certain variables and thresholds were identified as reliable predictors of past crises, market

---

15. Theorists modeling these coordination problems acknowledge this in the language they use, referring to outcomes as "sunspot equilibria." Furman and Stiglitz (1998) rightly note that insofar as countries are vulnerable to these sorts of self-fulfilling attacks only when they enter a danger zone of economic and financial fragility, it should still be possible to predict crises *on average* (in the stochastic sense). But, as they conclude, the fact that the top quartile of countries can be eliminated as plausible candidates for self-fulfilling attacks is not very helpful for policy.

16. Other reviews of this literature, which make similar points, are Berg and Pattillo (1998) and Furman and Stiglitz (1998).

17. Corsetti, Pesenti, and Roubini (1998), Berg and Pattillo (1998), and Furman and Stiglitz (1998) all demonstrate this point by updating the sample analyzed by Sachs, Tornell, and Velasco (1996a) and showing that few of the results continue to hold.

participants cognizant of them and aware of the tendency for macroeconomic variables to be slow-moving and persistent would sell their claims before those thresholds were breached. Thus, the crisis would occur before the flashing yellow light was observed.[18]

None of this is to deny the value of studies seeking to deepen our understanding of past crises. But the success of current papers in explaining past crises does not mean that they will succeed in predicting future crises.

An International Debt Insurance Agency

George Soros has recommended creating a public corporation to insure investors against debt default (Soros 1997, 1998). In the same way that deposit insurance averts the danger of depositor runs, the credit insurance issued by this corporation would avert the danger of a loss of creditor confidence in which investors refuse to roll over their maturing loans and precipitate self-fulfilling debt and currency crises. The herd behavior that roils capital markets would be reduced; like insured bank depositors, insured foreign creditors would have less incentive to scramble for the exits. Moreover, pension funds, mutual funds, and insurance companies precluded from holding low-rated bonds would not be forced to sell into a declining market if the country issuing them suddenly experienced financial difficulties.

Countries would underwrite the cost of Soros's insurance by paying a fee when floating loans. To ensure that the scheme was actuarially sound, each country's access would be limited to a ceiling set by the IMF on the basis of its assessment of the country's macroeconomic and financial condition. Loans in excess of the ceiling would not be insured. The IMF would make clear that it was not prepared to aid countries having difficulty servicing uninsured loans. Lenders would consequently charge countries borrowing in excess of that ceiling higher interest rates to compensate for the risk of default. And because the Fund would determine the amount of insured borrowing and reject pleas for aid from countries experiencing difficulty in servicing uninsured loans, there would be no prospect of a bailout to encourage excessive borrowing and lending.

But to assert that the international community will be able to stand aside in the event of default on uninsured loans, in disregard of the systemic consequences, is to assume a solution to the problem.[19] In prac-

---

18. Not that this would be entirely bad: if early-warning exercises led investors to sell before those critical thresholds were breached, market discipline would be strengthened and welfare would be enhanced (assuming, of course, that early-warning exercises focused on the right variables in the first place!).

19. The dilemma is analogous to that which arises in connection with narrow banking (as described in chapter 4).

tice, those worried that debt problems in one country might spread contagiously to others, endangering the stability of the international system, are sure to be worried most about uninsured bonds. Information about uninsured issues will be least, accentuating the tendency for their prices to move together. Uninsured issues will be perceived as especially risky, causing their prices to suffer most in periods of generalized financial turbulence. Institutional investors that specialize in holding uninsured issues will have the greatest need to meet margin calls in a crisis, forcing them to liquidate their holdings in other countries.

Nor is it clear how the IMF would determine the cutoff for the loans that qualified for insurance. In theory, the Fund would determine the safe, economically sound level of debt for each of its members and insure only that amount. But not only do bureaucrats lack a convincing model of the optimal level of debt, it is far from clear that the decision would be taken on the basis of economic rather than political considerations. The Fund would presumably insure more borrowing by countries with sound economic and financial policies and use that fact as leverage to encourage policy reform. But what would happen when a less reform-minded government took office or policy otherwise took an unexpected turn? Would the Fund then lower the ceiling for insured loans? Would insurance for previously insured loans be revoked? Would insurance be available only for foreign-currency loans, or would loans denominated in the home currency also qualify? If the demand for foreign funds exceeded the ceiling, what would determine which loans were insured? Would insurance be allocated on a first-come-first-served basis? Who would decide which of several competing loans was insured and which was not?

Above all, there is the question of why the world needs a *public* insurance corporation. If the idea is so attractive, why can't investment banks and other underwriters set it up as a self-financing operation?[20] The answer presumably has something to do with the tendency for private insurance markets operating in an impacted information environment to break down. Perhaps adverse selection and moral hazard would undermine the viability of private insurance. These problems would not arise if all countries were required to participate in an IMF-run program, if the Fund had better information than the private sector on the creditworthiness of potential borrowers, and if its conditionality could guarantee that insured borrowers would not embark on riskier policies. Unfortunately, these assumptions are either economically implausible or politically unrealistic.

---

20. Mann (1998) attacks this question head-on, arguing the need for private market-based insurance instruments.

A Tobin Tax

Each episode of turbulence in international financial markets prompts calls for taxing foreign-exchange transactions.[21] Some proponents of this tax question the rationality and efficiency of the market. They suggest that currency traders buy and sell in disregard of fundamentals, which introduces unnecessary volatility into foreign-exchange markets and capital flows (see, e.g., Felix 1995). Others acknowledge the rationality of currency traders but characterize their activities as socially counterproductive, invoking second-generation models of currency crises and arguing that unregulated financial markets make it too easy for speculators to shift the economy from the good to the bad equilibrium.[22] It follows that a tax on foreign-exchange transactions that makes it more difficult for investors to speculate against currencies could in principle reduce the incidence of crises and enhance the social welfare.

Some critics of the Tobin tax deny the existence of these and, for that matter, all problems in financial markets. They warn that a transactions tax would disrupt the market's ability to carry out its financial functions. Recent experience makes it hard to take seriously the strong efficient-markets view. As for the objection that a Tobin tax would seriously worsen resource allocation, it is hard to see how the modest tax most proponents have in mind, on the order of 5 or 10 basis points, could be so disruptive.

The more compelling objection is on grounds of feasibility. In times of crisis, currency traders would simply disregard the tax. Under these conditions, a tax of 5 or 10 basis points is a negligible deterrent. And a larger tax—throwing boulders instead of sand in the gears—would seriously disrupt the operation of financial markets.

Moreover, the tax could be evaded by booking foreign-exchange transactions in tax-free jurisdictions.[23] This ability to move transactions offshore means that the tax would have to be implemented simultaneously by all the leading centers of foreign-exchange trading. This may be only a handful of locations, but the fact that it includes countries as diverse as the United States and Hong Kong suggests that easy agreement, not to mention vigilant enforcement, cannot be assumed.

---

21. The original argument is Tobin (1978). It has been revived recently by a number of commentators (see, e.g., Kuttner 1998).

22. See, for example, Eichengreen, Tobin, and Wyplosz (1995) and, more recently, Wyplosz (1998a, b). The idea is that introducing a cost of international capital mobility can moderate the interest rate increases needed to defend the currency and thereby tip the balance for a government deciding whether or not to raise interest rates in a concerted defense at the cost of aggravating various internal economic problems.

23. This possibility is analyzed by Kenen (1996), Garber and Taylor (1995), and Garber (1996b).

In addition there is the problem that new foreign-exchange trading centers would then spring up in remaining tax havens—the Cayman Islands, for example.[24] This tendency would be limited by the additional costs incurred by traders when the transaction was undertaken and booked in an offshore center. Currency traders would be hesitant to move their transactions to a locale of uncertain reputation where counterparty risk is significant—where they are uncertain that their transactions will in fact be booked at the contracted price and their funds will be collected promptly. If banks attempt to solve this problem by moving their own operations offshore, they will first have to invest in trading rooms and personnel at the new dealing site. It may not be attractive for any of them to do so unless other banks do so simultaneously.[25] That said, the danger of offshore centers developing will surely increase over time. Universal adoption, through an amendment to the IMF's Articles of Agreement, and effective enforcement, no mean task, would be essential for a Tobin tax to be more than a temporary expedient.

Even if market migration were slowed, there would remain the danger that the tax could be evaded by the simple relabeling of transactions. Traders betting on changes in the exchange rate don't merely trade national currencies; they trade any one of a number of assets denominated in different currencies. If currency transactions were defined for tax purposes as the exchange of bank deposits in different currencies, traders could substitute the exchange of treasury bills denominated in those currencies and then sell those treasury bills for deposits.[26] Tax avoidance is a problem with all taxes, of course, not just with taxes on foreign

---

24. The French government's proposal for reforming the international financial architecture alludes to the need to deal with the problem of offshore centers, and this has long been a favorite theme of IMF Managing Director Michel Camdessus. The problem was highlighted by the Long Term Capital Management debacle, when those who advocated stronger regulation of hedge funds by national authorities were quickly reminded that many hedge funds were already legally domiciled offshore and that many others would simply move offshore in response to tighter regulation. None of these observations, however, prompted realistic proposals for dealing with the problem of offshore financial centers, which would seem intractable; some free rider will always have an irresistible incentive to free ride, and there is little that can be done about this problem.

25. If, as Kenen (1996) suggests, the tax were levied at twice the normal rate when the counterparty was in a tax-free jurisdiction, more than one bank would have to move simultaneously to that jurisdiction for relocation to pay.

26. This point is made by Garber (1998). Substitution is not without costs, of course. Most obviously there is the increase in the number of transactions, as traders first sell bank deposits for securities, then trade the securities, and finally repurchase bank deposits. And holding stocks or bonds even for an instant entails an element of price risk not shared by bank deposits. This will be especially true of currencies issued by countries whose stock and bond markets lack liquidity. But the ability of financial engineers to develop synthetic assets to hedge these risks and more generally to evade foreign-exchange taxation should not be underestimated.

exchange transactions. The tax authorities should have the power to reclassify transactions if they suspect them to be motivated mainly by tax avoidance. But there is good reason to think that the markets will always remain one step ahead of the authorities.

Seen in this light, a tax on all capital inflows, similar to Chile's deposit requirement, has two signal advantages over a Tobin tax. First, it would apply to all financial transactions between residents and nonresidents and therefore be less subject to asset substitution.[27] Second, it would limit countries' vulnerability to the destabilizing effects of sudden capital outflows not by attempting to staunch those outflows, which is unlikely to be effective, but by taxing capital at the inflow stage, when the incentive for evasion is less. To be sure, a Chilean-style inflow tax will make no difference when it is residents who are fleeing the currency. But where excessive capital inflows, such as those prompted by government guarantees that permit domestic banks to lever up their bets, create the problems that lead ultimately to that outflow risk, there is a sound rationale for the policy.

An International Court for Sovereign Debts

A recurrent strand of academic thought invokes the idea of an international bankruptcy court.[28] Motivation stems from the observation that there exists no international analog to domestic bankruptcy procedures, in particular no international court for the orderly restructuring of sovereign debts.

The notion of an international bankruptcy court raises complex issues, because insolvency provisions differ across countries and specialists do not agree on the particulars of an efficient bankruptcy code. That said, it is possible to discern something of a consensus on basic principles. First, bankruptcy procedures should empower the courts to impose a stay on payments. This will prevent a grab race in which creditors scramble after the remaining assets of the troubled enterprise, forcing it to be dismantled even when it would be profitable if restructured and, more generally, heightening the costs of adjustment.

With this standstill in place, fundamentally insolvent enterprises can be liquidated and viable ones reorganized. Debtors and creditors should

---

27. There will still be other possible channels of evasion, such as over-invoicing imports, as described in chapter 5. But as explained there, these too may have nonnegligible costs.

28. See, inter alia, Kampffmeyer (1987), Raffer (1990) Sachs (1994), Miller and Zhang (1997, 1998), and Radelet and Sachs (1998b) for variants of this idea.

be encouraged to negotiate a mutually acceptable reorganization plan.[29] If the parties are unable to reach an agreement within a reasonable period, the courts should then have the power to impose it. To discourage debtors from resorting to bankruptcy as a way of shedding their financial obligations and managers from stripping the enterprise of assets while negotiations are underway, the courts may also have the power to seize control of the firm's financial affairs and replace its management, if necessary.[30]

Finally, some national bankruptcy procedures allow distressed debtors to tap the markets for interim financing—to obtain what is referred to in the United States as debtor-in-possession financing. Even a firm whose assets are worth more in place than when dismantled may be unable to continue operating unless it obtains working capital. The courts can facilitate this by giving postpetition creditors priority over existing claimants. Those existing claimants will benefit as well if the enterprise is worth more as a continuing concern than if wound up.[31]

In contrast to these national arrangements, there is no international bankruptcy court to which countries can appeal. Even if the creditors' claims are collectively maximized when they renew their maturing loans and give governments, banks, and corporations time to reorganize their financial affairs, each individual creditor still has an incentive to scramble for the exit if he can attach the available collateral.[32] The absence of an international authority with the power to impose a standstill leaves unre-

---

29. This agreement may have to satisfy certain legal constraints, such as the priority of claims. In other words, creditors who receive preferential treatment outside of bankruptcy also receive preferential treatment in it.

30. Similarly, some national bankruptcy procedures give the courts or the administrator the power to nullify transfers made by management to related parties in the period immediately preceding the bankruptcy filing.

31. Taken together, these provisions are designed to maintain a balance between creditor and debtor rights—to balance the benefits of strict enforcement of debt contracts (strengthening the bonding role of debt) against the gains from maximizing the ex post value of the enterprise (clearing away unviable debts and removing debt overhangs that distort investment incentives). They are intended to encourage and if necessary impose the kind of agreement that creditors and debtors would reach in a world free of information and transactions costs. Hence, there is the well-known proposition that there would be no need for a court-enforced bankruptcy procedure in a world where borrowers and lenders could write provision for all the relevant contingencies into the original loan contract and where enforcement was costless. Existing procedures may be criticized for failing to get the balance between the interests of debtors and creditors quite right, but the fact that no one is inclined to abolish prevailing arrangements suggests that they are still preferable to a world in which the courts have no power to expedite negotiations.

32. Forbearance that is in the collective interest may not also be in the individual interest if there is no mechanism to enforce collective action. With luck, individual creditors might be brought to recognize their collective interest. But when information on compliance is incomplete and the creditors do have a long-standing relationship with one another, the incentive (and ability) to chisel on an agreement may be stronger still.

strained this destructive incentive to scramble for the exits. Similarly, the fact that there is no international court or arbitrator charged with coordinating negotiations and cramming down settlement terms means that talks can drag on, aggravating the macroeconomic and financial losses caused by default.

These observations motivate calls for a mechanism for imposing an internationally recognized standstill and creating an international court with the power to oversee negotiations and, if necessary, impose settlement terms. The analogy is drawn with Chapter 9 of US insolvency law, under which the debts of insolvent municipal governments are restructured. Kunibert Raffer's proposal for an international court of arbitration in a "neutral" country (one that is neither an active lender nor a borrower), empowered to impose a standstill and cram down settlement terms, is representative of the genre (Raffer 1990).

The objections to this idea are overwhelming. Most obviously there is the question of whether there really is the need to create a new entity with the ability to impose a standstill, because governments can already declare a unilateral moratorium. Dissident creditors have pressed lawsuits and sought to attach sovereigns' assets, but governments have generally had few attachable assets in the relevant jurisdiction.[33] Then there is the moral hazard that would flow from the fact that the international tribunal would not possess the other powers of a national bankruptcy court, which can seize control of the bankrupt firm's financial affairs and, in some cases, replace its management. Above all there is the political question of whether the creditor countries would be prepared to vest such formidable powers in the hands of an international tribunal of officials. For all these reasons, even the kind of limited scheme floated by the Canadian government, that the IMF Executive Board would give a Good Housekeeping Seal of Approval to countries that declared a 90-day standstill or moratorium on all cross-border or cross-currency debt contracts, is patently unrealistic (Canada, Department of Finance 1998).[34]

---

33. Thus, even Peru, which was a particularly confrontational debtor under socialist President Alan Garcia, did not see any of its exports seized or its foreign assets attached (Cohen 1989). Note that Lehman Brothers' successful action in London courts freezing $113 million in assets of two Russian banks in September 1998 related not to Russia's domestic debt default but to the failure of Russian counterparties to settle their forward foreign-exchange contracts.

34. It is not clear what the advantage would be of having the IMF Executive Board "officially approve" that moratorium, as suggested in Radelet and Sachs (1998b), unless there was some assurance that its approval would be recognized by national courts, which would use it as a basis for overriding other considerations. If the IMF lent into sovereign arrears, creditors might be tempted to press lawsuits in an effort to attach the Fund's resources. But this is a separate problem and it admits of a more limited solution (amending the IMF's Articles to give immunity from legal action to its own financial transactions and encouraging countries to amend their own sovereign immunities laws, as explained in chapter 5).

And if it is unrealistic to think that the IMF or another international entity could be empowered to impose a standstill on payments, it is pure fantasy to suggest that the Fund could be given the power to impose settlement terms on debtors and creditors. Insofar as the main function of any new body will boil down to facilitating communication between debtors and creditors, this can be provided by a standing committee of creditors with no enforcement powers, as described in chapter 5. If there is a need for further measures to ease restructuring negotiations, this is best done by adding sharing, majority-voting, minimum-legal-threshold, and nonacceleration clauses to bond contracts, again as explained in chapter 5. And if there is a need to provide debtor-in-possession financing, this is best done by IMF lending into arrears, as also explained there.

Global Moneys and Global Monetary Institutions

Schemes for an international bankruptcy court may be unrealistic, but they are realism exemplified compared with recent proposals for a world financial regulator, a world central bank, and a single world currency. The impulse for these castles in the air is understandable. Financial institutions do business globally. Hedge funds invest globally. Financial markets are integrated globally. For all these reasons, crises originating in one country or region can quickly infect other parts of the globe. But the institutions of monetary and financial policymaking are segmented nationally; policies are framed with national rather than global conditions in mind, and the international coordination needed to cope with global problems remains difficult to arrange. Hence, Henry Kaufman (1998a, b) proposes a single superregulator of financial institutions and financial markets to set and enforce prudential regulations. Jeffrey Garten (1998) proposes a world central bank with responsibility for maintaining global financial stability that would act as a true international lender of last resort to stabilize currencies and financial systems. Despair over the undesirable properties of both fixed and flexible exchange rates has led a number of recent commentators to resuscitate Richard Cooper's idea of a single world currency (1984).

Those who take such proposals seriously might pay just a little bit more heed to the fact that politics are local. Nations remain jealous of their prerogatives. Even in Europe, where there is a strong integrationist tradition with intellectual roots stretching back centuries, nation-states continue to jealously guard their responsibility for the regulation of domestic financial markets and hesitate to turn this over to an international entity. Better coordination of national regulatory policies is possible and desirable, but it is hard to imagine 182 IMF member countries ceding responsibility for the operation of their domestic financial markets and institutions to an international superregulator.

Europe's experience also discredits the notion that exchange rate and financial problems could be solved by creating a world central bank and a world currency. A world central bank to loan foreign exchange to national central banks but without a world currency, as Garten seems to suggest, would be pointless. An international central bank that "would not be able to override the decisions of the national central bank," as he acknowledges would inevitably be the case when discussing any new global monetary institution's relationship to the US Federal Reserve, would in practice extend only limited loans. Just as no commercial bank is willing to extend unlimited credit to a customer whose behavior it cannot control, no central bank is willing to extend unlimited support to other central banks whose actions it cannot control for fear of creating a runaway engine of inflation and aggravating problems of moral hazard.[35] This is a clear lesson of the European Monetary System (EMS): the provision in the EMS Articles of Agreement requiring countries with strong currencies to provide "unlimited support" to their weak-currency counterparts was not credible because the inflation-averse Bundesbank predictably obtained the German government's agreement that it could opt out when it saw fit. The notion that intra-European exchange rates could be pegged by unlimited interventions proved to be an illusion. Europe was forced to conclude that the only way to make the extension of unlimited interventions credible was by creating a true European Central Bank, and that so long as it was doing that it might as well create a single currency.

Thus, the logic for a world currency is impeccable; the only way to eliminate exchange rate problems once and for all, as Europe has learned, is by eliminating the exchange rate. But this is not the same as eliminating crises. Indeed, some critics warn that European Monetary Union (EMU) may end up increasing rather than reducing the incidence of financial crises. Insofar as the inflationary costs of a monetary bailout of a national government experiencing a debt run or of a national banking system experiencing a depositor panic will now be borne by the residents of all EMU countries, not just by those of the country experiencing the crisis, there arises a free-rider problem that tends to encourage lax regulation. The specific illustration may be exaggerated, but the general principle is valid: the elimination of exchange rates does not necessarily mean the elimination of crises; it may simply shift the pressure from the exchange rate to other variables.

Moreover, Europe has cultivated the political consensus to take the momentous step of ceding responsibility for its monetary policy to the

---

35. This is also the critique of proposals to turn the IMF into a true international lender of last resort, as discussed in chapter 7.

European Central Bank only after 50 years of economic and political institution building that have no counterpart in other parts of the world. European monetary unification is a political as well as an economic bargain, as its critics are especially quick to observe. Only because the members of the European Union have taken very significant steps down the road toward political unification are they prepared to accept the authority of a transnational monetary institution. And they are prepared to take those political steps only because the recent impulse to do so (the "lesson of World War II," that Europe must integrate to avoid a recurrence of war) was superimposed on a venerable integrationist tradition. William Penn proposed a European parliament, Jeremy Bentham a European assembly, Jean-Jacques Rousseau a European federation, Henri Saint-Simon a European monarch. The Pan-European Union, founded in 1923 to lobby for a European federation, counted among its members Konrad Adenauer and Georges Pompidou. One could go on. The point is that there exist no comparable tradition and support for political integration in other parts of the world.

To be sure, dissatisfaction with existing exchange rate arrangements and the desire to insulate customs unions from the disruptive effects of intraunion currency swings will encourage expansion of Europe's monetary union to incorporate additional members. The Mercosur countries will surely contemplate a single currency to insulate their customs union from exchange rate instability.[36] One can imagine a phased transition starting with a series of regional monetary unions and ending with the creation of a world central bank and a world currency. But even the first step in this process assumes a degree of political consensus and a commitment to political integration that, at present, simply does not exist. Ideas such as these are useful for focusing thought on the shortcomings of existing monetary and financial arrangements and for helping to identify the global functions that coordination among national policy institutions must try to simulate. But to take them more seriously than this would be a diversion from the work at hand.

---

36. Argentine President Carlos Menem raised the idea at the beginning of 1998 and again at a regional summit in the summer. The idea has also been mooted in Asia, for example, in the Association of Southeast Asian Nations (ASEAN).

7

What the IMF Should Do (and What We Should Do about the IMF)

Since the Asian crisis erupted, the IMF has been at the center of the storm. Some have criticized it for pushing currency devaluation on its developing-country members, with generally disastrous consequences, while others have denounced it for demanding that countries hike interest rates to defend their currencies, precipitating deeper recessions and aggravating financial problems. Some criticize its lending for eroding market discipline and only heightening the likelihood of future crises, while others attribute its inability to stabilize the crisis economies to a failure to lend more freely. Some criticize the microeconomic and structural conditions that the Fund attaches to its loans as meddling in the internal affairs of countries that has the perverse effect of undermining investor confidence, while others insist that it has no choice but to insist on institutional reform because this is essential for the restoration of investor confidence and that to lend without such conditions would be to throw good money after bad.

This disagreement about whether the IMF should be expanded, restricted, abolished, or restructured is understandable insofar as changes in the environment in which it operates are forcing its mission and operating procedures to be rethought. Public debate is a healthy part of that process. The confusion surrounding that debate is not so healthy.

Why Radical Reform Won't Work

In a world where not all information problems are remediable, crises will still occur. And in a world of highly levered financial institutions, serious crises can still threaten systemic stability and spill across countries. These are convincing grounds on which to dismiss the extreme recommendation to abolish the IMF (see Shultz, Simon, and Wriston 1998; Schwartz 1998). While there is no question that the Fund will have to become more involved in standard setting and debt restructuring, they are grounds on which to dismiss the idea that it should get out of the lending business entirely in order to concentrate on these other tasks (see, inter alia, Wolf 1998). To be sure, the financial safety net that the Fund provides is a source of moral hazard, but moral hazard cannot be the sole concern of policymakers. Moral hazard risk must be balanced against meltdown risk. We do not abolish central banks' discount facilities or national deposit insurance schemes because they create moral hazard for domestic financial institutions. We do not abolish fire departments because they encourage people to build their houses out of wood. We do not prohibit motorists from using seat belts because they encourage some to drive faster. For drivers as for financial markets, we worry about more than just moral hazard. We worry also about the sudden stop.

This means that there will remain a role for IMF lending to countries that experience a sudden stop—where there is a shock to investor confidence, where capital inflows dry up, and where the exchange rate has to be unpegged or devalued, resulting in financial distress. Using IMF resources to replenish their international reserves will allow central banks forced to devalue to continue intervening in the foreign-exchange market to prevent the shock to confidence from wholly destabilizing the currency and precipitating a complete financial meltdown that creates severe problems not just in the country of origin but also abroad. It can give the government the fiscal resources to support the banking system and expand the social safety net without going on an inflationary binge. Properly administered, IMF support can help governments to respond to a crisis in ways that limit the financial distress, shock to confidence, and recession that tend to occur in its wake. And it can bolster political support for reform.

What the IMF cannot do is to follow Walter Bagehot's classic advice for a domestic central bank to lend freely against good collateral at a penalty rate. Compared to a domestic central bank, its resources are too limited, as is its leverage over the recipient. Unlike a domestic lender of last resort, the IMF cannot print money, nor would its principal shareholders let it (see Schwartz 1998). Compared to a government dealing with a problem bank, the IMF has less ability to force corrective action on its members. Because the Fund does not possess the other legal and regulatory powers of a government, it lacks the leverage to ensure that it will get its money back. This is why the IMF is endowed with fewer resources, why it lends less freely, and why it relies more heavily on continuing performance criteria when providing funds. It is why the IMF hesitates to front-load its disbursements, requiring evidence that policy reforms are in train before releasing each additional bit of finance.

The Clinton Proposal

Because the IMF does not have the powers of a government is also why the provision of contingent credit lines to countries in advance of financial difficulties is not in general a feasible IMF response to the crisis problem. This idea was advanced by the United States during the IMF annual meetings in October 1998 as a response to the problems facing countries such as Brazil. Later that month it was embraced by the G-7 in its declaration on strengthening the financial system. As described there, IMF members would agree to establish a new facility to provide a contingent short-term line of credit for countries pursuing strong IMF-approved policies and exposed to the danger of contagion (G-7 1998).

The problem is that contingent credit lines, to be effective, would have to be large, and once extended they would have to be unconditional. But while this approach might be practicable for countries such as Argentina, which is small relative to global markets and whose policies are exceptionally strong, there is reason to doubt that it could be used to meet the needs of the Brazils and South Koreas. The November 1998 loan to Brazil was not a contingent credit line; rather, it was a conventional 36-month standby arrangement. To be sure, that loan has some special features: the first tranche is large, and the date of disbursal of the second can be advanced in the event of need. But availability is still tied to ongoing performance criteria—that is, to evidence that Brazil is meeting a variety of fiscal conditions.

The reason is not hard to see. Embracing the precautionary credit proposal with open arms would mean, for the G-7 countries, effectively giving the IMF a blank check. The IMF's traditional approach to standby lines of credit implies a specific, determinate financial obligation: the Fund calculates the current-account deficit consistent with the budgetary target and provides a standby in this amount (net, typically, of other available sources of finance). A precautionary credit, in contrast, would not be tied down in this way. It would have to be large enough to offset all sales of domestic and foreign assets that financed outflows over the capital account of the balance of payments. Inevitably, the resources of the IMF are small relative to those of the relevant financial markets. How many $42 billion Brazilian-sized credits could be provided by an IMF whose lending capacity is still less than $200 billion even with the approval of an additional $90 billion by the US Congress and its foreign counterparts?[1] This budget

---

1. Some observers—Guillermo Calvo, for example—have argued that contingent credits adequate to head off a crisis will have to be significantly larger even than the $42 billion extended to Brazil.

constraint naturally renders the Fund concerned to husband its limited resources and reluctant to disburse resources without attaching (and therefore having to negotiate) new conditions that maximize the probability of repayment. Moreover, questions about the recipient's willingness to adjust will inevitably lead the IMF to insist on additional conditions at the time of disbursement. Like any lender, the Fund would regret having preapproved a credit line were the economic policies and performance of the borrowing countries to take a turn for the worse. Not only might repayment be jeopardized, but were the Fund to then revoke its preapproval, its negative signal could precipitate a crisis (see Goldstein and Calvo 1996, 271). And credit lines that could not be revoked—that were not conditioned on ongoing performance criteria—could give rise to *very* serious problems of moral hazard.

It is revealing that there was some discussion in 1994 of the creation of a short-term financing facility under which the IMF would disburse funds to countries experiencing temporary payments problems and whose eligibility had been determined in advance (see Williamson 1998). These discussions were not informed, however, by an appreciation of the magnitude of the funds that might have to be disbursed to restore confidence, given the rapid growth of the liquidity of private financial markets. Once the Mexican crisis revealed the extent of the commitments that would be required, the idea of contingent credit lines receded from view.[2]

The G-7 declaration itself provides veiled acknowledgments of these problems. Acknowledging that the IMF will not have the resources to provide contingent credit lines to several significantly sized emerging markets simultaneously, it suggests that G-7 countries might have to activate bilateral contingent financing lines alongside the IMF facility. Acknowledging implicitly the difficulty of extending and revoking access to contingent credit lines, it says nothing about whether countries would be prequalified or about how qualification would be determined. Nor does the G-7 raise the possibility that the Fund might take its cue from the private sector. This is the idea that it could take guidance on the availability and pricing of the facility from the banks, charging the same

---

2. The Supplemental Reserve Facility (SRF) approved by the IMF's Executive Board in December 1997 is in fact a small step in the direction of exceptional credit lines. It is designed to provide financial assistance to a member suffering from a temporary loss of market confidence and exceptional balance of payments problems (presumably reflecting turbulence in other countries), where there is the expectation that the problem can be corrected in short order. The idea is that these extra funds, sufficient to offset the impact on domestic markets of a sudden decline in market confidence, would be disbursed quickly (in conjunction with an existing standby or extended arrangement). Note, however, that access is not negotiated in advance, which is the critical point given the argument in the text about the Fund's limited ability to provide standby lines of credit.

fees and requiring the same collateral.[3] Only if a country qualified for a credit from the commercial banks would this be supplemented by the Fund. The problem the G-7 presumably worried about is that access would be limited to a few countries with exceptionally strong economic policies (the Argentinas of the world), and that politicians would lose their discretion to decide whether or not to extend a loan.

For a variety of reasons, then, these kind of schemes can operate only on a limited scale. They are not a silly idea, but they can provide only limited insurance against financial shocks.

The Calomiris Proposal

Charles Calomiris suggests that the Fund could square the circle by lending only to countries that accept a long list of conditions for strengthening their financial systems. Eligible countries would have to agree to raise capital requirements to 20 percent of assets so that bank stockholders would suffer a "credible first tranche of private loss . . ." in the event of an international rescue, mitigating the moral hazard problem (Calomiris 1998b, 16). They would have to require banks to issue subordinated debt and to hold substantial shares of their assets in cash and liquid securities. They would have to allow free entry into the domestic market by foreign banks and to adopt limited programs of deposit insurance. The Fund would lend only to countries that met these (and several additional) criteria.[4]

Calomiris's proposal is essentially an international variant of the narrow-banking proposals for domestic bank regulation described in chapter

---

3. See Gavin and Hausmann (1998) and Feldstein (1998b). As described by Gavin and Hausmann, the regional development banks, along possibly with the World Bank, would participate as members of syndicates along with commercial banks, with all of them agreeing to provide standby lines of credit; in Feldstein's variant, the IMF would do the same. Official cofinancing would give the credit lines effective seniority in repayment that would make them attractive to private lenders. The financial structure would be analogous to a private-sector "A/B loan," in which the Inter-American Development Bank (IDB) is the lender of record but agrees with private participants in the facility to share all payments with other lenders. Drawings would have to be repaid in three to five years. In one variant of the proposal, the mechanism would rely more on price and less on collateral than would existing commercial credit lines. The credit line would be renewed and the price would be adjusted at regular intervals (say, every 12 months). The IDB and allied multilaterals would extend such credit lines only to countries whose economic policies satisfied certain strong policy conditions. It would be possible, for example, to make eligibility for drawing on the facility contingent upon a good report in the IMF's Article IV consultations.

4. In a sense, these other preconditions for IMF support are designed to buttress the stability of the domestic financial system, providing the international analog to Bagehot's rule that a domestic lender of last resort should lend only against good collateral—in other words, insuring against the collapse of the domestic financial system and maximizing the probability that the Fund will get its money back.

4. Just as narrow-banking proponents argue that the moral hazard associated with the domestic financial safety net can be mitigated if it is extended only to banks that are subject to strict limits on their use of leverage and the composition of their investment portfolios, he assumes that the moral hazard created by IMF assistance can be contained by extending it only to countries that place similar restrictions on the entire banking system. The two proposals are open to the same objections. In the case of narrow banking, it is implausible that the failure of finance companies and other financial intermediaries operating outside the regulatory fence will be free of systemic implications. As the case of Long Term Capital Management reminds us, this makes it implausible that the authorities will really be prepared to stand by idly. In the case of IMF lending, it is similarly implausible that a crisis in a country that did not follow Calomiris's prescriptions would be free of systemic repercussions. In turn this renders it questionable that the time-consistent policy for the Fund would be to stand aside.

The reality is that simple rules for IMF lending are no more feasible than simple rules for intervention by national central banks. In both cases, there will inevitably be an element of discretion involved. Calomiris's proposal has the merit of at least highlighting the role of the Fund in promulgating international financial standards. But it does not finesse the fact that IMF resources will always be scarce and that the Fund will never be in the position to lend freely even to its most creditworthy members. And it assumes a willingness to ignore potential systemic repercussions that simply does not exist.

This means that as capital markets continue to expand, the Fund will have to rely less on lending and more on other levers. It will have to redouble its efforts at crisis prevention, promoting the promulgation of standards, strengthening its surveillance, and pressing its members to adopt sensible policies toward the exchange rate and the capital account. Inevitably, however, crises will still occur, and it will not be possible (or, for that matter, desirable) to meet them all with large-scale financial assistance. The Fund will then have play a more prominent role in debt workouts, acting as honest broker and attempting to bring debtors and creditors together. It can provide institutional incentives for the establishment of creditors' committees by working with those committees and financial incentives for the incorporation of renegotiation-friendly provisions into loan contracts by lending to countries that adopt the relevant contractual provisions at relatively favorable interest rates.

The Edwards Proposal for Breaking Up the IMF

The need for the IMF to concentrate on these new tasks and the unrealism of assuming that it can simply stand aside when countries fail to meet a formidable list of conditions for receiving standby credits have been acknowledged by Sebastian Edwards (1998c). These realizations lead Edwards to propose three new entities to supersede the Fund: a Global Information Agency to rate the health and stability of countries' economies and financial systems, a Contingent Global Financial Facility to provide contingent credit lines to countries meeting minimum standards of information disclosure and transparency as well as economic health, and a Global Restructuring Agency to provide conditional lending and advice on debt restructuring to crisis countries. Each of the new agencies would be "small and efficient" compared to the IMF and would have clearly defined responsibilities.

While this institutional division of labor has the merit of clearly delineating the tasks of each of the hypothetical agencies, it would do so at the cost of creating some potentially serious coordination problems. One can readily imagine, for example, confusion between the agencies responsible for contingent credits and conditional loans about who should provide assistance to a country such as Brazil. And it makes little sense for one international agency to set standards for financial transparency and disclosure and an entirely different agency, with no say over the design of those standards, to condition its lending on them. (Even worse would be for the Contingent Global Financial Facility to condition its lending on an entirely different set of standards than those set down by the Global Information Agency.) The proposal assumes that the transparency- and disclosure-rating function should be taken on by a multilateral, where this is best left wherever possible to the private sector.[5] It assumes the international community's willingness to underwrite much more generous international financing than heretofore; otherwise, the idea of contingent credit lines will remain impractical. It assumes a willingness to pay the salaries of additional international civil servants, because these three entities will have to be staffed not only by current IMF employees but also private-sector experts in debt restructuring and financial regulation, as Edwards acknowledges. Moreover, the premise that this global rating agency would improve on the performance of Moody's and Standard & Poor's assumes that these salaries would be more attractive than those offered by the private sector (so that the best analysts would choose to work for the multilateral). It assumes that national governments would accept the uncertainty that would come with establishing new international institutions that lack a track record. For all these reasons, Edwards's proposal is a nonstarter.

IMF Exchange Rate Advice

The Asian crisis raised obvious questions about the wisdom of the IMF's advice—for that matter, about the wisdom of everyone's advice—regard-

---

5. As argued in chapter 3.

ing the management of exchange rates. The *Wall Street Journal* view, that only pegged exchange rates are compatible with monetary and financial stability, is vulnerable to the criticism that pegged rates are strongly associated with crises. Pegged rates create one-way bets for speculators, making sitting ducks of the central banks and governments seeking to operate them. On the other hand, the view that high capital mobility should and will lead most countries to float their currencies must confront the fact that floating was a disaster in Asia, where currencies, rather than adjusting smoothly downward, collapsed abruptly, bankrupting financial and nonfinancial firms with debts denominated in foreign currency.

Why did the Asian devaluations have such devastatingly negative effects?[6] If there is one explanation, it is that governments failed to prepare the markets for the change in the exchange rate. The currency peg having been the centerpiece of their economic policy, jettisoning it was a heavy blow to their policy credibility. It raised doubts about their competence and about their commitment to their stated policy goals. Their stated commitment to the peg lulled banks and firms into the mistaken belief that there was no need for costly insurance against exchange rate fluctuations. Debtors saw no need to use forward and futures markets to hedge against exchange rate fluctuations. Hence, when the inevitable adjustment came, it was devastating not just to confidence but to the solvency of banks and corporations with unhedged foreign exposures. Investors, having been lulled into complacency by official assurances that the exchange rate was fixed, scrambled for the exits once they realized that those promises were empty. Banks and corporations with unhedged foreign liabilities scrambled for cover, purchasing the additional foreign exchange needed to service their debts and to hedge against further currency fluctuations. Both responses pushed the exchange rate down still further, which pushed yet additional banks and firms into bankruptcy. This only fed investor fears, further weakening the exchange rate and aggravating the difficulty of servicing private-sector debts.

Recommending that countries operating exchange rate pegs avoid these land mines by warning the markets that the peg can be changed, thereby encouraging banks and corporations to hedge their exposures, is disingenuous. Any government operating a peg that sends the message that it is prepared to change the rate invites a speculative attack. The first priority of any government seeking to peg the currency is to convince the markets that it is committed to maintaining that peg. To protect its reserves it will be forced to deny that it is contemplating an adjustment in the level of the exchange rate or change in the regime. Inevitably, its statements will discourage banks and corporations with liabilities denominated in foreign

---

6. This section summarizes the more elaborate discussion of Asia's experience with devaluation in appendix C.

currency from undertaking costly transactions in currency forward and futures markets to hedge that foreign exposure. Consequently, when the change in the exchange rate eventually and inevitably comes, its effects will be devastating.

It follows that in a world of high capital mobility there are only two feasible approaches to exchange rate policy. One is not just to peg the exchange rate but to lock it in—the Argentine strategy. In this case it matters little whether banks and firms hedge against exchange rate fluctuations because there is a negligible probability that the exchange rate will change. Of course, credibly locking in the exchange rate is easier said than done. Doing so requires abolishing the central bank and its discretionary powers in favor of a currency board and creating high hurdles to reversing that change (e.g., by putting the currency-board statute into the constitution).

Closing off all avenues for discretionary monetary policy not just for a time but for the foreseeable future is something that few societies are prepared to do. The vast majority of countries will consequently have to follow the other alternative of allowing their currencies to fluctuate. If the exchange rate moves regularly, banks and firms will have an incentive to hedge their foreign exposures, and they will then possess insurance against the negative financial effects of unexpectedly large currency fluctuations if and when these occur. By implication, the vast majority of emerging markets should move to greater exchange rate flexibility sooner rather than later.

The IMF should therefore push more of its members to adopt policies of greater exchange rate flexibility before they are forced to do so in a crisis. Even if this evolution is inevitable, it will be associated with financial distress, as in Asia, if it is forced on reluctant governments that fail to prepare banks, firms, and households for the eventuality. If, on the other hand, the authorities move gradually toward greater exchange rate flexibility while capital is still flowing in, banks and firms will hedge their exposures and not suffer catastrophic losses when the exchange rate moves by an unexpectedly large amount. If the government does not link its entire economic-policy strategy to the maintenance of a fixed currency peg but develops a more diversified portfolio of intermediate targets and anchors, it will not lose all credibility when it bows to the inevitable.

Hence, the IMF needs to more forcefully encourage its members to move to policies of greater exchange rate flexibility, and the sooner the better. With few exceptions it should pressure its members, in the context of Article IV consultations and program discussions, to abandon simple pegs, crawling pegs, narrow bands and other mechanisms for limiting exchange rate flexibility before they are forced to do so by the markets.

This does not mean that countries that reject the currency-board option will have to allow their exchange rates to float freely; they can still intervene in the foreign-exchange market to dampen temporary fluctuations and limit the volatility that a freely floating exchange rate entails. What they should not do, by this argument, is commit to an explicit exchange rate target that would force them to issue misleadingly reassuring statements likely to lull banks and firms into a false sense of complacency and set the stage for an ugly crisis. Floating, even dirty floating, is uncomfortable because of the volatility that it tends to entail. It is that volatility and not the obtuseness of policymakers, of course, that leads many governments to continue to attempt to peg their exchange rates. But the globalization of financial markets both makes it easier to live with volatility (by creating additional opportunities for banks, firms, and households to hedge their exposures) and heightens the difficulty of operating a peg, strengthening the association between currency pegs and crises. Witness the case of Mexico, whose currency declined against the US dollar by more than 20 percent in the final quarter of 1998. The peso's depreciation has created problems for certain segments of the Mexican economy, to be sure, but it has not precipitated a crisis. Surely, most countries, given a choice between Mexico's situation and the dilemmas of the Brazilian authorities desperately seeking to defend their currency peg, would prefer the former, and with good reason.

Is There Still a Case for a Peg as a Nominal Anchor in Disinflation?

Some otherwise strong proponents of greater flexibility still concede a temporary role for pegged rates in countries that are trying to bring down high inflation (e.g., Sachs 1998c; Bruno and Fischer 1990). If the country, having brought down inflation, can then smoothly exit the currency peg before being forced to do so in a crisis, the peg will have been worth the candle.

The problem is the same as with using heroin or morphine to treat a patient in pain; once the suffering subsides, the patient is still hooked. And open markets offer no padded cell into which to place the country until it kicks the habit. Smooth exits from currency pegs, whatever the original rationale for the peg, are very much the exception to the rule.[7] In fact, the secret to a successful exit is not that mysterious: governments can move to greater exchange rate flexibility without precipitating a crisis if they do so before capital stops flowing in—while the pressure is still for appreciation, not depreciation. Firms and banks will then learn to hedge their exposure to currency fluctuations before being taught that lesson by a devastating crisis. But the fact of the matter is that few governments are willing to move while there is still time. Having made the currency peg the touchstone of their anti-inflationary policy, they fear

---

7. This pattern is documented in Eichengreen and Masson (1998).

that investors will interpret its relaxation as opening the door to a new round of financial excesses (Sachs 1998d). Almost without exception, they tend to put off the day of reckoning. Hence, when the exit finally occurs, it comes in the context of, and in turn tends to aggravate, a crisis.

This problem is intrinsic to the strategy of pegging the exchange rate in the early stages of inflation stabilization, when the government makes the currency peg the cornerstone of its economic-policy strategy. It is disingenuous to simply assume it away. The evidence that exchange-rate-based stabilizations are associated with pegs that outlive their usefulness, which are in turn associated with crises, is too compelling to be denied. It follows that the Fund should be much more cautious than heretofore to endorse exchange-rate-based stabilization strategies and should do more to push its members toward greater exchange rate flexibility.

The Currency-Board Option

The only exception to this rule is countries that are prepared not just to fix the exchange rate but to lock it in for the foreseeable future.[8] Such countries will be few in number. Locking in the exchange rate means abolishing the central bank and its discretionary monetary powers. It means making those steps difficult to reverse. The currency board will have to be created by a parliamentary law or constitutional amendment that can be overturned only by a supermajority. It means starting down that path only when there exists broad and deep support for putting monetary policy on autopilot, rendering it a very low probability event that a supermajority can be marshaled to reverse the policy. Otherwise, when times are tough, speculators will anticipate mounting public opposition to monetary austerity, perhaps leading to abandonment of the currency board and the exchange rate peg, and thereby giving rise the generic pegged-rate problem of self-fulfilling speculative attacks.

The idea that more than a few countries in exceptional circumstances will be prepared to fix the exchange rate once and for all flies in the face of theory and evidence. Since the mid-1970s, the share of developing countries with managed or floating exchange rates has risen from 10 percent to more than half the total (see figure 7.1). The trend is more impressive still if one calculates the share of developing country GDP (measured at purchasing power parity) accounted for by each arrangement (see figure 7.2). There are reasons to expect the trend to continue. For one thing, international capital mobility sharpens the tradeoff between domestic and international objectives. Capital controls and transaction costs that once insulated the domestic economy from financial conditions

---

8. The discussion here of currency boards is necessarily abbreviated. For the definitive study see Williamson (1995).

Figure 7.1   Evolution of exchange rate regimes, 1975-97
(percentage of total number of developing countries)

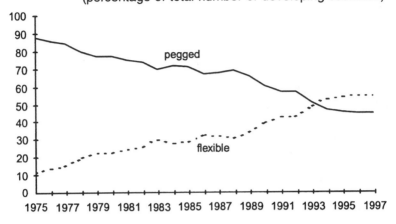

Source: Eichengreen (1998).

Figure 7.2   Evolution of exchange rate regimes, 1975-96
(output-weighted share of total output of developing countries)

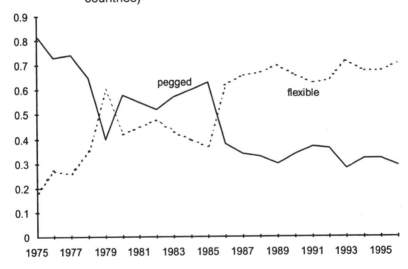

Source: Eichengreen (1998).

abroad now do so to a much lesser extent. A fixed exchange rate, in conjunction with high capital mobility, means that a country must rigidly conform to the monetary and financial conditions prevailing in the rest of the world. In addition, the liberalization of financial markets and the growth of international capital flows heighten the need for a lender of last resort, a service the central bank can provide only if it is not constrained by the need to defend a fixed currency peg. Both factors create strong pressure for greater exchange rate flexibility.

Only countries in which investors harbor exceptional distrust of discretionary monetary policy, where the economy is sufficiently flexible and resilient to adapt to whatever monetary and financial conditions are implied by a fixed exchange rate, and where there exists deep-seated public support for the policy, however painful its consequences, can sustain the currency-board alternative. Argentina can, given the profound distrust of discretionary policy that exists there as a result of the country's repeated bouts with hyperinflation, which in turn provides broad-based public backing for its "convertibility law."[9] Hong Kong can, given the province's highly internationalized banking system and flexible labor markets, the economy's extreme openness to international trade, and the Hong Kong Monetary Authority's insulation from political pressures. But in few other countries is public support for putting monetary policy on autopilot as deep and broad.[10] Again, the implication for the IMF is that it needs to push the vast majority of its members to install regimes of greater exchange rate flexibility. The failure of recent official reports on measures to enhance the stability of the international financial system to make this point shows a regrettable lack of consensus and political will.[11]

Fiscal and Monetary Policies

The IMF came under withering fire for asking Thailand, Indonesia, and South Korea to hike interest rates and tighten fiscal policies following the onset of their crises. It was accused of blindly taking a page from its Latin American debt crisis cookbook, where the setting was one of budget

---

9. Another popular explanation for the viability of the Argentine currency board is the country's increasingly effective prudential supervision and regulation, which the authorities have strengthened precisely in order to render their fixed exchange rate more defensible.

10. In Asia, the flash point for this debate was the question of whether a currency board was appropriate for Indonesia when the country was in the throes of its crisis. Fear of inflation and distrust of the monetary authorities were there, but the IMF and other commentators questioned whether the other conditions for fixing the exchange rate and putting monetary policy on autopilot were in place. For one thing, the banking system was weak, and if investors tested the authorities' commitment to the peg, the government might not have been able to sustain the higher interest rates needed to defend it at the price of further bank failures and financial distress. For another, there was the question of whether the public would support these official efforts, especially if exchange-rate stabilization was seen as a temporary expedient to support the rate only until the ruling elite had succeeded in removing their assets from the country.

11. Thus, G-7 (1998, 5) speaks only of the need to consider "the elements necessary for the maintenance of sustainable exchange rate regimes in emerging economies."

deficits and inflation, making monetary and fiscal retrenchment necessary parts of the solution. It was criticized for neglecting the fact that Asian countries entered their crises with high savings, low inflation, and government budgets in balance or surplus, hardly suggesting that excessively expansionary policies were at the root of the problem and that monetary and fiscal austerity were needed for its solution. In fact, the critics argue, the IMF should have encouraged Asian governments to employ all of their available macroeconomic-policy instruments to prevent the onset of recession or to minimize its severity.

Fiscal Policy

There is no question that absorption had to be reduced once capital stopped flowing in and it became necessary to eliminate the current-account deficit. It being undesirable for the entire burden of adjustment to fall on the private sector, there was a presumption in favor of fiscal cuts. In addition, there was the need to recapitalize the banking system. Bonds might be issued to spread those costs over time, but additional tax revenues would still be needed to service the additional obligations. Business cycle considerations notwithstanding, this pointed to the need for a significant tightening of fiscal policy. And to the extent that it anticipated some slowdown in Asian economic growth, the IMF saw the need to temper that advice.

The problem was that the Fund failed to adjust for the cycle. It failed to anticipate the severity of the Asian downturn or see that the restrictive fiscal policies it recommended would themselves make that downturn worse. Once this realization dawned, it modified its advice. Subsequent adjustments to its initial programs acknowledged the need for governments to use fiscal policy to provide countercyclical stimulus to neutralize the deepening recession and to provide a social safety net for the poor. In Indonesia, for example, the second program of January 1998 revised the target for fiscal policy from a surplus of 1 percent of GDP to a deficit of 1 percent of GDP; the second revision widened it to 3 percent of GDP, the third to 8.5 percent. The 4 March 1998 revision of the Thai program excluded the 3 percent of GDP interest costs of the financial-sector cleanup. Successive revisions of the South Korean program adjusted the deficit target from essentially 0 to 2 percent of GDP (Cline 1998, table 2; World Bank 1998, table 2.9). With hindsight, it is nevertheless clear that the Fund's fiscal targets were too tight and that larger deficits should have been encouraged.[12] The Fund now appears to have acknowledged its error, which provides some reassurance that it will not be committed again (e.g., Neiss 1998).

---

12. In fact, there may have been some cases where the IMF pushed for larger budget deficits than governments themselves were prepared to accept.

Figure 7.3 Short-term interest rates, January 1997-March 1998

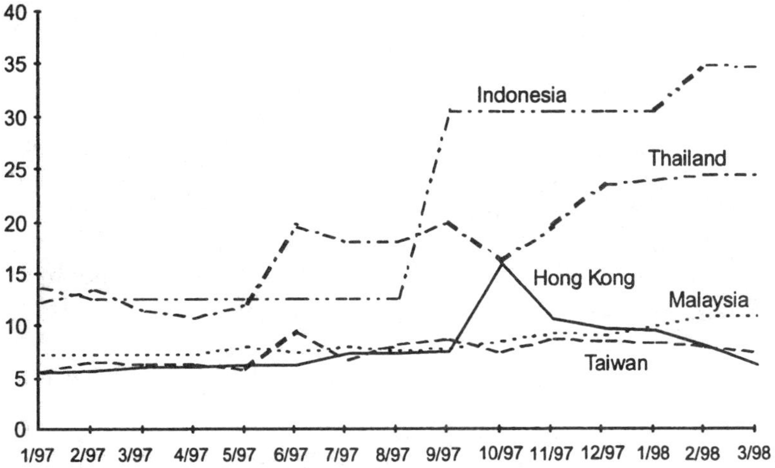

Source: The Economist, *Emerging Market Indicators* (various issues).

Monetary Policy

In each country, the IMF recommended sharp increases in interest rates to restore investor confidence, stem capital flight, and stabilize the currency. This, it argued, was the only way for the authorities to quickly reassure investors, given the time needed to push through other reforms. Only if they signaled their resolve to defend the exchange rate by rendering short-term money-market instruments more attractive could confidence be restored.

That the medicine did not work is clear. The IMF's own explanation is that governments did not push up interest rates and hold them there with adequate resolve (see figure 7.3). Indonesia raised rates to 30-40 percent in August but reduced them to 20-30 percent in September despite the rupiah's continued decline. South Korea maintained an official ceiling on interest rates as late as December despite the deterioration of the foreign-exchange market. These half-hearted measures, it is argued, were insufficient to restore confidence.

The Fund's critics argue that interest rates were not too low but too high. High rates plunged Asia's highly geared corporations into bankruptcy. As failures cascaded through the manufacturing sector and banks were rendered insolvent by the inability of their customers to service their loans, the exchange rate weakened, reflecting this further damage to the financial system. Flight capital, rather than being attracted back by higher yields, was repelled by additional defaults. Thus, higher interest rates weakened the exchange rate rather than strengthening it as the IMF had forecast.

The effect of interest rates on the exchange rate, while an empirical question, is one on which there exists exactly zero convincing evidence, forcing both the Fund and its critics to rest their cases on arguments rather than statistics. Both sides can agree that in theory there exists an "interest rate Laffer Curve." While modest interest rate increases are likely to strengthen the currency, if taken to excess they may so damage the financial condition of banks and firms that confidence deteriorates and the currency weakens. The empirical question is where the point of inflection lies and whether IMF-inspired policies surpassed it. It is plausible that the critical turning point should be lower in Asia than in less debt-dependent countries, given the high gearing ratios of corporations in the region. Reflecting the underdevelopment of the equity market and its bank-centered financial system, South Korea's ratio of debt to GDP, for example, is 30 to 50 percent higher than in the United States (e.g., Wade and Veneroso 1998). The capacity of nonfinancial firms to absorb increases in debt-servicing costs is consequently more limited.

While there is no question about the fact, its implications for the interest rate/exchange rate nexus are uncertain. Assertions that interest rates were pushed to the point where they weakened the exchange rate rather than strengthening it remain just that—assertions.

Some of the harshest critics of IMF policy, while insisting on the need for lower interest rates for domestic reasons, acknowledge that these would not have lured back flight capital and strengthened the exchange rate—to the contrary. The right choice may have been to reduce rates in order to relieve the distress among heavily indebted firms and reflate the economy, but there would have been a price, namely the need to suspend service on the external debt and impose Malaysian-style capital controls. Lower interest rates might have been the right remedy for South Korea, for example, but they would have rendered the country unable to roll over its maturing debts. Robert Wade and Frank Veneroso (1998, 13) are explicit about this tradeoff: "Why should not Korea, for one, not just declare a debt moratorium and set about exporting it way out of trouble?" they ask. "The vast increase in the servicing and repayment costs of foreign loans due to the devaluation is a national disaster, the costs of which should be borne collectively. Let belts be tightened, to the extent of refusing any new reliance on external finance."

This is the unfortunate reality: there was a choice between reducing interest rates on the one hand and maintaining capital-market access on the other, and governments could not have it both ways. Lower rates might have facilitated much-needed domestic reflation, but they would have also required countries to suspend service on their external debts. And that last step was something that governments, in their wisdom, were reluctant to take. Their belief was that debts, once suspended, are difficult to restructure, and that, in the interim, access to working capital and trade credits will be disrupted. Thus, calls for the IMF to amend its advice to encourage lower interest rates in crisis economies will remain impractical absent other changes in capital markets to make the process of restructuring and renegotiation more efficient.

Measures to Encourage Debt Restructuring

The most important changes to facilitate restructuring and renegotiation, as noted in chapter 5, are the incorporation of sharing, majority-voting, minimum-legal-threshold, nonacceleration, and collective-representation clauses into loan contracts. This is a task for national regulators. But there is also a role for the IMF. By lending at relatively favorable rates to governments that incorporate such provisions into their own loan contracts and that require domestic banks and corporations to do so and by making a commitment to adopt such clauses a condition for the continued disbursal of financial assistance, the Fund can provide incentives for contractual innovation.[13] By lending after a country has suspended debt payments and before it has cleared away its arrears, the Fund can encourage recalcitrant creditors to come to the bargaining table. Insofar as the large number of creditors and rules requiring their unanimous assent to the terms of a restructuring plan create problems of collective action that hinder negotiations, lending into arrears can jump-start the process. To be sure, the Fund should lend into arrears only when a government is prepared to make a serious adjustment effort and to engage in good-faith negotiations with its creditors.[14] But insofar as sovereign debtors and the international community generally see the temporary suspension of payments as too difficult and costly a route to pursue, the IMF needs to use its lending power to tip the balance, opening up restructuring negotiations as a viable alternative to regular IMF rescues designed to avert default.

Transparency

The difficulty of developing reliable early-warning indicators is the obvious reason why it is unrealistic to ask the IMF to be more transparent about its own views—to more aggressively "blow the whistle" on coun-

---

13. In a hypothetical world, one might wish the Fund to lend only after countries' adoption of the relevant provisions. The problem is that demanding immediate action of this type from countries in a crisis would likely alert the market to their institutional shortcomings and disrupt their market access.

14. When these conditions do not hold, the policy will delay crisis resolution, not expedite it. This is why lending into arrears should be considered on a case-by-case basis.

tries courting financial crises. Its capacity to predict crises being imperfect, the Fund will inevitably blow its whistle in error. Failing to warn of crises is one thing, but warning of crises that might not otherwise happen is more serious still.

In contrast, bank regulators detecting balance-sheet problems in domestic financial institutions are able to blow the whistle because they can halt the operation of the problem bank; otherwise, their warnings would provoke a depositor run. Because the IMF possesses no analogous powers vis-à-vis its members, by blowing the whistle it could therefore precipitate a crisis.

The same objection applies to the idea that the IMF should publicly rate its members' vulnerability to currency and banking crises (e.g., Kaufman 1998a, b). If there is value in such ratings, there is nothing to prevent their sale by commercial agencies less subject to political pressure. There is an argument for the Fund to assume a rating-agency role only if one believes that it has better access to information than the markets and that this additional information has significant value for predicting crises.[15] Neither premise is transparently correct.

None of this is to deny that the Fund can and should be more forthright in its assessment of financial problems. But it must walk a fine line between swallowing its fears and exciting already skittish markets.

Nor does any of this weaken the general case for greater IMF transparency. Without transparency there cannot be accountability, and without accountability there will be neither political support nor additional funding for the IMF. At present, summaries of Executive Board discussions appear only once a year in the Fund's *Annual Report*, and program documents can be embargoed for 30 years.[16] Such confidentiality is excessive. At the same time, no one would suggest that all IMF staff analyses should be placed on the world wide web as soon as written or that Executive Board meetings should be broadcast on cable television, because this would simply shift all meaningful conversations between staff and management to the telephone and all Executive Board decision making to the cloakroom. Immediate release of all program documents is not feasible either; when these contain financially damaging information, as in the case where confidential IMF documents leaked to the public revealed that

---

15. And even then there is the objection that governments will withhold such information if they believe that the Fund is prepared to release it to the public or to publish credit ratings based upon it.

16. Some countries—Thailand, Indonesia, and South Korea, for example—choose to release letters of intent voluntarily, at which point the Fund posts them on its website. In addition, the Fund now releases "press information notices" (PINs) summarizing the conclusions of Article IV consultations, but only with the authorization of the member. In its first year of operation, roughly half the members subject to Article IV consultations authorized the release of a PIN.

the Bank of Korea had tied up a substantial share of its foreign-exchange reserves by loaning these to foreign branches of domestic banks, the effect can be destabilizing.

Here, the US Federal Reserve Board, which has struck a balance between confidentiality and transparency, offers a model to follow. The Open Market Committee releases minutes of each meeting with a lag of about six weeks. (Full transcripts, with a small amount of confidential information regarding foreign central banks, businesses, and persons deleted, are released with a lag of five years.) The six-week lag prevents market participants from using the minutes as a source of inside information on future interest rate movements but at the same time forces governors to articulate the rationale for their decisions. Perhaps summaries or minutes of Executive Board discussions should be released with a somewhat longer lag on the grounds that while decisions to change discount rates are implemented when taken, the decision to disburse IMF assistance will in contrast be stretched out over a period of weeks and months. But a lag of 52 weeks is excessive. The same is even more true of 30 years for program documents.

The IMF should also regularize the external review and evaluation of past programs (see Sachs 1998b, 21). It has already constituted an Evaluation Group, chaired by a member of its Executive Board, which commissions ad hoc external evaluation exercises with the consent of the Executive Board. To date, these have focused on broad issues: the first evaluated the IMF's enhanced structural adjustment facility; the second, announced on 30 June 1998, seeks to evaluate the effectiveness of the IMF's surveillance over members' policies under Article IV of the Articles of Agreement; and the third, announced in December, will review the Fund's research function. This process should be regularized and should no longer require the approval of the Executive Board. It should accompany each country program, and it should be initiated within a fixed period of time.

The Fund and the Capital Account

Many criticisms of the IMF reflect more fundamental doubts about its response to the emergence of an increasingly integrated international financial market. Since its creation, the Fund's core responsibility has been to oversee the operation of the international monetary system, which for many years meant focusing on its members' policies toward the current account. With the growing integration of financial markets, however, the international monetary system is now increasingly shaped by international capital flows. IMF staff has long favored openness to capital flows, arguing the case for capital mobility by analogy to the case for free international trade. In 1996 the Interim Committee requested that the Fund analyze the costs and benefits of capital flows and consider changes to the Articles of Agreement that would give the IMF jurisdiction over its members' policies toward the capital account. In April 1997 the Interim Committee concluded that there would be benefits from amending the Articles to enable the Fund to promote the orderly liberalization of capital movements, a view that it reiterated at the September 1997 Annual Meetings of the World Bank and IMF in Hong Kong, where it stated that capital-account liberalization should be made one of the "purposes" of the Fund (Camdessus 1998b, 1).

These statements look less than astute in the wake of the Asian crisis, which unleashed a barrage of criticism of IMF-led efforts to encourage capital-account liberalization. The analogy with current-account liberalization, many critics now insist, was fundamentally flawed. While the positive effects of trade liberalization for economic growth have been extensively documented, the evidence of comparable benefits of capital-account liberalization is more limited, if it exists at all (see Bhagwati 1998).[17]

It is easier to levy criticisms at this level of abstraction than it is to suggest concrete alternatives. Practical recommendations must acknowledge the powerful forces promoting the growth of capital flows. The information and communications revolutions, and the manifest desire of governments to partake of the advantages of liberalized domestic financial markets, mean that administrative controls, in order to retain their effectiveness, will have to become increasingly onerous and distortionary. At the least, governments seeking to shape the extent and composition of international capital flows will have to do so in more market-friendly ways.

Prudential Regulation of the Capital Account

To say that there are pressures for the liberalization of international financial transactions and that there is something inevitable about the process does not mean that these transactions should be left unregulated. In the domestic context it is understood that banks are fragile, prompting governments to impose prudential regulations on financial intermediaries' transactions and positions in assets whose liquidity and risk characteristics have implications for systemic stability. Such regulations are especially strict where the techniques of risk management are least well developed, where auditing and accounting practices leave most to be desired, and where financial disclosure is least adequate, weakening market discipline.[18]

---

17. The question is debated at length by the contributors to Kenen (1998).

18. The existence of systemic risk has also led governments to provide deposit insurance and lender-of-last-resort services (mechanisms "for converting highly illiquid portfolios into liquid ones, in extraordinary circumstances," in the words of Greenspan [1998b, 4]). Stronger

These same grounds justify the regulation of international financial transactions even more strongly than they justify the regulation of domestic transactions. Information asymmetries are more pervasive in international financial markets. The difficulties of raising liquidity in emergencies is greater, as is the scope for contagion. And insofar as the liabilities of banks and other borrowers are denominated in foreign currency, the domestic central bank (not being able to print foreign currency) has limited ability to undertake lender-of-last-resort operations.

This does not mean that international financial transactions should be prohibited but that their cost should be influenced by regulation that takes into account their implications for systemic risk. As explained in chapter 4, banks should be required to purchase cover in currency forward or futures markets for their open foreign positions, better aligning the private and social costs of foreign funding. They should be required to close their open positions by matching the currency composition of their assets and liabilities—when borrowing in foreign currency, making only loans denominated in foreign currency.[19] Capital requirements should be adjusted to take into account not just the implications for systemic risk of banks' investments but also the special risks of foreign funding. Banks borrowing abroad should be required to put up additional noninterest-bearing reserves with the central bank, while banks lending abroad (notably US, European, and Japanese banks) should be required to attach higher risk weights to short-term claims on banks in emerging markets. And where there is reason to doubt the effectiveness of supervision and regulation in containing systemic risk, the authorities should reinforce these other measures by imposing taxes or nonremunerated deposit requirements on capital inflows.

Sequencing

The implications for sequencing the liberalization of capital-account transactions flow from the potential for dangerous interaction between international capital movements and domestic banks. The most important point is the risk of precipitous liberalization, namely liberalization that precedes the removal of blanket government guarantees for the banking system and the implementation of international standards for auditing and accounting, financial disclosure, corporate governance, and supervision and regulation. FDI should be liberalized first, politics permitting, because

---

prudential regulations are then seen as necessary to mitigate the tendency for financial-market participants to take on additional risk in response to the provision of this safety net.

19. Additional measures would be required to the extent that this only transformed currency risk into credit risk (in other words, to the extent that banks were still vulnerable because their customers were no better able to manage foreign-exchange risk than the banks themselves, raising the specter of loan defaults, as explained in chapter 4).

inward FDI is unlikely to immediately turn into outward FDI in response to a deterioration in macroeconomic and financial conditions. This can happen, to be sure, but FDI tends to be less responsive to the conjuncture than financial capital, given the costs of liquidating tangible assets, and therefore has a lesser tendency to precipitate a crisis.[20] Foreign investment in equity and bond markets should be liberalized before, or at least not after, the removal of barriers to offshore funding by the banking system. Thailand's and South Korea's experiences in 1997 provide ample warning of the dangers of removing restrictions on inflows into the banking system while retaining those on sales of domestic stocks and bonds to foreign investors.

Is There Still a Case for Amending the Articles of Agreement?

Where does all this leave proposals to amend the Articles of Agreement to make capital-account convertibility a goal of IMF policy and to give the institution authority to encourage the orderly liberalization of capital flows? There is no contradiction between using taxes and tax-like instruments to manage capital flows and the desideratum of capital-account convertibility. Convertibility means shunning prohibitions and quantitative restrictions that prevent market participants from undertaking certain transactions at any price but is compatible with taxes that better align private and social costs. A blanket prohibition on foreign borrowing is more distortionary than a capital-import tax, which still permits those with especially attractive investment projects to finance them externally so long as they are willing to incur the additional costs of a public policy designed to make them internalize the implications of their decisions for systemic stability.

This is the same distinction the IMF has traditionally drawn regarding the current-account. Current-account convertibility is a goal of IMF policy under the Articles of Agreement. But while current-account convertibility is defined under Article VIII as freedom from restrictions on payments and transfers for current international transactions, that article does not proscribe the application of import tariffs and taxes to the underlying transactions. Correspondingly, capital-account convertibility, while implying the removal of controls and prohibitions, does not mean abjuring taxes and tax-like levies on the underlying transactions.

In principle, amending the Articles of Agreement to give the IMF jurisdiction over the capital account would enable an enlightened Fund to encourage its members to implement this important distinction. It would

---

20. The empirical results of Frankel and Rose (1996) clearly support this conclusion.

position it to give guidance to its members on the optimal speed and sequencing of capital-account liberalization. It could lend legitimacy to taxes and tax-like instruments designed to limit the level and shape the term structure of foreign debts. And it would give the Fund leverage to encourage countries utilizing taxes on inflows to accelerate financial-sector reforms. Against this should be weighed the danger that an IMF with expanded powers might push its members to liberalize prematurely and that it would oppose any and all tax and tax-like policies toward capital flows. It might require countries seeking to adopt Chilean-style holding-period taxes to first obtain the authorization of the Executive Board, or it might authorize countries to restrict capital-account transactions on prudential grounds only after it was convinced that other, more capital-account-friendly measures were not available.[21] If the amendment to the Articles of Agreement giving it jurisdiction over capital-account policies regarded taxes and controls on inflows as permissible only when adopted temporarily or for a limited transitional period, IMF staff might then become knee-jerk opponents of the indefinite use of such measures for prudential reasons. Even if countries were permitted to limit capital flows as a form of prudential regulation, staff might argue that a measure had actually been adopted for other reasons (e.g., that a differential reserve requirement was in fact being used for purposes of monetary control) and was therefore not acceptable. As Jacques Polak (1998, 8) has put it, an IMF-given jurisdiction over capital-account restrictions might become "the enforcer of the new code, making sure at every step that any policy it recommends or endorses can pass the test of the new Article."

Experience with Article VIII, which obliges members to establish the convertibility of their currencies for purposes of current-account transactions, does not suggest that the IMF will automatically become the rigid enforcer of a new code. In enforcing Article VIII, the Fund has in fact recognized a wide range of mitigating circumstances. Still, to reassure the skeptics, the IMF needs to articulate its strategy for capital-account liberalization, explaining its approach to the problem of sequencing and its policy toward the taxation of capital inflows. It needs to make clear that amending the Articles of Agreement does not mean eliminating Article VI, Section 3, which gives members the right to apply capital controls. Only then, having dismissed fears that it will push for precipitous liberalization and that it will oppose taxes on capital inflows as prudential measures, might its efforts to amend the Articles deserve support.

Conclusion

The notion that the IMF should be abolished flies in the face of a century and more of experience with the operation of financial markets. Accidents

---

21. Thus, one could imagine the Fund withholding its approval of a capital-import tax on these grounds in the case of a country that had not yet succeeded in meeting the Basle

can happen, and preventing fatal consequences requires the provision of a financial safety net. IMF loans can play a useful role in limiting the systemic consequences. But IMF resources will always be small relative to those of the markets. This, and the fact that government commitments to policy reform will always be uncertain, will limit the Fund's ability to extend standing lines of credit. But proposing that the Fund should loan only to countries that meet a long list of economic and financial preconditions assumes away the fact that crises in other countries can have serious adverse consequences for their neighbors and for the stability of the global financial system as a whole.

This means that there will remain a role for IMF lending and that when loans should be extended will remain a judgment call. This is not to deny that the IMF can go about this better. The Fund can make a more concerted effort to round up private credits to supplement its own. It can encourage the creation of private committees of creditors. And it can contribute to efforts to create a third alternative to ever-larger bailouts and devastating defaults. This means pushing not just for the creation of creditors' committees but also for the incorporation of new provisions in loan contracts, something it can do by lending on more favorable terms to countries agreeing to this step. It can lend into arrears as a way of providing debtor-in-possession financing and bringing the creditors to the bargaining table.

Of course, the IMF should continue to strengthen its surveillance of financial markets, institutions, and supervision. It should continue to cultivate contacts with market participants as a way of obtaining independent assessments of financial risks. It should continue to pursue its data dissemination initiatives, extending the coverage of economic and, particularly, financial variables. But it should not lull itself or market participants into the mistaken belief that improved surveillance and additional data will allow crises to be foreseen and prevented. The unexpected will still happen. Even the most reliable data will have to be revised in response to new developments.

Given the impossibility in this day and age of effectively segmenting domestic and international financial markets, the IMF's surveillance activities will ineluctably draw it deeper into issues of financial-market structure and regulation. To an extent this has already happened, rendering moot the objections of those who would have the Fund refocus on its traditional monetary and fiscal concerns. But the Fund has not dealt adequately with its resource constraint—that it lacks the personnel and expertise needed to provide detailed analysis and advice on bank regulation, auditing and accounting, insolvency and reorganization procedures, and corporate governance—or with the backlash that is understandably elicited by its ever deeper incursions into the domestic legal and economic arrangements

---

Capital Standards, where in fact this is precisely the sort of country that most needs to resort to a capital-inflow tax.

of its clients. It needs to better articulate the case for involvement in these areas. It needs to approach them not by attempting to provide detailed advice on institutional reform to each of its members, something of which it is not capable and which its members would not accept, but by working more systematically with private-sector organizations and other multilaterals in the promulgation of international standards.

These changes in the way the IMF goes about its business will help, but they will not profoundly alter the international financial architecture. The most important changes—in the provisions of loan agreements, in exchange rate policies, and in policies toward the capital account—will occur elsewhere, at the national level and in the markets. It is there that the scope is greatest for reducing the risk of financial crises.

APPENDICES

Appendix A
Architecture Scorecard

Architectural reform is a crowded field, making it hard to tell the players without a scorecard. This appendix therefore provides a roster of the competing plans. For those most closely resembling that laid out above, it provides an evaluation as well as a description.

National Proposals

The UK Proposal

The UK government proposes creating a new permanent Standing Committee for Global Financial Regulation bringing together the IMF, the World Bank, the Basle Committee, and other regulatory groups (Brown 1998). Its main task would be to establish and implement international standards for financial regulation and supervision. The United Kingdom would push for the mandatory adherence to codes of conduct for fiscal policy, monetary policy, corporate governance, and social policy to be drawn up by the World Bank and the Fund.

The French Proposal

The French government proposes transforming the Interim Committee into a council that would serve as the ultimate decision-making body for the IMF (Government of France 1998). That council, made up of national finance ministers, would meet regularly in order to vote on matters concerning the IMF's major strategic decisions, including financial commitments.[1] The French government recommends that the IMF work for the adoption of a "Disclosure Charter" for private financial institutions. It urges regulators to adopt rules to rein in the financial activities of offshore centers. It suggests that countries should more slowly and prudently liberalize their capital accounts and recommends, without providing details, the creation of a "financial safeguard clause" for governments to invoke, "in consultation" with the IMF, to protect themselves against destabilizing capital flows.

The US Proposal

The United States recommends the creation of a contingency-finance mechanism "anchored in the International Monetary Fund" to extend credit lines to countries not yet experiencing a full-fledged crisis but whose stability is potentially threatened. This would provide countries with strong policy fundamentals relatively short-term money at high interest rates.

The Canadian Proposal

Canada's six-point plan emphasizes "vigilance on the part of G-7 central banks," the pursuit of strong policies by emerging-market economies, attention to the needs of the poorest countries, steps to strengthen national financial systems and international oversight, development of a specific strategy for prudent liberalization of the capital account, and mechanisms for involving private investors in the resolution of crises, specifically the negotiation of standing credit lines and modification of the terms of bond contracts. It points to the need to consider standstill mechanisms and suggests that countries legislate an "Emergency Standstill Clause" affecting all cross-border financial contracts. This clause would be invoked only if the withdrawal of short-term finance were threatening financial stability (Canada, Department of Finance 1998). Activating it would require the agreement of the IMF Executive Board.

Private Proposals

Soros's Credit Insurance Agency

George Soros has suggested the creation of a public corporation to insure investors against debt defaults (Soros 1997, 1998). Countries would pay

---

1. An allied proposal, due to Philippe Maystadt, former chairman of the Interim Committee, would allow that committee to create subcommittees to address specific issues of concern.

a fee when floating loans in order to underwrite the cost of insurance. Each country's debts would be limited to a ceiling set by the IMF on the basis of its assessment of the country's macroeconomic and financial condition. Loans in excess of the ceiling would not be insured, and the IMF would not aid countries having difficulty servicing uninsured loans.

Kaufman's International Regulator and Rating Agency

Henry Kaufman (1998a, b) would create a new international institution with supervisory and regulatory responsibilities over financial markets and institutions. It would supervise the investment and position-taking activities not just of traditional financial intermediaries but of nonbank financial-market participants (hedge funds, etc.). It would be empowered to harmonize minimum capital requirements, establish uniform accounting and disclosure standards, and monitor the performance of the financial institutions and markets of its members. Its board would be composed of investment professionals drawn from "all major industrial countries." It would provide public ratings of the credit quality of the market participants under its authority. The IMF would similarly provide ratings of the economic and financial strength of its members and make those credit ratings public.

Raffer's International Bankruptcy Court

Raffer's scheme for an international bankruptcy court is representative of a number of academic proposals along similar lines (Raffer 1990). Raffer would create an international court of arbitration, to be headquartered in a neutral country that is neither an active international lender nor borrower and give it the power to impose a standstill in the event of a crisis and impose settlement terms when debtors and creditors are unable to agree on voluntary restructuring terms.

Meltzer's "True International Lender of Last Resort"

Meltzer (1998) would limit IMF lending to short-term loans at high interest rates to countries following fundamentally sound economic policies and able to put up sound collateral. Central banks could borrow from the Fund only upon presenting internationally traded assets, and the Fund would be barred from making loans without receiving marketable collateral. In some forums he has suggested that the IMF might be closed and that the BIS, as the central bank for central banks, could instead serve in this function.

Calomiris' Rules for IMF Lending

Calomiris (1998b) would replace the Fund and the US Exchange Stabilization Fund with a reformed IMF that would offer a limited discount window lending facility. Loans would be at a "penalty" interest rate and for short periods only. The facility would be available exclusively to IMF members, and membership would require countries to (1) make their banks hold substantial amounts of capital and issue subordinated debt, (2) extend deposit insurance for other bank debt claims, (3) impose a liquidity requirement on their banks requiring them to hold 20 percent of their assets in cash or a close substitute, (4) require banks to hold a further 20 percent of their asset in liquid securities, (5) allow free entry by domestic and foreign institutions into the domestic banking market, (6) limit other government assistance to banks, (7) require banks to offer accounts denominated in both domestic and foreign currencies, (8) require banks to hold additional reserves if the exchange rate is pegged, and (9) require the government to follow certain debt management practices (e.g., limiting the share of short-term debt in total government obligations). IMF members would collateralize their discount window borrowing with government securities. Collateral would be in the amount of 125 percent of the hard currency borrowed, and 25 percent of the total would have to take the form of securities issued by foreign governments.

Garten's Global Central Bank

Jeffrey Garten (1998) would create a global central bank authorized to engage in open-market operations by purchasing the government securities of its members. Its operations would be financed by credit lines from national central banks or a modest tax on international merchandise transactions and/or certain global financial transactions. It would possess oversight powers over banks and other financial institutions and establish uniform standards for lending. It would be accountable to a committee of governors drawn from the G-7 and eight rotating emerging-market members.

Litan's Put Options in Bank Credits

Robert Litan would have countries receiving IMF assistance enact legislation imposing an automatic reduction of the principal of interbank deposits extended to banks in their countries (Litan et al. 1998). To discourage creditors from withdrawing their funds, haircuts would be imposed if creditors withdraw or fail to roll over their claims while an IMF program is in place. Countries that failed to enact this kind of creditor loss-sharing arrangement could be made ineligible for IMF assistance or required to pay a substantially higher penalty rate. Ideally, the IMF would make enactment of such legislation a condition for the disbursal of its assistance.

Edwards's Specialized Agencies

Sebastian Edwards would replace the IMF with a trio of specialized agencies, each with limited responsibilities (1998c). His Global Information Agency would concentrate on providing timely and uncensored information on countries' financial condition. It would publish public ratings of their financial systems and issue red alerts when countries were not providing it with adequate information. His Contingent Global Financial Facility would provide contingent credit lines for countries following fundamentally sound policies but with temporary liquidity problems that were certified by the Global Information Agency as complying with its standards. His Global Restructuring Agency would have the power to impose a stay of payments (for a "cooling-off period") and would provide official financing, subject to conditionality, for countries that were engaged in good-faith negotiations with their creditors and making a realistic effort to restructure their economies.

Bergsten's Target Zones

C. Fred Bergsten has criticized the G-7's neglect of the role of exchange rate issues in the crisis, arguing that swings in the dollar-yen and dollar-euro rates were critical in destabilizing emerging-market currency pegs. He therefore advocates target zones for exchange rates to prevent this problem from recurring.[2] Under his plan, G-7 governments would announce limits on the extent of permissible swings between their currencies, starting with plus-or-minus 15 percent around agreed currency midpoints. Long-term disequilibria due to ongoing inflation differentials would be avoided by regularly adjusting the ranges by very small amounts. In the absence of such disequilibria, central banks would defend the bands as necessary by intervening in foreign-exchange markets and, if necessary, adjusting monetary policies. Emerging-market economies would then find it attractive, Bergsten suggests, to similarly establish bands for their currencies, perhaps around a trade-weighted basket of G-7 currencies.

International Proposals

IMF Proposals

The IMF, via speeches by its managing director and elsewhere, has sketched five imperatives to be included on an agenda for reforming

---

2. See Bergsten (1998a) and, for an earlier incarnation that spells out the proposal in more detail, Bergsten and Henning (1996). Similar ideas have also been advanced by Paul Volcker

the international financial system (e.g., Camdessus 1998c). First, enhance transparency by encouraging governments to provide additional information about their financial affairs, requiring nonfinancial firms to comply with sound accounting and auditing standards, requiring financial institutions to adopt sound risk-management practices and acceptable disclosure standards, and having the IMF agree to release more information of its own. Second, develop standards and codes of good conduct for economies and financial markets. Third, liberalize the capital account, but in an orderly fashion that recognizes the importance of putting in place the necessary preconditions. Fourth, strengthen and reform the financial sector. Fifth and finally, find a way of dealing with the "complicated" problem of bailing in the private sector. To date, IMF officials have provided few concrete details on how these goals might be achieved.

G-7 Proposals

In October 1998, G-7 finance ministers and central bankers issued an extraordinary out-of-cycle declaration on strengthening the international financial system (G-7 1998). While repeating elements of other international declarations, that is, the need for international standards for minimally acceptable financial practices and for increased transparency, it also provided some specific if limited proposals for increasing the involvement of the private sector in crisis resolution.

G-7 ministers pointed to the need for heightened supervision of financial institutions in creditor as well as debtor countries (to be achieved by negotiating disclosure standards for nonbank financial intermediaries as well as banks and by having the IMF monitor its members' compliance and issuing a Transparency Report); to the need for greater transparency on the part of governments (which should strengthen the SDDS, release timely and accurate information on their international reserves, and comply with the IMF's Code on Fiscal Transparency and negotiate a companion code on Monetary and Financial Policy); and to the need for more transparency on the part of the IMF (which should release information "except where this might compromise confidentiality" and which should commission additional external evaluation exercises). To bail in the private sector, they embraced the idea of adding collective-action clauses in loan contracts (and for the G-7 countries themselves to consider their use in their own sovereign and quasi-sovereign bond issues), for the IMF to lend into arrears as appropriate, and for emerging economies to negotiate private contingent credit lines with commercial banks in the creditor countries.

(1995). The German government has also tabled a proposal for "the controlled flexibility of exchange rates" as its contribution to the architecture debate.

This declaration said little, however, about how the negotiation of international standards should be organized other than involving the IASC and the Basle Committee in finalizing accounting standards. It said nothing about discouraging excessive bank-to-bank lending or about the need for Chilean-style capital-import taxes to prevent excessive short-term capital inflows. It said nothing about exchange rate policy or IMF advice and conditionality toward it, aside from the need to consider "the elements necessary for the maintenance of sustainable exchange rate regimes in emerging economies." Other than offering to "consider" incorporating collective-representation clauses into bond covenants, it offered no commitments to solve the prenuptial-agreement problem that prevents emerging markets from unilaterally moving in this direction.

G-22 Proposals

The G-22 issued three reports in October 1998. Because these reports are currently the international community's definitive statement on reforming the international architecture, and there is considerable overlap with proposals advanced in this book, it is worth considering them in detail.

The Working Group on Transparency and Accountability

This group recommended establishing national standards for the disclosure of private-sector financial affairs and that regulators require banks and firms to adhere to recognized accounting standards. It recommended that countries that do not yet do so presently should report to the BIS data on their cross-border borrowing and lending, that governments should compile and disseminate data on the foreign-exchange position of the public financial and corporate sector, and that a working group should be established to explore the feasibility of gathering and publishing data on the international exposures of noncommercial-bank institutional investors. It urged the IMF to move toward greater transparency and asked national authorities to support the publication of Letters of Intent, background papers to Article IV reports, and Public Information Notices. It recommended that the IMF prepare a "Transparency Report" for each country in conjunction with its regular Article IV consultations.

The benefits of greater transparency are now widely accepted and are embraced in this book as well. However, the G-22 report (1998a) is more sanguine about governments' ability to gather information about private-sector behavior. It appears to assume, for example, that governments will be able to gather accurate information on the financial affairs of nonbank firms, that is, their foreign financial exposures, an assumption I do not share. It proposes that the Transparency Report should focus on compliance with disclosure standards and does not mention standards for financial supervision and regulation, corporate governance, and insolvency procedures, which are critical if the promulgation and monitoring of international standards are to make a difference for financial stability.

More generally, this working group says little about how international standards are to be set and enforced. It does not share my emphasis on the need to rely on private-sector resources in developing the relevant standards and to allow the private sector to take the lead wherever possible in monitoring compliance. Nor does it emphasize the need for international action to provide effective incentives for compliance. It does not suggest, as I do, that the IMF should condition its assistance to program countries on their taking specific steps to comply, that it make the interest rate charged on its loans a function of that compliance, or that it make eligibility for any preapproved credit lines a function of compliance status.[3]

The Working Group on Strengthening Financial Systems

This group endorses the Basle Core Principles for Effective Banking Supervision and points to the need for similar principles in the areas of internal controls, liquidity management, corporate governance, and insolvency procedures (G-22 1998b). In contrast to my conclusions, however, it does not emphasize the role of the private sector in developing internationally recognized principles, instead supporting the related efforts of the Basle Committee and the OECD.[4] Nor does it embrace the idea that the IMF should monitor compliance with these principles and issue a report evaluating its members' compliance status, reporting that its members are divided on the issue of published compliance ratings. In contrast to my approach, the working group displays more faith in the ability of capital, reserve, and subordinated-debt requirements to deter excessive risk taking in emerging markets and in the capacity of regulators to effectively surveil the funding and investment decisions of banks and to restrain socially counterproductive behavior.[5] Above all, it says nothing about the need for Chilean-style controls to reinforce prudential supervision and regulation in developing countries or of the need for greater exchange rate flexibility to encourage banks and corporations to hedge their foreign exposures.

---

3. Although some of these possibilities are raised by the working group concerned with strengthening financial systems.

4. It does acknowledge the need for the official sector to "initiate a dialogue" with the relevant private organizations and professional groups, but mainly with an eye toward determining how the private sector can more effectively utilize information that emerges from standard setting and prudential regulation rather than in how it can take the lead in the process of standard setting itself.

5. The section of the report on "Methods to Ring-Fence the Socialization of Risk and to Limit Forbearance" reiterates that providers of risk capital and subordinated debt should not be bailed out without addressing the political difficulties this presents.

The Working Group on International Financial Crises

This group recommends that lenders and borrowers explore the development of innovative loan contract provisions such as prenegotiated put options to enhance payments flexibility (G-22 1998c). It points to the desirability of incorporating collective-representation, majority action, and sharing clauses into loan contracts. To this end, it recommends that governments engage in "educational efforts" in the major financial centers and that the governments of creditor countries "examine" the use of such clauses in their own sovereign and quasi-sovereign bonds issued in foreign offerings. In contrast to my conclusions, it does not emphasize the need for the IMF to encourage its members to incorporate such provisions into their loan contracts and to key its lending rates and disbursements to their governments' willingness to do so. It does not stress the need for regulators in the leading creditor countries to make such provisions a condition for the admission of international bonds to trading on their markets. It is uncritical about the scope for introducing new provisions into cross-border bank credits. It does not acknowledge that the only effective way to contain the risks of bank-to-bank lending when the banks in the borrowing country are too big and important to fail is by using inflow taxes to prevent excessive reliance on short-term foreign bank credits in the first place. It fails to acknowledge the need for greater exchange rate flexibility to encourage banks and firms to hedge their foreign exposures and as a deterrent to excessive capital inflows.

To facilitate orderly workouts of sovereign debts, the working group suggests that the international community should signal its willingness to provide the crisis country with conditional financial support, where appropriate, through IMF lending into arrears. However, it does not acknowledge the need for standing committees of creditors to facilitate restructuring negotiations.

Appendix B
How Economists Understand Crises

Proposals for reforming the international financial architecture make sense only if they address the fundamental causes of financial crises. Putting the point less positively, observers find it difficult to agree on reforms to better prevent and contain financial crises because they do not agree about their underlying causes. This appendix therefore lays out the different ways in crises are conceptualized. My ulterior motive, naturally, is to provide theoretical justification for the approach to reform taken in the text, although I try to provide enough detail on the alternative theoretical schools to permit readers to make up their own minds.

Macroeconomic Imbalances

Financial crises are not new. Nor are scholarly studies of the phenomenon. What is new about recent crises, compared to those of the preceding 50 years, is their violence and the damage they do. And what is new about the scholarly studies is the systematic way in which currency and banking panics are modeled and analyzed.

Connoisseurs distinguish three generations of theoretical work on the dynamics of currency crises. (Some, including the present author, less impressed by the novelty of recent contributions, would be more inclined to say two and one-half.) The first and still most influential contribution, Krugman (1979), uses a simple model to show how attempts to defend a fixed exchange rate can collapse in the face of a speculative attack. Krugman shows how a series of persistent balance of payments deficits can precipitate a run on the authorities' stock of international reserves and destroy their capacity to defend the exchange rate by robbing them of the ability to intervene in the foreign-exchange market. His contribution is to demonstrate how an attack collapsing the exchange rate peg can occur before reserves would have been exhausted otherwise and to pin down its timing.[1]

Like all good models, this one is streamlined by the strategic use of simplifying assumptions.[2] The key assumptions are what lies behind the balance of payments deficits making reserves decline toward the danger point, and what governments can do about it. Krugman assumed that payments imbalances and the currency crises to which they gave rise resulted from the tendency for governments to run excessively expansionary monetary and fiscal policies. Governments ran deficits that they financed by printing money. Investors, not wishing to hold the additional money that the authorities injected into circulation, exchanged it for foreign assets, which the central bank was forced to supply out of its dwindling stock of reserves. The central bank had no ability, again by assumption, to replenish its reserves by borrowing abroad. It followed that reserves marched steadily downward until they approached the danger point where the crisis erupted and the currency collapsed. The leading indicators of a crisis thus were budget deficits, excessive rates of growth of the money supply, and dwindling reserves. As extended by other authors, the model also predicted that countries vulnerable to a speculative attack would show signs of excessive inflation, real exchange rate overvaluation, and rising interest rates.[3]

These were sensible assumptions for their time, namely, the early 1980s. Governments in many of those countries that succumbed to crises were in fact prone to large budget deficits. It was plausible to attribute their crises to a lack of fiscal discipline. In this inflationary environment and with bond markets in developing countries still at rudimentary stages of development, it was plausible that governments would seek to finance

---

1. The timing was pinned down by the assumption that the relative rate of return on assets denominated in domestic and foreign currency was simply the expected rate of depreciation of the domestic currency. Because that rate was zero prior to the attack but positive thereafter, maximizing investors would want to trade some share of the assets denominated in domestic currency in their portfolios for foreign assets in the same amount. Once official reserves fell to just that amount, those reserves were wiped out by speculators in one fell swoop as they reconfigured their portfolios.

2. Thus, the assumption that relative rates of return on domestic and foreign assets were simply the expected change in the exchange rate suppressed an independent role for interest rates. Similarly, the assumption that domestic and foreign goods were perfect substitutes and that their prices were governed by purchasing power parity eliminated all role for relative prices.

3. For example, on a role for interest rates see Willman (1988). For a model with inflation and relative prices, see Goldberg (1993).

their deficits by printing money. And with capital markets disinclined to lend after the debt crisis struck, it was plausible that central banks should be unable to replenish their reserves by borrowing abroad.

Economic and Political Fragility

With time, circumstances changed and these assumptions were called into doubt. In the crises that nearly toppled the Exchange Rate Mechanism of the European Monetary System in 1992-93, not all of the afflicted countries displayed large fiscal and current-account deficits; increasingly it seemed that currency crises could occur in the absence of these indicators of excessive demand and external disequilibrium. As capital controls were lifted and international financial markets continued to expand, it became less plausible to assume that central banks could not borrow abroad to replenish their reserves. Above all, assuming that governments were dumb but speculators were smart (that governments made no effort to adjust their policies to circumstances and mindlessly defended the exchange rate until their reserves were exhausted) grated on the refined sensibilities of theorists.

This dissonance motivated the development of a second generation of crisis models.[4] Second-generation models add the assumption that governments balance the benefits of continuing to defend the currency peg, through the maintenance of tight monetary policies and high interest rates, against the costs of giving up the ghost. Typically, the benefits take the form of enhancing the credibility of the authorities' commitment to defending the currency and to pursuing policies oriented toward the maintenance of price stability. The costs come in the form of the adverse impact of high interest rates on the economy and the financial system. The level of reserves and the authorities' ability to borrow abroad play no role in these calculations.[5] What matter are the condition and resilience of the domestic economy—whether the interest rate hikes needed to

---

4. See, for example, Obstfeld (1997) and Ozkan and Sutherland (1998), which were first circulated as working papers in 1991 and 1994.

5. It is possible to introduce channels through which the level of reserves can matter. Imagine a scenario in which a government of a country with a weak economy and a fragile financial sector is not prepared to sharply hike interest rates to defend the currency in response to a speculative attack. If it has sufficient reserves to simply finance capital outflows for a time, putting off the need to raise interest rates, there is the possibility that the economy or the financial system will strengthen sufficiently that interest rate increases, when rendered necessary to defend the currency by the exhaustion of reserves, become more palatable. Knowing that the government is now in a position to use interest rates to defend the currency, the speculative pressure should recede. Note the word "possibility" in this story; it is possible only if there occurs a sufficiently rapid improvement in the domestic economic and financial situation.

defend the currency, by depressing demand, will add to a painfully high unemployment rate, for example; whether raising interest rates, by forcing bank borrowers into default, will aggravate the condition of an already weak banking system; and whether higher interest rates will increase the burden on an already overtaxed government of servicing a large short-term debt. If, for any of these reasons, the costs of defending the currency exceed the benefits, the authorities will cave in. There is no technical reason why they must give up (no exhaustion of reserves that eliminates their capacity to intervene in the foreign-exchange market, as in first-generation models). Rather, they choose to abandon their defense of the currency as a matter of economic and political self-interest.[6]

In the standard first-generation model, the crisis is preceded by evidence of overly expansionary monetary and fiscal policies and the progressive depletion of reserves. Because the timing of the attack is governed by the technical condition that the authorities lack reserves with which to intervene in the foreign-exchange market, the decline of reserves makes its eruption predictable.[7] In second-generation models, in contrast, susceptibility to crises will depend on subtler, less-easily measured conditions such as the strength of the banking system, the prospects for economic growth, and domestic political support for the government and its policies. The hardest factor of all to measure when gauging the likelihood of a successful attack will be the government's resolve. The success or failure of an attack on the Hong Kong dollar, for example, will depend not just on such obvious indicators as the strength of Hong Kong's banking system and flexibility of its labor market (and thus on the amount of unemployment produced by higher interest rates) but also on how ready the authorities in Hong Kong (and in Beijing) are to defend it.

A corollary of the introduction of self-interested governments is the possibility of self-fulfilling balance of payments crises. In first-generation models, the attack on the currency merely anticipates the inevitable. Devaluation is coming with or without the attack. In second-generation models, in contrast, the speculative attack can itself precipitate a devaluation that would not have occurred in its absence. Consider a government that is tempted to indulge in a more accommodating, inflationary mone-

---

6. Thus, whereas first-generation models focused exclusively on the determinants of external balance and on technical reasons why a government's ability to defend its currency peg might be undermined, second-generation models shift the focus to the decisions of governments concerned with internal balance and to fundamentally economic reasons why they might be unwilling to mount a sustained defense.

7. More complicated versions of the model (e.g., Krugman and Rotemberg 1990) allow the money supply to evolve stochastically rather than deterministically. While this reintroduces some uncertainty about the exact timing of the crisis and makes both the average rate of growth of the money supply and its variance relevant for predicting crises, the fundamental insights from the model remain intact.

tary policy in the hope of stimulating economic growth but that concludes in its wisdom that the costs of continued monetary austerity, in the form of gloomier prospects for the banking system and employment growth, are dominated by the benefits of the greater credibility of its reputation for pursuing policies of price stability, which hinges in turn on its continued defense of the currency peg. Absent any change in market conditions, the government will maintain the currency peg indefinitely. Imagine now a speculative attack in which investors sell the currency for foreign exchange, draining liquidity from the market and forcing the authorities to raise interest rates. Suddenly, the costs of defending the peg, in the form of additional unemployment and even more damage to the banking system, have risen relative to the benefits. The balance having shifted, it may now make sense for the authorities to abandon their defense of the currency in favor of more accommodating policies where doing so made no sense before. In this setting, a speculative attack can precipitate the collapse of the currency peg (it can succeed, in other words, even if that peg could have been maintained indefinitely in its absence). The attack is self-validating because it can induce a shift in policy in a more accommodating, inflationary direction.

The introduction of high international capital mobility (equivalently, the relaxation of controls) has particularly profound implications in second-generation models. In first-generation models, the only effect of capital controls was to alter the timing of the attack. By making it harder for investors to shift between domestic and foreign assets, controls delayed the day of reckoning, but not indefinitely (see Wyplosz 1986; Sachs and Park 1987). In second-generation models, in contrast, controls can tip the balance between the collapse of a currency peg and its maintenance forever. This is because controls break the link between domestic and foreign interest rates. In the absence of capital-account restrictions, domestic interest rates equal foreign interest rates plus the expected rate of depreciation of the currency over the holding period.[8] In their presence, domestic rates equal foreign rates plus the expected rate of depreciation *minus* the cost of evading the controls (and shifting from domestic currency into foreign exchange). Lower interest rates will now be needed to leave speculators indifferent between holding domestic and foreign assets and to rebuff the attack. And insofar as the costs of sustaining a defense rise with the level of interest rates, that defense becomes more palatable. An attack that would have neither occurred nor succeeded in the presence of capital controls may do both in their absence.

Academics have endlessly debated the realism of these models. Some disparage the accuracy of the assumptions and warn that tales of self-fulfilling attacks and multiple equilibria are too easily used to absolve

---

8. Assuming domestic and foreign assets to otherwise be perfect substitutes for one another.

governments of all blame for currency crises, which are more than just runaway trucks flattening innocent bystanders.[9] Others insist that these models capture the essence of modern currency crises.[10] A reasonable reconciliation is that self-fulfilling crises and multiple equilibria are possible only when the economy has entered a zone of vulnerability.[11] When unemployment is high, the banking system is weak, or short-term public debt is large (so that higher interest rates imply a painful increase in debt-servicing costs), the authorities may find themselves unable to bear the pain associated with the need to raise interest rates further. But if unemployment is low, the banking system is robust, and short-term debt is minimal, they may be prepared to defend the currency peg against any and all attacks. In this sense, models of multiple equilibria and self-fulfilling attacks cannot be used to absolve the authorities of responsibility; their policies still determine whether or not the economy strays into the zone of vulnerability. If it does, whether and when an attack occurs then depends on when currency traders decide to test the government's resolve.

Crony Capitalism and Moral Hazard

Asia, having spawned the most recent round of currency crises, has predictably spawned the latest generation of crisis models. Some observers insist that events there are readily explained in familiar first- and second-generation terms. They cite Thailand with its overvalued exchange rate and large current-account deficit as an example of first-generation dynamics, and South Korea with its high and rising levels of short-term debt as an example of the mechanisms highlighted by second-generation models.[12] What is striking about the Asian crisis, though, is that prior to its outbreak few of the stricken countries displayed either the monetary and fiscal excesses and balance of payments problems identified in first-generation models as leading indicators of currency crises or the slow growth and domestic financial problems emphasized by their second-generation counterparts as sources of vulnerability. To the extent that such problems appeared, they did so only after the fact. There is the feeling among observers of the Asian crisis that something more was involved.

That something more is now given the label "crony capitalism and implicit guarantees." As the story is told by Dooley (1997) and Krugman

9. See Krugman (1996) and Dornbusch, Goldfajn, and Valdes (1995) for two such criticisms.

10. See, for example, Obstfeld (1996) and Wyplosz (1998).

11. This is the direction in which the modern literature has moved; see, for example, Sachs, Tornell, and Velasco (1996a, b), Calvo and Mendoza (1996), and Cole and Kehoe (1996).

12. That this was debt of the banking system rather than the government was of little moment, they continue, because the authorities moved quickly to guarantee the obligations of the banking system as soon as the crisis struck.

(1998a), banks were the financial tools used by Asian governments to further their economic development strategies, leading the owners of banks and industrial conglomerates on the one hand and political leaders on the other to develop ties of mutual dependence. Those ties left governments loath to let banks fail. Once the capital account of the balance of payments was opened, the implicit guarantees provided by governments to the banks were an irresistible lure to foreign investors. Normally, those investors would have balanced the high interest rates offered by Asian banks against the risk of losses and invested just to the point where the incentive offered by the former equaled the disincentive posed by the latter. But with governments guaranteeing the banks against failure, the specter of losses was removed. Foreign capital flooded into the economies and banking systems of the region as a consequence of this moral hazard. This is one way of understanding why economies with some of the highest savings rates in the world were such enthusiastic foreign borrowers. McKinnon and Pill (1997) argue that this borrowing was so excessive and that funds were so poorly allocated that the capital inflow may have actually reduced the growth rates of the countries involved.

Eventually, something brought these uncomfortable facts to light, and investors responded by withdrawing their money from the region. Banks being threatened, governments stepped in. To every depositor who now wished to convert his domestic-currency deposits into foreign currency, the government provided foreign exchange. But—and here is the crucial assumption—guarantees could be provided only once. Why is not clear: perhaps by revealing the "I'll scratch your back if you scratch mine" relationship between the bankers and politicians, guarantees provoked a populist backlash that brought down the crony capitalists. Or, as Dooley (1997) assumes, perhaps the countries concerned damaged their international creditworthiness so seriously that they were rendered unable to borrow abroad, and lacking foreign exchange they now found themselves unable to guarantee the banks' foreign liabilities. Given that foreign bank deposits were no longer guaranteed, foreigners found it less attractive to hold these now more risky assets. The stock of foreign capital fell once and for all to a lower level. This capital outflow posed wrenching difficulties for the economies of the region, which are still suffering adjustment problems. And among the consequences of that capital outflow and the deteriorating balance of payments has been pressure on the currency. As the authorities leapt to the rescue of the banking system, pumping in additional domestic credit, they were forced to disregard the constraints on liquidity implied by their commitment to peg the exchange rate. Thus, currency collapses were one consequence of the Asian banking crisis. Put another way, this approach shows why banking crises and currency crises go together (see Kaminsky and Reinhart 1996).[13]

---

13. A detailed theoretical treatment of this connection between banking and currency crises is in Chang and Velasco (1998a). These authors show how lender-of-last-resort intervention

Although certain elements of this story are new and expressly tailored to circumstances in Asia, the model shares key assumptions with those that preceded it. With first-generation models it shares the assumption of myopic governments that follow silly policies. It shares the assumption that once the authorities have expended their international reserves in paying off bank creditors, they are no longer able to defend the banking system or the currency. With second-generation models it shares the assumption that a speculative attack can provoke a change in policies that would have remained constant in its absence. If investors do not take fright, the guarantees do not have to be invoked. So long as they are there to reassure, the level of foreign investment remains high. But if an investor panic does ensue, the guarantees must be activated, after which they are withdrawn once and for all. Foreign investment falls to permanently lower levels, reflecting the change in the policy regime induced by the crisis itself. Thus, the investor panic produces a result that would have not occurred in its absence. This is a classic second-generation result involving multiple equilibria and self-fulfilling crises. As in earlier second-generation models, a crisis can result because the government follows inappropriate policies, in this case by adopting a poorly designed financial safety net (rather than by pursuing unsound monetary and fiscal policies).[14]

Implications

Theorists are prone to exaggerate their differences. If they did not claim that their latest article was a fundamental challenge to all that preceded it, they would have that much more trouble publishing it. In fact, their differences are less than meets the eye. What emerges from their competing models and interpretations is a single, synthetic understanding of why crises occur. Crises do not occur randomly. Rather, they afflict countries whose governments set themselves up for the fall. Some have done so by following inconsistent policies, running recklessly expansionary monetary and fiscal policies that are inconsistent with their intention of pegging the exchange rate, or providing implicit guarantees to the banking system that encourage reckless lending and lead to a banking crisis that undermines confidence in the currency and the economy. In these extreme cases, the leading indicators of currency and banking crises are obvious. The writing is on the wall.

---

to prop up the banking system may avert the danger of self-fulfilling banking panic but at the same time transform the banking panic into a currency crisis.

14. In the end, then, I do not really view the new models developed in response to the Asian crisis as analytically distinct from the first- and second-generation models that preceded them but rather as interesting special cases of those more general frameworks.

More commonly, the evidence of vulnerability is subtler. Growth may be slow, unemployment high. The banking system may be weak. The government may have issued a large amount of short-term debt that must be rolled over at interest rates that are sensitive to the state of market confidence. None of these conditions is necessarily fatal; policymakers successfully navigate these dangerous straits without being blown off course by speculative gales. But if an attack is unleashed, they will be unable to withstand it. Their weak economy, weak banking system, or weak finances may lead them to conclude that the most sensible response is to throw in the towel.

Whether they do depends, first, on whether or not they are attacked and, second, on how energetically they are prepared to defend the currency. Once again it is not hard to point to sources of vulnerability (i.e., weak economy, weak banking system, and weak finances), though their presence does not necessarily imply a crisis, nor do they contain much information about its timing. Such problems imply a crisis only if combined with two additional elements: a loss of investor confidence and inadequate political resolve on the part of the government. Not only are these factors hard to measure—even the most dedicated designer of leading indicators would be hard-pressed to construct numerical indicators of the mental state of the government and the markets—but they can change abruptly. Crises occur for good reasons, but this does not mean that they are predictable.

Appendix C
Understanding Asia's Crisis

A framework for understanding currency and financial crises will convince only if it sheds light on the Asian crisis—"the first financial crisis of the twenty-first century." That crisis illustrates well the difficulty of using simple models to make sense of complex economic events. It shows how counterproductive it is to think of Asia's financial collapse as a single event. The causes and consequences differed across countries. New financial crises unfolded upon old ones; by the spring of 1998, the IMF's managing director, Michel Camdessus, routinely referred to "crises within crises." To be sure, these difficulties were related. But attempting to explain them all in terms of a single set of factors or to use them as turf on which to run a horse race between competing theoretical models is unlikely to be helpful. Rather, the Asian crisis suggests that understanding twenty-first-century crises will require one to weave together strands from different approaches. Correspondingly, proposals for reform must address the problems highlighted by each of the relevant models.

Background

One sign that the Asian crisis was both complex and distinctive is that the period leading up to it was characterized not by economic difficulties but by robust rates of economic growth. Table C.1 shows that GDP growth rates in 1996 ranged from 8 percent in Indonesia to more than 6 percent in Thailand. This achievement continued a pattern that had held since the early 1980s. Rapid growth was fueled by high rates of saving and

Table C.1 Growth, inflation, equity prices, and current-account balance, 1990-97

	Real GDP			Consumer prices			Equity price index			Current-account balance		
	1990-95	1996	1997	1990-95	1996	1997	1990-95	1996	1997	1990-95	1996	1997
			Annual percentage change							As a percentage of GDP		
Indonesia	7.2	7.8	4.6	8.7	8.0	6.6	5.7	15.0	-76.1	-2.5	-3.7	-2.9
Thailand	8.9	6.4	-0.4	5.0	5.8	5.6	9.1	-45.8	-78.7	-6.7	-7.9	-2.0
South Korea	7.8	7.1	5.5	6.6	4.9	4.4	-0.6	-35.7	-69.8	-1.2	-4.8	-1.9
Malaysia	8.8	8.6	7.8	3.7	3.5	2.7	15.2	17.0	-73.5	-5.9	-4.9	-5.1
Philippines	2.3	5.7	5.1	11.0	8.4	5.1	27.0	14.6	-63.2	-3.8	-4.7	-5.2
Singapore	8.6	6.9	7.8	2.7	1.3	2.0	10.6[a]	-5.2	-35.0	12.7	15.5	15.2
Hong Kong	5.0	5.0	5.2	9.3	6.0	5.7	37.8	33.5	-20.3	3.3[b]	-1.7[b]	-3.8[b]
China	10.6	9.7	8.8	12.4	8.3	2.8	13.8[c]	81.5	32.5	0.9	0.9	2.3
Taiwan	6.4	5.7	6.8	3.8	3.1	0.9	-9.2	46.5	-8.3	4.0	4.0	2.7

a. From company reports and stock exchange of Singapore, various issues.

b. Balance of goods and nonfactor services.

c. Average for 1991-95.

Sources: BIS (1998, table III.1); Emerging Stock Markets Factbook, International Finance Corporation, World Bank (various years).

investment (as high as 40 percent), sound macroeconomic policies, and outstanding rates of export growth. Government budgets were in surplus, and economies were successfully restructured along export-oriented lines. References to the East Asian "miracle" became commonplace.[1]

More than a year after the fact, it is now possible to discern disquieting signs. The growth of export revenues decelerated in 1996, reflecting slower growth of demand in the region's principal export markets, a slowdown in the global electronics industry, and competition from mainland China.[2] (The rate of growth of East Asian export markets in the period leading up to the crisis is shown in figure C.1.) Current-account deficits were large in Thailand and Malaysia (refer to table C.1). Equity prices declined, foreshadowing lower profits in the manufacturing sector. Indonesia, South Korea, Thailand, and even Singapore had large amounts of short-term debt relative to foreign-exchange reserves (see table C.2). Legions of financial analysts now justify their livelihood by pointing to these leading indicators of problems that came later. But this is wisdom after the fact.

The one exception is Thailand. Not only had Thailand's current-account deficit risen to an alarming 8 percent of GDP, but its export performance was disappointing. By pegging the baht to a basket with a heavy weight on the US dollar, which was itself strengthening against other major currencies, the Thai authorities allowed their trade-weighted real exchange rate to be pulled up significantly (see figure C.2). While the currency-pegging policy was not limited to Thailand, only there did leading investment analysts expect a sustained slowdown in exports (Radelet and Sachs 1998a; D. Park and Rhee 1998). Reflecting these problems, Thai equity prices trended downward (see figure C.3) and the real estate bubble burst. With the country's finance companies heavily exposed to the property and stock markets, the decline in asset values posed an obvious threat to their solvency and, in turn, to the government's commitment to the maintenance of the currency peg.

The managing director of the IMF wrote letters of warning to the Thai authorities. IMF officials traveled to Bangkok to convey the message in

---

1. The classic reference, of course, is World Bank (1993).

2. While some have gone so far as to cite Beijing's devaluation of the yuan in 1994 as setting the stage for the crisis, most observers agree that not too much weight should be attached to this event: Chinese competition was but one of a number of factors intensifying the pressure on the crisis countries, and devaluation of the yuan was but one of a number of factors contributing to the intensification of Chinese competition. The depreciation of the yuan was largely offset by (and was itself designed to offset) the relatively rapid rise in yuan-denominated export prices. Analysis of these issues is provided by Fernald, Edison, and Loungani (1998). Radelet and Sachs (1998b) emphasize also surging Mexican exports of electronics, apparel, and automotive components to the United States following the North American Free Trade Agreement and the depreciation of the peso in 1995.

Figure C.1   Growth of export markets of the East Asian economies,[a] January 1992-July 1997
(percentages)

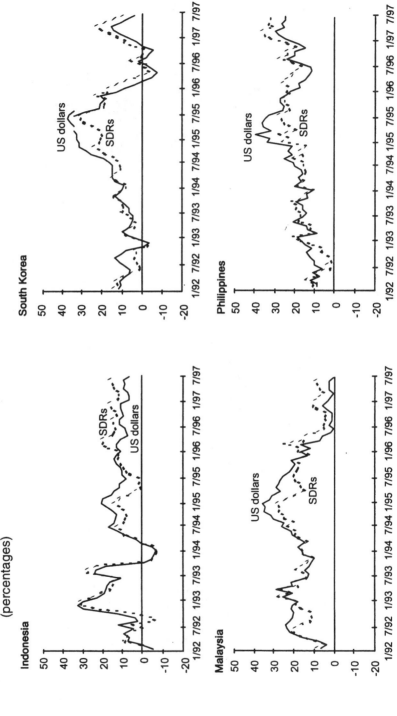

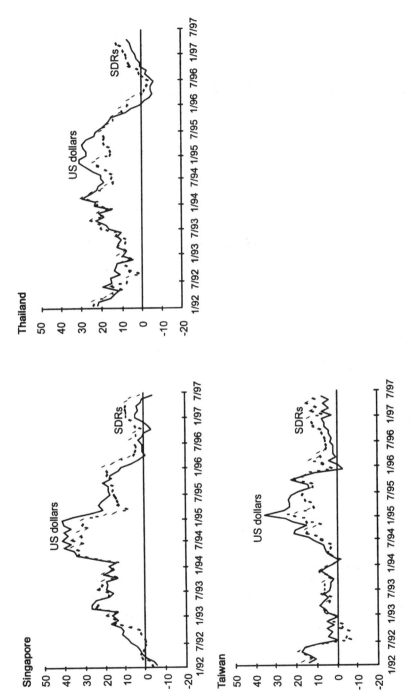

a. Percent change in export revenues from 12 months earlier; 3-month moving averages.

147

Table C.2 Short-term debt, second quarter of 1997

	Short-term debt	Total reserves	Short-term debt ratio
	Billions of US dollars		As a percentage of total reserves
Indonesia	34.25	20.34	168
South Korea	67.51	34.07	198
Malaysia	11.18	26.59	42
Philippines	7.74	9.78	79
Singapore	175.23	80.66	217
Taiwan	18.87	90.02	21
Thailand	45.57	31.36	145

Sources: BIS (1998); IMF, *International Financial Statistics* (various issues).

Figure C.2 Thai baht real exchange rate, January 1990-October 1998

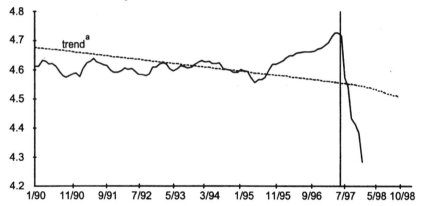

a. Linear trend from January 1979 to June 1997.

Source: Chinn and Dooley (1998).

person. The markets, if not the Thai officials, took heed. One hedge fund manager reported to me that he was first alerted to problems in Thailand by a presentation at the annual meetings of the Fund and the World Bank in September of 1996.[3] There was pressure against the baht as early as July of that year following the collapse of the Bangkok Bank of Commerce. In the nine months leading up to its 2 July 1997 devaluation, the baht was hit by three more speculative sell-offs. But even in Thailand, there

---

3. The other obvious indicator of Thailand's mounting problems, namely, the steady decline of the central bank's foreign reserves, is another example of wisdom after the fact, if only because the country did not release timely information about changes in the extent of its spot- and forward-market positions.

Figure C.3 Thai equity index, January 1996-March 1998

Source: *Emerging Stock Markets Factbook*, International Finance Corporation, World Bank (various issues).

was no indication that the market anticipated the severity of impending problems in the spreads on syndicated bank loans, in the spreads on bond issues on primary and secondary markets, in the sovereign debt ratings issued by Standard & Poor's and Moody's, or in the forecasts of the leading commercial and investment banks.[4]

Course of the Crisis

The crisis opened with Thailand's devaluation on 2 July 1997 and deepened with the spread of difficulties to neighboring countries in Southeast Asia. Although the Thai, Indonesian, Malaysian, and Philippine currencies all depreciated by 25 to 33 percent in the third quarter of 1997, the crisis could still be seen at this time as limited to these countries. This was no longer true starting in October with the devaluation of the Taiwan dollar, which led to a speculative attack on Hong Kong (whose economic structure was similar to Taiwan's and which competed with it in many markets), and with the spread of the crisis to South Korea. The first half of 1998 was dominated by the continued deterioration of economic, financial, and political conditions in Indonesia, with strongly negative impacts on investor confidence and, hence, on the prospects for the other crisis economies. The most recent phase was ignited by the worse-than-expected economic performance of Japan, which came to light in the second quarter

---

4. Radelet and Sachs (1998a) present and discuss these data. For example, spreads on emerging-market bonds only began to widen *following* the Thai devaluation (Cline and Barnes 1997).

of 1998, and by Russia's default in August and the spread of turmoil to still other emerging markets.

The Trigger

Given the palpable nature of Thailand's difficulties and the subtler problems of its neighbors, it was possible at first to see the devaluation of the baht as an isolated event. The fact that the large international investors (hedge funds, commercial banks, investment banks) with short positions against the baht did not typically also have large short positions against other Southeast Asian currencies is a clear sign that this is how they perceived the situation.[5] And the fact that the Thai authorities responded to mounting speculative pressure by intervening in the forward market rather than by attempting to correct the fundamentals made the devaluation seem both unavoidable and fully justified.

Following its devaluation, the baht continued to depreciate at an alarming rate. On 29 July the Chavalit government approached the IMF for help. Within two weeks, Japan convened a meeting of supporting countries who agreed to supplement the resources provided by the Fund. But Thailand's weak government was unprepared to take bold measures either to reassure investors or to halt debt-servicing payments and reflate the economy. Increases in gasoline taxes designed to raise revenue for use in recapitalizing the banking system were reversed in response to public protests, heightening uncertainty about the orientation of policy. The finance minister resigned on 19 October. The baht continued to decline, losing nearly 50 percent of its value against the US dollar by the end of the year despite the installation of a new government committed to the terms of the IMF agreement. Only in early 1998, after the new government demonstrated its resolve by moving on the issue of bank restructuring, did the baht begin to recover some of the ground lost previously and did the equity market stabilize.

The Spread

While the fact of Thailand's difficulties hardly came as a surprise to informed observers, the same cannot be said of their extent and, especially, their repercussions in other countries. The stock market fell and pressure against the currency was felt almost immediately in Indonesia, Malaysia, the Philippines, Singapore, and Taiwan. The Philippines responded on 11 July by abolishing its fluctuation band for the peso, and Indonesia widened its band for the rupiah later that same day. Along with Thailand,

---

5. This is documented in Eichengreen and Mathieson (1998) and Brown, Goetzmann, and Park (1998).

Indonesia was most strongly affected. Its stock prices, currency values, and international reserves fell sharply, and the Suharto government was forced to abandon its defense of the widened fluctuation band for the rupiah after little more than four weeks.

The spread of the crisis to Indonesia was unexpected because the country's growth had been unusually rapid and its macroeconomic fundamentals were strong. More generally, it was hard to see what the countries hit by the contagion had in common other than physical proximity. Levels of income and economic development were disparate. Some, such as Malaysia and Singapore, did modest amounts of business with Thailand, but others, such as Indonesia and Hong Kong, sold virtually nothing there. Some countries depended heavily on exports of primary commodities, while others produced and sold high-tech goods. Their industrial structures ranged from the large industrial groups of Indonesia to the small export-oriented firms of Taiwan. Except with benefit of hindsight, the virulence and scope of the contagion was, in truth, very much a surprise.[6]

With the crash of the Hong Kong stock market in October and the spread of instability to South Korea, the crisis went global. The world's 11th largest economy, South Korea was far larger than those stricken previously. Its banks had extensive investments around the world. Market participants being cognizant of these facts, fears mounted for the stability of currencies as far away as Russia and Brazil.

Just as the spread of the crisis to Indonesia had been a surprise, so too was the virulence with which it infected South Korea. South Korea had been recovering from a slowdown in 1996, when the prices of semiconductors (its single biggest export item) had declined sharply. The government had brought down the current-account deficit from 5 percent of GDP to a more manageable level of 2 percent. But slower growth and depreciated currencies elsewhere now raised questions about whether this progress could be sustained. They heightened fears about the financial difficulties of the country's industrial conglomerates. The Hanbo Group (the 14th largest conglomerate, or *chaebol*) had collapsed in January 1997, taking $6 billion of domestic bank loans with it. Sammi Steel (the lead firm of the Sammi Group, the 26th largest *chaebol*) failed in March, the Kia Group (the 8th largest *chaebol*) in July. As business failures mounted, concern spread for the viability of the banks to which the *chaebol* were linked. South

---

6. A representative opinion is Chase Manhattan Bank's research circular dated 1 October 1997 (Chase Manhattan Bank 1997, 8-9), whose analysts concluded that it was unlikely that any of the other countries in the region "faces an imminent financial crisis" and who forecast growth rates for 1998 of 7 percent for Indonesia, 7 percent for Malaysia, and 6 percent for Thailand. Statistical studies support this distinction between Thailand and the other crisis countries: the leading econometric studies of crisis incidence have some success in predicting the Thai crisis, but not so the crisis in other Asian countries (see Berg and Pattillo 1998).

Korean banks thus found it increasingly expensive to fund themselves abroad. Meanwhile, foreign investors suffering losses elsewhere in Asia liquidated their investments in South Korea in order to rebalance their portfolios and raise cash, intensifying the pressure on the financial system.

South Korea's negotiation of an IMF package, an exceptional step for an OECD country, brought only temporary respite. Revelations through the publication of leaked IMF documents that the country's short-term debt was significantly higher than previously thought, combined with the government's reluctance to close troubled banks, undermined confidence among international investors.[7] Commercial banks refused to renew their maturing short-term loans and took their money out of the country even faster than the IMF and G-7 governments pumped it in. With short-term foreign debt maturing at the rate of $1 billion a day, it seemed inevitable that South Korea's reserves would be exhausted by the end of December.

The week between Christmas and the New Year saw emergency negotiations between the foreign commercial banks with credits to South Korea and the newly elected government of Kim Dae Jung, under the stewardship of G-7 central banks. Forced to acknowledge their collective-action problem, US, Japanese, and European banks agreed to roll over their short-term loans, giving the government time to negotiate a more comprehensive financial restructuring package. On 28 January, South Korea and the banks reached an agreement on the rescheduling of $24 billion of debt and on a plan to replace the bank loans with long-term bonds. Inducing investors to take up those bonds required the country to maintain high interest rates, with adverse implications for the economy. The consequences became known in May, when it was announced that the South Korean economy had shrunk by nearly 4 percent in the first quarter of 1998.

The Crisis within the Crisis

Yet the dominant events of the first months of 1998 were not those in South Korea but rather those affecting Indonesia and Japan. The IMF had unveiled a $23 billion rescue package for Indonesia in October. With the situation there continuing to deteriorate, the Suharto government and the Fund signed a second agreement on economic reform in January. Against

---

7. In addition, there was the rumor, later shown to be true, that the Bank of Korea had deposited a portion of its reserves with foreign branches of domestic banks, rendering those reserves unusable. Japanese banks were first to call in their short-term debts due to mounting problems in the Japanese financial system, such as the failure of Yamaichi Securities, the fourth largest securities firm in the country, and the bankruptcy of several regional and city banks. Kim and Rhee (1998) suggest that because Japanese banks were thought to be particularly well informed of the South Korean financial situation, their refusal to roll over their short-term credits precipitated similar actions on the part of other banks.

the backdrop of the government's continued indecision regarding the fate of major public-investment projects and insolvent banks, investor doubts rendered IMF loans and conditions less than effective.[8] The rupiah fell to Rp17,000 to the dollar on 22 January (down more than 80 percent compared to a precrisis level of Rp2,434), before recovering. Indonesian banks and corporations having been left unable to service their foreign-currency debts, the country was forced to suspend debt-service payments. Banks stopped lending, and trade credits evaporated. The economy ground to a halt.

Against this backdrop, evidence of the severity of Japan's economic difficulties had a devastating impact on confidence. Japanese corporate leaders warned at the beginning of April of the gravity of the economic situation. Moody's downgraded Japan's sovereign debt on 3 April. Asia's "locomotive" having stalled, investor confidence in the other crisis countries suffered. Indonesia was hit hardest. A third agreement on economic reform with the IMF had little effect. In early May, the continued deterioration of economic and financial conditions spilled over into street demonstrations, forcing President Suharto's resignation two weeks later. Hopes that this might set the stage for stabilization and recovery were then dashed by more bad news from Japan. On 8 June the yen fell below 140 to the US dollar. On 12 June the government reported that first-quarter GDP had fallen by more than 5 percent at an annual rate. Fears that further weakening of the yen might so aggravate the competitive difficulties of Japan's Asian neighbors that they (and China) would succumb to another round of competitive devaluations prompted US and Japanese intervention in the foreign-exchange market to prop up the Japanese currency.

When the first anniversary of the Asian crisis was "celebrated" on 2 July 1998, there were still few signs of the kind of recovery that had developed in Mexico within six months of the 1994-95 peso crisis. While most Asian currencies had recovered from their early 1998 troughs, there were still few firm indications of economic growth. The IMF forecast renewed growth in South Korea and Thailand in 1999, but even this was far from assured. And it seemed highly unlikely that Indonesia, mired in debt and political problems, would glimpse the light at the end of the tunnel even then. Antigovernment riots continued to flare up, raising questions about the sustainability and direction of future policy.

The Crisis Goes Global

The latest in this series of events was the most dramatic, or at least it had the most far-reaching repercussions. In mid-August, Russia surprised

---

8. These problems were then compounded by a serious drought and by rumors of President Suharto's ill health.

the markets by devaluing the ruble and at the same time unilaterally suspending payments on most of its debts. The impact on confidence was devastating for investors who had come to see Russia as too big and important to fail. Its default consequently triggered a fundamental reevaluation of the risks of lending to emerging markets and of the price of risk more generally. It ignited a collective scramble out of risky assets in favor of safe havens such as US Treasury securities. Once this flight to quality was under way, investors who had purchased Brady bonds in order to hedge their Russian exposure were forced to liquidate their Latin American holdings in order to raise liquidity and meet margin calls; the crisis thus immediately leapfrogged from Russia and Asia to Latin America. The simultaneous collapse of the prices of virtually all risky assets put institutional investors at risk: it precipitated the collapse of the US hedge fund Long Term Capital Management and created fears for the stability of other hedge funds, hedge fund counterparties, and the very markets in which they had positions.

These events prompted fears of a global recession, or even a depression, eliciting a series of extraordinary policy responses to contain the crisis. The US Federal Reserve Board cut its lending rate three times, including an exceptional reduction between its regularly scheduled meetings; this led other G-7 central banks to follow suit. The IMF provided an unusually large, front-loaded package of financial assistance to Brazil in an attempt to create a firebreak wide enough to prevent the crisis from spreading further. The US Congress finally voted additional funding for the IMF. Japan accelerated its program of banking-sector recapitalization and restructuring and announced additional fiscal stimulus. Together, these measures sufficed to restore calm to financial markets, although not to restore the flow of capital to emerging markets. Whether that calm would endure remained, at the time of writing, very much an open question.

Causes

The Asian crisis that was the trigger for this series of events is best understood as a financial crisis with self-fulfilling features afflicting countries whose governments lacked the economic and political wherewithal to defend their currencies. And the weakness of governments, in turn, reflected three sources of vulnerability.

Macroeconomic Imbalances

Macroeconomic factors contributed to this vulnerability, however strange this might seem for countries where growth was proceeding at 5 to 8 percent a year. The region's rapid growth was sustained in part by capital inflows that had as by-products increasingly overvalued real exchange rates, accompanied in some cases by ballooning current-account deficits. The appreciation of real exchange rates was not large by the standards of, say, Argentina and Brazil, and the current-account deficit reached truly alarming levels only in Thailand and Malaysia, but both the real appreciation and the current-account deficit were sources of vulnerability. They could be transformed into serious problems if foreign investors decided one morning that the deficit would no longer be financed. Eliminating a large current-account deficit requires the large-scale redeployment of resources from nontraded- to traded-goods sectors, something that can occur smoothly, without a recession, only if it is allowed to take place gradually over time. Eliminating that deficit quickly, in contrast, requires radically compressing demand, disrupting production, and almost certainly inducing a recession. If capital suddenly stops flowing in, bridge financing is required to avoid this, and if foreign reserves are not sufficient to provide capital, attracting it requires high interest rates.

Financial-Sector Weaknesses

This is where Asia's second source of vulnerability came into play, in the form of the weakness of the financial system. Financial systems in the crisis countries were in a delicate condition, and high interest rates only served to compound their problems. In particular, the now higher interest rates needed to attract foreign capital and stabilize the balance of payments threatened to destabilize the banking system. Because banks are in the business of liquidity transformation, higher interest rates raised their funding costs relative to their incomes. And passing on those higher funding costs to their customers precipitated loan defaults that further damaged their balance sheets. Put another way, sustaining capital inflows required draining liquidity from domestic financial markets, but draining domestic liquidity threatened to knock the props out from under the banking system. International investors were understandably skeptical that governments were prepared to stay the course. Rudiger Dornbusch put the point colorfully, as usual (1998, 16): "To keep the money coming in to finance the Ponzi game and hold the exchange rate, interest rates had to go up to reward foreign lenders for the risk, but that made real estate and banks even worse. To keep banks alive, interest rates had to go down. The government could not have it both ways. They cut rates, made it free to speculate against the currency and that is what happened."[9] After Samprasong Land missed a payment on its foreign debt in February 1997, the Bank of Thailand lent more than $8 billion to distressed financial

9. This is the theoretical dilemma modeled by Chang and Velasco (1998), as noted above in chapter 2.

Table C.3 Short-term borrowing as a percentage of total capital inflow
(percentages)

	Between 6/90 and 6/94	Between 6/94 and 6/97
Indonesia	78.72	56.71
South Korea	78.26	63.79
Malaysia	91.90	53.96
Philippines	12.17	69.50
Thailand	80.92	56.08

Source: Calculations based on data in Chang and Velasco (1998c).

institutions through its Financial Institutions Development Fund, despite mounting pressure on the baht, which it supported by intervening in the foreign-exchange market. Speculators drew the obvious conclusion.

Short Maturity of Debt

This leads to the third element of the story, the short-term nature of Asian banks' and corporations' foreign funding. Between 1990 and 1996, roughly 50 percent of net private portfolio capital inflows into Thailand took the form of short-term borrowing (see Bhattacharya, Claessens, and Hernandez 1997). Sixty-two percent of net capital inflows in South Korea consisted of short-term borrowing in the three years 1994-97, compared with 37 percent in 1990-93 (Y. Park 1998, 14) (see table C.3). Net interbank lending rose from $14 billion in the five years ending in 1994 to $43 billion in the subsequent seven quarters. Forty percent was denominated in yen, the rest in dollars. More than two-thirds of these loans matured in less than a year (BIS 1998, 122-23).

Hence, the Asian economies had not just a *flow* problem—a continued need to attract capital in*flows* to finance their current-account deficits— but a *stock* problem as well. They had accumulated large stocks of short-term debt denominated in foreign currency that needed to be rolled over regularly. If confidence were disturbed, it would be necessary to raise interest rates to induce foreign investors to renew their maturing loans. And given the weakness of the banks, there were obvious questions about the willingness and ability of governments to do so. To the contrary, the authorities might feel compelled to guarantee the foreign liabilities of the banks, creating additional claims against their thinly stretched foreign-exchange reserves and ensuring that the banking crisis also provoked a currency crisis.[10]

---

10. Here, then, is where the factors emphasized in "third-generation" models of currency crises, such as Dooley (1997) and Krugman (1998a), came into play.

These three elements—modest macroeconomic imbalances, serious banking-sector problems, and mismanagement of the maturity structure of the debt—placed governments in an untenable position. Painful policies were required to sustain confidence if it were disturbed, but financial systems could not bear the pain. There was nothing inevitable about the crisis, except in Thailand perhaps, in the sense that better luck (and better policies) might have enabled countries to grow out of their current-account deficits, lengthen the maturity structure of their debts, and strengthen their banking systems before a shock to confidence occurred. As it turned out, Thailand's devaluation disturbed investor confidence before its neighbors succeeded in escaping the zone of vulnerability, and the rest, as they say, is history.

Delving Deeper

This interpretation suggests that the turmoil in Asia in 1997 was a self-fulfilling crisis in which countries had entered a zone of vulnerability where governments were unable to sustain a credible defense of their currencies. In particular, the combination of modest macroeconomic imbalances, banking-system weaknesses, and the short maturity of foreign debts resembled problems in Mexico and in other countries that had felt the Tequila effect three years before.[11]

A deeper question is how the crisis countries allowed themselves to get into this bind in the first place. The obvious answer is that their crucial blunder was failing to upgrade bank supervision and regulation when liberalizing their financial systems, a failure that left them unable to raise interest rates and to mount a sustained defense of the currency (see, e.g., Goldstein 1998). Specifically, the inadequacy of supervision and regulation allowed the banks to rely excessively on high-cost foreign funding, to overcommit to the property market and industry, and to saddle themselves with nonperforming loans. Banks took on excessive short-term debt denominated in foreign currency because they were allowed to continue operating despite a weakened financial condition and the perverse risk-taking incentives it implied.

What remains to be explained is why the authorities were prone to these policy mistakes. Why did they fail to strengthen financial supervision and regulation? Why did bank owners with their own capital at stake fail to manage risks to avert such disastrous outcomes? And why were the markets so inclined to provide the short-term foreign funding that ultimately proved so disastrous?

---

11. These parallels are emphasized by Tornell (1998).

Banks as Instruments of Industrial Policy

The answer to these questions is that banks enjoyed government guarantees that promised to bail them out of any and all difficulties, which in turn encouraged them to take on excessive risk. Such guarantees were part and parcel of an economic development strategy in which the banks were the instruments of industrial policy. The banks were given franchises—alternative channels of intermediation were suppressed—in return for committing to accept government instructions regarding the allocation of credit.[12] Guarantees were the banks' quid pro quo for allowing themselves to be used as the instrumentality for public policy—as governments' quasi-fiscal agents. In this bank-led financial system, banks were too big and too important to fail. Knowing that they would not be allowed to fail, owners and managers had an incentive to take on additional risk.

One can see how this provided opportunities for crony capitalism. It was devilishly hard to determine whether the decision to extend credit to a particular industry or enterprise reflected the priorities of the economics ministry or the self-interests of political leaders' extended families. So long as there was an abundance of high-return projects waiting to be financed, the distinction was of little moment. But once high-return investments had been exhausted and the period of extraordinarily rapid growth drew to a close, that distinction became critically important, for now the extension of preferential credits in disregard of market signals placed the solvency of the banks at risk. This may not have been exactly what the Malaysian Prime Minister Mahathir Mohammad meant when he said that rapid growth, like high water, submerges rocks that can otherwise punch holes in the sturdiest boats, but the comment could not have been more apposite.

And when the water began to recede, revealing the rocks below, the banks navigated the shoals by borrowing abroad and only ending up in whiter water. Governments consorted in this decision to roll the dice. The Thai and South Korean governments liberalized the capital account exactly backwards. South Korea maintained stringent controls on FDI inflows into the country and limited opportunities for foreigners to purchase bonds and equities issued by South Korean corporations. It restricted the ability of those corporations to borrow on international markets.[13] The banks, meanwhile, were freed to borrow abroad, rendering the *chaebol* dependent on their debt. This policy was not one of incompe-

---

12. Other means of enhancing franchise values included interest rate ceilings on deposits and restraints in interbank competition in the loan market. In return, banks were subject to regulations requiring them to allocate certain portions of their loan portfolios to particular industrial sectors (Reisen 1998, 24).

13. With the exception of certain short-term trade-related credits.

Table C.4 Foreign liabilities of the banking system, 1990-96
(as a percentage of GDP)

	1990	1991	1992	1993	1994	1995	1996
Indonesia	6.5	5.2	6.2	6.2	6.5	6.0	5.6
Thailand	5.0	4.9	5.9	11.1	21.6	28.4	26.8
South Korea	4.1	4.9	4.8	4.5	5.5	6.9	9.3
Malaysia	7.0	9.1	12.7	19.5	9.2	7.4	9.2
Philippines	6.2	4.4	5.6	5.5	6.7	8.8	17.2

Source: Radelet and Sachs (1998a).

tence, as sometimes suggested; it was a logical outgrowth of the government's cultivation of a bank-centered financial system. Similarly, this is the only way to understand the decision of the Thai government to promote the growth of the Bangkok International Banking Facility (BIBF), which permitted Thai banks to borrow offshore and onloan the receipts to domestic customers in the form of loans denominated in foreign currency.[14] Thus, the foreign liabilities of the South Korean banking system more than doubled between 1993 and mid-1997, reaching nearly 10 percent of GDP. In Thailand, following the establishment of the BIBF, this ratio reached a remarkable 28 percent of GDP in 1995 (Radelet and Sachs 1998b, 25) (see table C.4).[15]

Accommodating Global Credit Conditions

It takes two to tango. These Asian policies would not have had such powerful effects had they not coincided with global conditions encourag-

---

14. The original intention had been to promote the development of Bangkok as an international financial center by financing "out-out" transactions in which Thai banks borrowed offshore and onlent only to offshore customers. Soon, however, the binding restrictions on domestic onlending were relaxed. Foreign banks were encouraged to abet this process by official intimations that the enthusiasm with which they helped to fund Thai banks' loans would affect their chances of eventually receiving a license permitting them to set up shop domestically.

15. Malaysia is a revealing comparison. In contrast to these other countries, its central bank sought to limit short-term foreign inflows through the banking system starting in 1994 by limiting banks' holdings of foreign funds, raising the cost of holding foreign deposits, and imposing ceilings on the net external liabilities of domestic banks. For details, see Glick and Moreno (1995). The foreign liabilities of deposit-money banks thus fell from a high of nearly 20 percent of GDP in 1993 to less than half that in 1996. While Malaysia hardly escaped the crisis unscathed, the fact that the initial impact was milder than in Thailand is plausibly ascribed to these policies. Indonesia provides another case where the authorities imposed quantitative controls on offshore borrowing by banks in 1991 as well as tightening limits on their open foreign-exchange positions and limiting their foreign-exchange swap positions as a percentage of capital. In this case, however, these restrictions merely caused offshore borrowing to be rerouted from the banking system to the corporate sector. And finally there is the Chilean case, considered in chapter 4 above.

ing US, European, and Japanese banks to lend. The consequences of Asian financial weaknesses could be contained so long as intermediaries there had limited access to funding. What changed in the mid-1990s was not just the relaxation of regulatory limits on their borrowing abroad but also structural and macroeconomic changes in the rest of the world that allowed Asian banks to freely indulge their appetites for foreign funding.

Financial deregulation in Europe was one of these changes: it encouraged bank lending to Asia by squeezing domestic margins, which encouraged European banks to seek higher yields in other parts of the world, and by removing regulatory limits on the ability of European commercial and investment banks to branch into new lines of business, notably in emerging markets. More important, low interest rates and yields in the major money centers encouraged institutional investors to borrow in the United States or Japan in order to purchase higher-yielding bank deposits or fixed-income securities in middle-income Asia.[16] The appearance of this "carry trade" in Malaysia in 1991-92 coincided with the US Federal Reserve Board's policy of low interest rates to stimulate the recovery of the US economy from its early-1990s recession and to strengthen the US banking system.[17] It was fueled by the decline of money-market rates to unprecedentedly low levels in Japan as that country descended into its mid-1990s economic funk.[18]

Understanding the flow of capital to East Asia does not require invoking technical terms such as "the carry trade" when one observes that there was an incentive to borrow where interest rates were low and invest where they were high so long as the exchange rate was pegged. Capital flows reflected the tendency toward interest parity, a condition that should hold in an environment of high capital mobility. An implication of this high capital mobility was that the authorities in capital-importing countries had little ability to restrain the growth of domestic credit once the US Federal Reserve Board opted for a more expansionary monetary policy to revive the US banking system (table C.5). Because exchange rates were

---

16. In addition, some critics suggest that the US- and IMF-led rescue of Mexico in 1995 was an important source of moral hazard, which, by allowing foreign investors to get out whole, encouraged them to rush back to emerging markets, including those of Asia. It is hard to know how much weight to attach to this explanation given the number of other forces also at work.

17. The carry trade is described in IMF (1998a).

18. In addition, the strength of the yen over much of this period stimulated investment both by making East Asian exports more competitive relative to those of Japan and by encouraging Japanese investment in the region (Y. Park 1998, 6; BIS 1998, 118). The rapid rise of stock markets in the United States and many European countries, itself a concomitant of the low level of interest rates, further encouraged investors in the advanced industrial countries to search for higher-yielding assets in middle-income Asia. Given their limited access to domestic securities markets, they funneled their cash through Asian banks.

Table C.5 Bank credit to the private sector, 1981-97[a]

	Annual rate of expansion[b] (in percent)		As a percentage of GDP
	1981-89	1990-97[c]	1997[c]
Indonesia	22	18	57
Thailand	15	18	105
South Korea	13	12	64
Malaysia	11	16	95
Philippines	- 5	18	52
Singapore	10	12	97
Hong Kong	13	8	157
Taiwan	15	13	138

a. Annual average.
b. Deflated by consumer prices.
c. 1997 data are preliminary.
Source: Bank for International Settlements (1998, table VII.1).

linked, monetary policies were linked. As David Hale (1997, 1) has put it, "As a result of the exchange rate link which east Asia had to the US dollar, America's expansionary monetary policy helped to encourage rapid credit growth in countries such as Thailand, Malaysia, Indonesia and the Philippines."

Thus, the exchange rate is a key part of the story. The operation of exchange rate bands and governments' stated commitment to their maintenance meant that there was little perceived exchange rate risk to deter capital inflows. Larger capital inflows meant larger current-account deficits, given the difficulty of sterilizing those inflows, and more real exchange rate appreciation. Both the deficits and the large real appreciation were sources of vulnerability when financial-market conditions were disturbed. Moreover, the absence of exchange rate variability left nothing to insulate money and credit conditions from those prevailing abroad. The loose monetary policies appropriate for a US economy recovering from a banking crisis and a Japanese economy still mired in one were not appropriate for Asian economies in which the problem was instead the risk of overheating. There, higher real interest rates were needed because there existed many attractive investment projects that could not all be undertaken at once. High interest rates were the rationing mechanism to force the market to choose among them. But the pegged exchange rate made it all but impossible to keep interest rates at a sufficient premium over foreign levels. Excessive credit expansion and an unsustainable real estate boom were the inevitable results.

To be sure, pegging the currency was not the only option for Thailand, Malaysia, Indonesia, the Philippines, and South Korea. By the time the crisis struck, South Korea had already moved cautiously in the direction of greater flexibility, and Indonesia, Malaysia, and the Philippines, as we have seen, did so soon after Thailand's devaluation. But limiting the flexibility of the exchange rate vis-à-vis the country's principal export markets was a logical policy for governments whose economic development strategies had been predicated on the promotion of exports. It was part of the bargain with export-oriented industries. Pegging to the dollar was also seen as a way of facilitating external financing of domestic investment projects (see Corsetti, Pesenti, and Roubini 1998). It was another legacy of Asia's development strategy that had outlived its usefulness.

Long-Term Historical Forces and Short-Term Financial Policies

Thus, Asia's crisis can only be understood in terms of a conjuncture of long-standing historical forces and short-term financial policies. Ultimately, the explanation for the crisis lies in the region's history and economic development trajectory, which relied on bank-centered financial systems, the use of the banks as instruments of industrial policy, and close connections between banks and politicians, all of which were designed to sustain high rates of investment and rapid economic growth. This was not a formula that could work forever: by the second half of the 1990s it had been in place for several decades and was showing growing signs of strain. At another level, the explanation lies in financial errors committed in the mid-1990s. Growth may have been slowing, but the day of reckoning was delayed by the selective liberalization of capital accounts to facilitate short-term financial flows, aided and abetted by the low level of interest rates in the major money centers and by the migration of US and European investment banks to middle-income Asia. These developments on the borrowing and lending sides enabled the newly industrializing countries to borrow their way out of their difficulties for a time. In the end, however, this only set them up for a harder fall.

Why Was the Crisis So Severe?

While these insights help one to understand the speculative attacks, they do not explain the full-blown economic and financial meltdown that followed. Something more is needed to account for the exceptional severity and scope of the crisis.

Unhedged Foreign Exposure

One factor, surely, was the extent of the foreign-currency exposure of the banking and corporate sectors. Mexico had foreign exposure as well, in the form of the notorious *tesobonos,* but these were liabilities of the government, not of firms and banks. When the peso began to decline, this created financial problems first and foremost for the Mexican government. In Asia, in contrast, the gravest problems were those created for the private sector. With so many banks and firms involved, the absence of an effective mechanism for coordinating debtor-creditor negotiations was a more serious problem than when there had been only the government on the debtor's side of the table. In comparison with Mexico, investors could look forward to a much longer period during which the debt overhang would continue to discourage potential lenders.

Critically, the foreign debts of Asian banks and firms were unhedged. The exchange rate having been pegged for so long, borrowers saw little reason to insure themselves against its depreciation by purchasing relatively expensive currency futures and forwards. Ironically, Asian governments' very success at pegging their exchange rates was one factor behind the severity of the crisis, for it lulled domestic banks and corporations into a false sense of security. And when the exchange rate began to move, it threw the banks and firms with the heaviest foreign exposures into bankruptcy.

One of the classic preconditions for a contractionary devaluation is the existence of a stock of foreign-currency denominated debt, the service on which grows heavier as the exchange rate declines.[19] The operation of this mechanism is clearly evident in Asia. As the exchange rate fell, debt denominated in foreign currency became more expensive in domestic currency terms, leaving domestic residents poorer. Firms, facing a heavier burden, invested less. Banks, facing a heavier burden, lent less. And as demand fell, there was downward pressure on output. Meanwhile, more domestic output had to be devoted to servicing the same external debt. This meant freeing up a larger share of domestic resources for debt-servicing purposes, which required using policy to restrict demand still further. But this only depressed output still more, in turn putting further downward pressure on the exchange rate and further elevating debt servicing costs in a vicious spiral.[20]

The Scramble for Cover

In addition, banks and firms that had previously left their foreign exposures unhedged scrambled for cover when the exchange rate began to

---

19. See Krugman and Taylor (1978) for a theoretical exposition.

20. Those who emphasize the depressing effects of the high interest rates applied by Asian central banks (and required by the IMF as a condition for its assistance) and argue that these may have depressed rather than strengthening currencies presumably have in mind something along these lines (see, e.g., Radelet and Sachs 1998a; Furman and Stiglitz 1998).

move. Not only did they find it more costly to purchase the foreign exchange needed to meet their current obligations, but they also scrambled after additional foreign exchange to protect themselves against the possibility of future exchange rate depreciation, pushing the exchange rate down in a self-fulfilling prophecy. Once it became clear that governments' stated commitments to stabilize exchange rates were worthless, banks and firms with debts denominated in foreign currency sought cover at any price.[21]

Other Sources of Positive Market Feedback

The scramble for cover was not the only reason why the initial decline in Asian exchange rates and asset prices fed on itself. The collapse of East Asian asset values and the fall of the Nikkei tightened the screws on already distressed Japanese banks, which responded by calling in their loans. And once asset prices began to fall, hedge funds and other investors who had purchased emerging-market securities on margin were forced to raise cash to pay back their borrowed funds. The dynamics of margin calls forced them to sell into a falling market, and the further the market fell the more frequent the margin calls became.

In addition, when Moody's downgraded Thailand, South Korea, and Indonesia's sovereign debts in December to below-investment-grade status, many portfolio managers were required to liquidate their holdings of those securities. The assumption that the debts of corporate and financial issuers cannot have a better credit rating than the sovereign (the "sovereign ceiling") meant that these other securities became junk bonds as well. Finally, a number of bond contracts contained acceleration provisions allowing creditors to call for immediate repayment in the event that the issue was downgraded (Radelet and Sachs 1998a, 13). The existence of these options was not well known to other investors or, for that matter, to officials.

Cascading Defaults

Another factor contributing to the severity of the crisis was the absence in most Asian countries of adequate bankruptcy and insolvency procedures and independent judiciaries. Anticipating that the firms to which they had lent would experience serious financial problems and lacking

---

21. As Alan Greenspan (1998, 4) put it, "The belief that local currencies could, virtually without risk of loss, be converted into dollars at any time was shattered. Investors, both domestic and foreign, endeavored en masse to convert dollars, as confidence in the ability of the local economy to earn dollars to meet their fixed obligations diminished. Local exchange rates fell against the dollar, inducing still further declines."

confidence that they would be treated fairly under Asian countries' insolvency codes, creditors scrambled to liquidate their claims in an asset grab race, illustrating a phenomenon described in chapter 3. Even where forbearance was in their collective interest, they had an incentive to scramble for the enterprise's remaining assets before these were stripped by insiders and other more politically influential claimants. And when borrowers began to default, the inability of lenders to repossess collateral produced a cascade effect where the debtor's nonperformance threatened to force its creditors into default. Where those creditors included banks, banking panics were the result. Specialists suggest that the dangers posed by inadequate bankruptcy procedures may not be apparent in periods of rapid growth when few firms experience financial distress, but that they will surface with a vengeance if and when growth slows (see, e.g., LaPorta and Lopez-de-Silanes 1998). Asia's experience is consistent with this view.[22]

The Contagion

Yet another factor contributing to the severity of the crisis was the speed and extent of the contagion. Exporting its way out of the crisis may have been possible for one stricken country, but it was not possible for an entire group of crisis economies, all of which could not significantly boost their exports to one another and to the same third markets. This suggests that one channel for contagion was competitive devaluation operating through bilateral and third-country trade linkages (for evidence, see Eichengreen and Rose 1998; Glick and Rose 1998). Thailand may have exported little to Indonesia and Malaysia, but these countries all sold into the same markets in other parts of the world. Thailand's devaluation therefore worsened the balance of payments prospects of all its neighbors and competitors.

That said, trade links seem insufficient to explain the speed and virulence with which the crisis spread. And the contagion seems to have infected countries that exported primary commodities and high-tech products equally, without discriminating between them.

This points to the operation of other channels, notably the generalized revision of expectations prompted by the devaluation of the baht and reinforced by the spread of financial upheavals to Indonesia and Malay-

---

22. Thus, authors such as Sachs (1994b) argue the need for an international bankruptcy court, or its equivalent, with the power to impose an automatic stay or standstill to halt the creditor grab race. Asia's experience suggests that the institutional lacuna giving rise to this socially counterproductive behavior was as much at the national as the international level. I discuss this point in chapter 6.

sia.[23] Not only did the Thai devaluation reveal that promises regarding Asian exchange rate pegs could not be taken at face value, but it alerted investors to the existence of deeper problems. Morris Goldstein (1998, 18) refers to this as the "wake-up-call" hypothesis. The term is both evocative and revealing of the limits of the interpretation. Rarely is an effort made to explain why this particular wake-up call was so loud and startling. As commonly invoked, this explanation for the contagion simply begs the question.

Guillermo Calvo (1997) suggests that globalization itself explains why investors were sleeping so soundly. Globalization makes it possible to diversify investment portfolios internationally. But diversification reduces the incentive for each investor to sink the costs of learning about conditions in each national economy, because investments there now account for only a small fraction of his or her portfolio. Lacking information, investors are more likely to draw inferences from the actions of other investors— that is, to run with the herd.[24] Unfortunately, it is not clear why investors would not solve this problem by turning to mutual funds and other collective investment vehicles that are in the business of acting as delegated monitors because of the existence of information costs. Nor is it clear why the Thai devaluation should have been regarded by investors with stakes in other Asian countries as having such important information content.

A more compelling potential explanation goes back to the bank-based nature of Asia's financial system.[25] The region had developed few financial *markets* on which information was impounded into the prices of exchange-traded financial assets. Rather, this business was done by banks possessing relatively favorable access to information on their customers' financial position. Those banks were understandably reluctant to share their proprietary knowledge with their competitors. They were entrusted, for better or for worse, to act as delegated monitors and generated few price signals such as those provided in other economies by bond and equity markets. Because there was little independent information on the quality of loans, bad news served to discredit them as a group.

Moreover, the lack of transparency of bank balance sheets, reflecting the failure of supervisors to require banks to follow rigorous auditing and accounting practices, heightened the difficulty of distinguishing good

---

23. An additional factor was the rebalancing of portfolios by commercial and investment banks and other institutional investors when the crisis struck. Losses on Thai investments encouraged them to sell off holdings in other Asian countries in order to rebalance their portfolios and to raise cash. The loan clauses described above provided one mechanism for doing so.

24. Bacchetta and van Wincoop (1998) show how herding behavior that amplifies market volatility can result from incomplete information.

25. This is the explanation suggested by Yellen (1998).

credit risks from bad ones, most obviously in Thailand but in South Korea as well. Lengthy delays were allowed to occur before banks revealed information about their nonperforming loans.[26] Information on individual banks and loans being lacking, the revision of confidence was general. And in this information-impacted environment, bank runs could lead to systemic banking crises and spill contagiously across countries.

Japan's Deepening Slump

If these are not enough explanations for the singular severity and scope of the crisis, finally there was the role of Japan. In 1994-95, when Mexico experienced its crisis, its principal trading partner, the United States, was growing strongly. In 1992-93, when much of Europe was in crisis, demand in Germany was strong, reflecting the effects of German unification. But in 1997-98, the opposite was true of the relevant regional power, Japan, which traded more than any other G-7 member with the crisis countries and which was growing, as it had for the whole of the 1990s, more slowly than any other G-7 economy. This further limited the ability of the crisis countries to export their way out of their difficulties and had obvious adverse impacts on investor confidence.

Similarly, the weakness of Japanese financial institutions left them little margin for error when their East Asian investments stopped performing. Japanese banks short of capital and required to meet the Basle Standards responded to problems in Thailand and Indonesia by liquidating their assets in other Asian countries, opening another channel for contagion.

Implications

This interpretation of the crisis has five lessons, all closely related to one another. First, large current-account deficits are not benign. Deficits have to be financed, placing a country at the mercy of its creditors. However admirable the uses to which foreign funds are put, the returns need to be balanced against risks in the form of a sudden curtailment of foreign lending and the need to eliminate that deficit overnight. Those of us who live in California appreciate the advantages of earthquake insurance. Policymakers need to similarly appreciate the importance of insuring themselves against financial tremors by avoiding excessive deficits.

Second, how the current account is financed is not a matter of indifference. Dependence on short-term funding, and short-term funding denomi-

---

26. And before regulators reclassified those assets as nonperforming.

nated in foreign currency in particular, is risky business.[27] If investors lose confidence for any reason and hesitate to roll over their short-term claims, the issuer's solvency can be cast into doubt. If those short-term foreign claims are claims on the financial system, macroeconomic stability will be threatened. And if those claims are denominated in foreign currency (or if the exchange rate is pegged), there will little that the government and the central bank can do about it.

Third, banks are a special source of vulnerability. Banks are particularly important in developing countries as a source of financial intermediation services. The securitized markets that are the modern alternative have more demanding information requirements and, historically, are later to develop. This dependence means that banks will be regarded as too big and important to fail. The knowledge that the government stands ready to run to their rescue is in turn a source of moral hazard that encourages excessive foreign funding of domestic banks. This provides a rationale on classic second-best grounds for policies to offset this distortion—for relating bank capital requirements to the source of their funding as well as the riskiness of their loans and more generally for regulating the flow of short-term foreign funds into the banking system. Regrettably, this is precisely the opposite of what Asian governments, seeking to use the banks as instruments of industrial policy and conduits for the transfer of foreign funds, did in the years leading up to their crisis.

Fourth, developing countries, with few exceptions, should move toward greater exchange rate flexibility.[28] A more flexible exchange rate gives banks and corporations an incentive to hedge their foreign exposures, which better positions them to cope with financial turbulence if and when it occurs. In Asia, currency depreciation was painful because it came all at once and banks and corporations were unprepared. Had governments allowed the exchange rate to exhibit more flexibility in the period while capital was still flowing in, banks and corporations would have hedged more of their exposure, and the subsequent sharp depreciation would not have been so disruptive. Asia is not evidence that greater exchange rate flexibility is undesirable, but it provides a graphic example of the importance of initiating that transition before problems arise.

Finally, it will not always be possible to prevent or predict financial crises. While investments in crisis prevention have a high payoff, there will be always financial surprises, implying the need for better mechanisms for

---

27. A corollary is that the absence of an external deficit does not mean the absence of a crisis; past deficits, if financed recklessly, continue to confer that danger long after they have been eliminated.

28. Those few exceptions are smaller, more open economies with strong reasons for wishing to put monetary policy on autopilot. A currency board may be attractive to these exceptional few. But the number of countries for which this alternative is viable is likely to be small. This is a point developed in chapter 7.

containing them. Unfortunately, the two options currently available for responding to crises—extending ever-bigger bailouts and standing aside and letting nature run its course—are equally unacceptable. This is why it is essential to create a third alternative.

References

Alesina, Alberto, and Roberto Perotti. 1994. Budget Deficits and Budget Institutions. Photocopy. Harvard University and Columbia University.

Allsopp, Chris, Gareth Davies, Warwick McKibbin, and David Vines. 1997. Monetary and
Fiscal Stabilization of Demand Shocks within Europe. *Review of International Economics*
5, no. 5 (November): 55-76.

Bacchetta, Philipe, and Eric van Wincoop. 1998. Capital Flows to Emerging Markets: Liberalization, Overshooting, and Volatility. Photocopy. Studinzentrum Gerzensee and Federal
Reserve Bank of New York.

Bank for International Settlements (BIS). 1997. *Core Principles for Effective Banking Supervision.
Basle Core Principles.* Basle: Basle Committee for Banking Supervision.

Bank for International Settlements (BIS). 1998. *68th Annual Report.* Basle: BIS.

Bardacke, Ted. 1998. Thais Agree on Debt Restructuring. *Financial Times* (11 September): 6.

Benston, George, and George Kaufman. 1988. Regulating Bank Safety and Performance. In
Restructuring Banking and Financial Services in America, ed. by William S. Haraf and Rose
Marie Kushmeider. Washington: American Enterprise Institute.

Berg, Andrew, and Catherine Pattillo. 1998. Are Currency Crises Predictable? A Test. Photocopy. International Monetary Fund.

Bergsten, C. Fred. 1998a. How to Target Exchange Rates. *Financial Times* (20 November).

Bergsten, C. Fred. 1998b. Missed Opportunity. *The International Economy* 12, no. 6 (November):
26-27.

Bergsten, C. Fred, and C. Randall Henning. 1996. *Global Economic Leadership and the Group
of Seven.* Washington: Institute for International Economics.

Bhagwati, Jagdish. 1998. The Capital Myth: The Difference between Trade in Widgets and
Dollars. *Foreign Affairs* 77: 7-12.

Bhattacharya, Amar, Stijn Claessens, and Leonardo Hernandez. 1997. *Recent Financial Market
Turbulence in Southeast Asia.* Washington: World Bank.

Brown, Gordon. 1998. And Impose New Codes of Conduct. *Wall Street Journal* (6 October): A22.

Brown, Stephen J., William Goetzmann, and James Park. 1998. *Hedge Funds and the Asian
Currency Crisis of 1997.* NBER Working Paper No. 6427 (February). Cambridge, MA:
NBER.

Bruno, Michael, and Stanley Fischer. 1990. Seniorage, Operating Rules, and the High Inflation Trap. *Quarterly Journal of Economics* 105: 353-74.

Bulow, Jeremy, and Kenneth Rogoff. 1989. Sovereign Debt: Is to Forgive to Forget? *American Economic Review* 79: 43-50.

Burnham, James B. 1990. *A Financial System for the Year 2000: The Case for Narrow Banking.* Center for the Study of American Business, Formal Publication Number 97 (February). St. Louis, MO: Center for the Study of American Business.

Calomiris, Charles. 1998a. The IMF's Imprudent Role as Lender of Last Resort. *Cato Journal* 17: 275-95.

Calomiris, Charles. 1998b. Blueprints for a New Global Financial Architecture. Photocopy. Columbia University.

Calvo, Guillermo A., and Morris Goldstein. 1996. What Role for the Official Sector? In *Private Capital Flows to Emerging Markets After the Mexican Crisis*, ed. by Guillermo A. Calvo, Morris Goldstein, and Eduard Hochreiter. Washington: Institute for International Economics.

Calvo, Guillermo A. 1997. *Rational Herd Behavior and the Globalization of Securities Markets.* Institute for Empirical Macroeconomics Discussion Paper No. 120 (August). Minneapolis: Institute for Empirical Macroeconomics, Federal Reserve Bank of Minneapolis.

Calvo, Guillermo A., and Enrique Mendoza. 1996. Reflections on Mexico's Balance of Payments Crisis: A Chronicle of Death Foretold. *Journal of International Economics* 41: 235-64.

Camdessus, Michel. 1998a. Report of the Managing Director to the Interim Committee on the International Monetary System. http://www.imf.org/external/np/omd/1001.98.htm.

Camdessus, Michel. 1998b. Capital Account Liberalization and the Role of the Fund. Remarks to the IMF Seminar on Capital Account Liberalization, Washington (9 March).

Camdessus, Michel. 1998c. Toward an Agenda for International Monetary and Financial Reform. Address to the World Affairs Council, Philadelphia (6 November). http://www.imf.org/external/np/speeches/1998/110698.HTM.

Canada, Department of Finance. 1998. Finance Minister Announces Six-Point Canadian Plan to Deal with Global Financial Turmoil. Press Release 98-094, Ottawa, Department of Finance (29 September). http://www.fin.gc.ca/newse98/98%2D094e.html.

Cardenas, Mauricio, and Felipe Barrera. 1997. On the Effectiveness of Capital Controls: The Experience of Colombia in the 1990s. *Journal of Development Economics* 54: 27-58.

Chang, Roberto, and Andres Velasco. 1998a. *Financial Crises in Emerging Markets: A Canonical Model.* NBER Working Paper No. 6606 (June). Cambridge, MA: NBER.

Chang, Roberto, and Andres Velasco. 1998b. *The Asian Liquidity Crisis.* NBER Working Paper No. 6796 (November). Cambridge, MA: NBER.

Chang, Roberto, and Andres Velasco. 1998c. The 1997-98 Financial Crisis: Why in Asia? Photocopy (July). Federal Reserve Bank of Atlanta.

Chase Manhattan Bank. 1997. Emerging Markets After Thailand: Guilt by Association or Flattered by the Comparison? New York: Chase Manhattan Bank (1 October).

Chinn, Menzie, and Michael Dooley. 1998. Why Latin America 1995 and East Asia 1997 Are Alike. Photocopy (June). University of California, Santa Cruz.

Cline, William R. 1995. *International Debt Reexamined.* Washington: Institute for International Economics.

Cline, William R. 1996. Crisis Management in Emerging Capital Markets. In *From Halifax to Lyons: What Has Been Done about Crisis Management?* ed. by Peter B. Kenen. Essays in International Finance No. 200 (October). Princeton, NJ: International Finance Section, Department of Economics, Princeton University.

Cline, William R. 1998. *IMF-Supported Adjustment Programs in the East Asian Financial Crisis.* Research Paper No. 98-1. Washington: Institute of International Finance.

Cline, William R., and Kevin J. S. Barnes. 1997. *Spreads and Risks in Emerging Market Lending.* Institute of International Finance Research Paper No. 97-1. Washington: Institute of International Finance.

Cohen, Benjamin. 1989. A Global Chapter 11. *Foreign Policy* 75: 109-27.

Cole, Harold L., and Timothy J. Kehoe. 1996. *A Self-Fulfilling Model of Mexico's 1994-95 Debt Crisis*. Research Report No. 210 (April). Minnesota: Federal Reserve Bank of Minneapolis Research Department.

Cooper, Richard. 1984. A Monetary System for the Future. *Foreign Affairs* 63: 166-84.

Corsetti, Giancarlo, Paolo Pesenti, and Nouriel Roubini. 1998. Paper Tigers? A Preliminary Assessment of the Asian Crisis. Photocopy. Yale University, Princeton University, and New York University.

Crockett, Andrew. 1994. Monetary Implications of Increased Capital Flows. In *Changing Capital Markets: Implications for Monetary Policy*. Kansas City: Federal Reserve Bank of Kansas City.

Dale, Richard. 1998. The Structure of Financial Regulation. Paper prepared for the Fourth Annual World Bank Conference on Development in Latin America and the Caribbean, San Salvador, El Salvador (28-30 June).

Darrow, Duncan, A. T. Chandler, and William R. Campbell. 1997. *Restructuring Eurobond Debt in Thailand*. New York: Orrick, Herrington & Sutcliffe, LLP.

De Gregorio, Jose, Sebastian Edwards, and Rodrigo O. Valdes. 1998. Capital Controls in Chile: An Assessment. Photocopy. Universidad de Chile, UCLA, and Central Bank of Chile.

Demirguc-Kunt, Asli, and Enrica Detragiache. 1997. Banking Crises around the World: Are There Any Common Threads? Photocopy. World Bank and International Monetary Fund.

Devenow, Andrea, and Ivo Welch. 1996. Rational Herding in Financial Economics. *European Economic Review* 40: 603-15.

Diamond, Douglas. 1984. Financial Intermediation and Delegated Monitoring. *Review of Economic Studies* 51: 393-414.

Dobson, Wendy, and Pierre Jacquet. 1998. *Financial Services Liberalization in the WTO*. Washington: Institute for International Economics.

Dooley, Michael. 1996. The Tobin Tax: Good Theory, Weak Evidence, Questionable Policy. In *The Tobin Tax: Coping with Financial Volatility*, ed. by Mahbub ul Haq, Inge Kaul, and Isabelle Grunberg. New York: Oxford University Press.

Dooley, Michael. 1997. *A Model of Crises in Emerging Markets*. NBER Working Paper No. 6300 (December). Cambridge, MA: NBER.

Dornbusch, Rudiger. 1998. The Asian Currency Crisis: What Happened and What Comes Next? Photocopy. MIT.

Dornbusch, Rudiger, Ilan Goldfajn, and Rodrigo O. Valdes. 1995. Currency Crises and Collapses. *Brookings Papers on Economic Activity* 2: 219-70.

Edwards, Sebastian. 1998a. Capital Flows, Real Exchange Rates, and Capital Controls: Some Latin American Experiences. Photocopy. UCLA.

Edwards, Sebastian. 1998b. Capital Controls Are Not the Reason for Chile's Success. *Wall Street Journal* (3 April): A19.

Edwards, Sebastian. 1998c. Abolish the IMF. *Financial Times* (13 November): A1.

Eichengreen, Barry. 1994. *International Monetary Arrangements for the 21st Century*. Washington: Brookings Institution.

Eichengreen, Barry. 1998. Kicking the Habit: Moving from Pegged Rates to Greater Exchange Rate Flexibility. *Economic Journal*. Forthcoming.

Eichengreen, Barry. 1999. The Baring Crisis in a Mexican Mirror. *International Political Science Review*. Forthcoming.

Eichengreen, Barry, Ricardo Hausmann, and Juergen von Hagen. 1996. Reforming Budgetary Institutions in Latin America: The Case for a National Fiscal Council. Photocopy. University of California, Berkeley, Inter-American Development Bank, and the University of Mannheim.

Eichengreen, Barry, and Paul Masson, with Hugh Bredenkamp, Barry Johnston, Javier Hamann, Esteban Jadresic, and Inci Otker. 1998. *Exit Strategies: Policy Options for Countries Seeking Greater Exchange Rate Flexibility.* Occasional Paper No. 168 (August). Washington: International Monetary Fund.

Eichengreen, Barry, and Donald Mathieson, with Bankim Chadha, Anne Jansen, Laura Kodres, and Sunil Sharma. 1998. *Hedge Funds and Financial Market Dynamics.* Occasional Paper No. 155 (May). Washington: International Monetary Fund.

Eichengreen, Barry, and Michael Mussa, with Giovanni Dell'Ariccia, Enrica Detragiache, Gian Maria Milesi-Ferretti, and Andrew Tweedie. 1998. Capital Account Liberalization: Theoretical and Practical Aspects. Occasional Paper No. 172 (October). Washington: International Monetary Fund.

Eichengreen, Barry, and Richard Portes. 1989. After the Deluge: Default, Negotiation, and Readjustment During the Interwar Years. In *The International Debt Crisis in Historical Perspective,* ed. by Barry Eichengreen and Peter H. Lindert. Cambridge, MA: MIT Press.

Eichengreen, Barry, and Richard Portes, with Francesco Cornelli, Leonardo Felli, Julian Franks, Christopher Greenwood, Hugh Mercer and Giovanni Vitale. 1995. *Crisis? What Crisis? Orderly Workouts for Sovereign Debtors.* London: Centre for Economic Policy Research.

Eichengreen, Barry, and Andrew Rose. 1997. Staying Afloat When the Wind Shifts: External Factors and Emerging-Market Banking Crises. In *Money, Capital Mobility, and Trade: Essays in Honor of Robert A. Mundell,* ed. by Guillermo Calvo, Rudiger Dornbusch, and Maurice Obstfeld. Cambridge, MA: MIT Press. Forthcoming.

Eichengreen, Barry, and Andrew Rose. 1998. Contagious Currency Crises: Channels of Transmission. In *Changes in Exchange Rates in Rapidly Developing Countries,* ed. by Takatoshi Ito and Anne Krueger. Chicago: University of Chicago Press. Forthcoming.

Eichengreen, Barry, Andrew Rose, and Charles Wyplosz. 1995. Exchange Market Mayhem: The Antecedents and Aftermath of Speculative Attacks. *Economic Policy* 21: 249-312.

Eichengreen, Barry, Andrew Rose, and Charles Wyplosz. 1996. Is There a Safe Passage to EMU? Evidence on Capital Controls and a Proposal. In *The Microstructure of Foreign Exchange Markets,* ed. by Jeffrey Frankel and Alberto Giovannini. Chicago: University of Chicago Press.

Eichengreen, Barry, Andrew Rose, and Charles Wyplosz. 1997. Contagious Currency Crises: First Tests. *Scandinavian Journal of Economics* 98: 1-22.

Eichengreen, Barry, James Tobin, and Charles Wyplosz. 1995. Two Cases for Sand in the Wheels of International Finance. *Economic Journal* 105: 162-72.

Eichengreen, Barry, and Charles Wyplosz. 1993. The Unstable EMS. *Brookings Papers on Economic Activity* 1: Washington: Brookings Institution.

Feldstein, Martin. 1998a. Refocusing the IMF. *Foreign Affairs* 77: 20-33.

Feldstein, Martin. 1998b. Self-Protection for Emerging Market Economies. Photocopy. Harvard University.

Felix, David. 1995. *Financial Globalization vs. Free Trade: The Case for the Tobin Tax.* UNCTAD Discussion Paper No. 108. New York: UNCTAD.

Fernald, John, Hali Edison, and Prakiash Loungani. 1998. *Was China the First Domino? Assessing Links between China and the Rest of Emerging Asia.* International Finance Discussion Paper No. 604 (March). Washington: Board of Governors of the Federal Reserve System.

Fletcher, Ian F. 1997. The European Union Convention on Insolvency Proceedings: An Overview and Comment, with U.S. Interest in Mind. *Brooklyn Journal of International Law* 23: 25-55.

Folkerts-Landau, David, and Carl-Johan Lindgren. 1998. *Toward a Framework for Financial Stability.* Washington: International Monetary Fund.

Frankel, Jeffrey, and Andrew Rose. 1996. Currency Crashes in Emerging Markets: An Empirical Treatment. *Journal of International Economics* 41: 351-66.

Furman, Jason, and Joseph Stiglitz. 1998. Economic Crises: Evidence and Insights from East Asia. *Brookings Papers on Economic Activity*. Forthcoming.

Gamble, William. 1998. *Restructuring in Asia: A Brief Survey of Asian Bankruptcy Law*. Providence, RI: Emerging Markets Strategies Company.

Garber, Peter. 1996a. Managing Risks to Financial Markets from Volatile Capital Flows: The Role of Prudential Regulation. *International Journal of Finance and Economics* 1: 188-95.

Garber, Peter. 1996b. Issues of Enforcement and Evasion in a Tax on Foreign Exchange Transactions. In *The Tobin Tax: Coping with Financial Volatility*, ed. by Mahbub ul Haq, Inge Kaul, and Isabelle Grunberg. New York: Oxford University Press.

Garber, Peter. 1998. *Derivatives in International Capital Flows*. NBER Working Paper No. 6623 (June). Cambridge, MA: NBER.

Garber, Peter, and Mark Taylor. 1995. Sand in the Wheels of Foreign Exchange Markets: A Skeptical Note. *Economic Journal* 105: 173-80.

Garten, Jeffrey E. 1998. In This Economic Chaos, a Global Bank Can Help, *International Herald Tribune* (25 September): 8.

Gavin, Michael, and Ricardo Hausmann. 1996. The Roots of Banking Crises: The Macroeconomic Context. In *Banking Crises in Latin America*, ed. by Ricardo Hausmann and Liliana Rojas-Suarez. Baltimore: Johns Hopkins University Press.

Gavin, Michael, and Ricardo Hausmann. 1998. A Contingent Facility to Promote Financial Stability and Strengthen Market Discipline, ed. by Ricardo Hausmann and Liliana Rojas-Suarez. Washington: Office of the Chief Economist, Inter-American Development Bank.

Gavin, Michael, and Roberto Perotti. 1997. Fiscal Policy in Latin America. In *NBER Macroeconomics Annual*. Cambridge, MA: NBER.

Glick, Reuven, and Ramon Moreno. 1995. Responses to Capital Inflows in Malaysia and Thailand. *Weekly Letter* (7 April). California: Federal Reserve Bank of San Francisco 95-14.

Glick, Reuven, and Andrew Rose. 1998. Contagion and Trade: Why Are Currency Crises Regional? Photocopy. Federal Reserve Bank of San Francisco and University of California, Berkeley.

Goldberg, Linda. 1993. Predicting Exchange Rate Crises: Mexico Revisited. *Journal of International Economics* 36: 413-30.

Goldsmith, Raymond. 1985. *Comparative National Balance Sheets*. Chicago: University of Chicago Press.

Goldstein, Morris. 1996. Avoiding Future Mexicos: A Post-Halifax Scorecard on Crisis Prevention and Management. In *From Halifax to Lyons: What Has Been Done about Crisis Management?* ed. by Peter B. Kenen. Essays in International Finance No. 200 (October). Princeton, NJ: International Finance Section, Department of Economics, Princeton University.

Goldstein, Morris. 1997. *The Case for an International Banking Standard*. POLICY ANALYSES IN INTERNATIONAL ECONOMICS No. 47. Washington: Institute for International Economics.

Goldstein, Morris. 1998. *The Asian Financial Crisis: Causes Cures and Systemic Implications*. POLICY ANALYSES IN INTERNATIONAL ECONOMICS No. 55. Washington: Institute for International Economics.

Goldstein, Morris, and Carmen Reinhart. 1999. *Forecasting Financial Crises: Early Warning Signals for Emerging Markets*. Washington: Institute for International Economics. Forthcoming.

Goldstein, Morris, and Philip Turner. 1996. *Banking Crises in Emerging Economies: Origins and Policy Options*. Economic Paper No. 46. Basle: Bank for International Settlements.

Gould, David, and José Amaro-Reyes. 1983. The Effects of Corruption on Administrative Performance. Photocopy. World Bank.

Government of France. 1998. *Facing International Instability: Twelve Proposals for a European Initiative*. Paris: Government of France.

Greenspan, Alan. 1998a. Testimony before the Committee on Banking and Financial Services, US House of Representatives (30 January). Washington: Board of Governors of the Federal Reserve System.

Greenspan, Alan. 1998b. Remarks before the 34th Annual Conference on Bank Structure and Competition (7 May). Chicago: Federal Reserve Bank of Chicago.

Group of Seven (G-7). 1998. *Declaration of G-7 Finance Ministers and Central Bank Governors.* G-7. http://www.imf.org/external/np/g7/103098dc.htm.

Group of 10 (G-10). 1996. *Resolving Sovereign Liquidity Crises.* Washington: G-10.

Group of 30 (G-30). 1997. *Global Institutions, National Supervision, and Systemic Risk.* Washington: G-30.

Group of 22 (G-22). 1998a. *Report of the Working Group on Transparency and Accountability.* Washington: G-22.

Group of 22 (G-22). 1998b. *Report of the Working Group on Strengthening Financial Systems.* Washington: G-22.

Group of 22 (G-22). 1998c. *Report of the Working Group on International Financial Crises.* Washington: G-22.

Hale, David. 1997. The East Asian Financial Crisis and the World Economy. Testimony before the Committee on Banking and Financial Services, US House of Representatives (13 November). Washington: Board of Governors of the Federal Reserve System.

Hardy, Daniel, and Ceyla Pazarbasioglu. 1998. *Leading Indicators of Banking Crises: Was Asia Different?* IMF Working Paper No. 98/91 (June). Washington: International Monetary Fund.

Hurlock, James. 1995. The Way Ahead for Sovereign Debt. *Euromoney* (August): 78-79.

Institute of International Finance (IIF). 1996. *Resolving Sovereign Financial Crises.* Washington: IIF.

International Monetary Fund (IMF). 1998a. *International Capital Markets.* Washington: IMF.

International Monetary Fund (IMF). 1998b. *IMF Announces an External Evaluation of Its Surveillance Role.* News Brief No. 98/21 (30 June). Washington: IMF.

International Monetary Fund (IMF). 1998c. *World Economic Outlook* (May). Washington: IMF.

Kaminsky, Graciela, Saul Lizondo, and Carmen Reinhart. 1997. *Leading Indicators of Currency Crises.* Policy Research Working Paper No. 1852 (November). Washington: World Bank.

Kaminsky, Graciela, and Carmen Reinhart. 1996. *The Twin Crises: The Causes of Banking and Balance of Payments Problems.* International Finance Discussion Paper No. 544. Washington: Board of Governors, Federal Reserve System,

Kaminsky, Graciela, and Carmen Reinhart. 1998. Currency and Banking Crises: A Composite Leading Indicator. Photocopy. Federal Reserve Board and University of Maryland.

Kampffmeyer, Thomas. 1987. *Towards a Solution of the Debt Crisis: Applying the Concept of Corporate Composition with Creditors.* Berlin: German Development Institute.

Kaufman, Henry. 1998a. Preventing the Next Global Financial Crisis. *Washington Post* (28 January): A17.

Kaufman, Henry. 1998b. Proposal for Improving the Structure of Financial Supervision and Regulation. Outline of remarks before the Brookings Institution Symposium on Limiting Moral Hazard in Financial Rescues (4 June). Washington.

Kenen, Peter B. 1996. The Feasibility of Taxing Foreign Exchange Transactions. In *The Tobin Tax: Coping with Financial Volatility,* ed. by Mahbub ul Haq, Inge Kaul, and Isabelle Grunberg. New York: Oxford University Press.

Kenen, Peter B., ed. 1998. *Should the IMF Pursue Capital Account Convertibility?* Essays in International Finance No. 207 (January). Princeton, NJ: International Finance Section, Department of Economics, Princeton University.

Kim, In-June, and Yeongseop Rhee. 1998. Currency Crises of the Asian Countries in a Globalized Financial Market. Photocopy. Seoul University and Sookmyung University.

King, Robert, and Ross Levine. 1993. Finance, Entrepreneurship, and Growth: Theory and Evidence. *Journal of Monetary Economics* 32: 513-42.

Krugman, Paul. 1979. A Model of Balance-of-Payments Crises. *Journal of Money, Credit, and Banking* 11: 311-25.

Krugman, Paul. 1996. Are Currency Crises Self-Fulfilling? In *NBER Macroeconomics Annual.*

Krugman, Paul. 1998a. What Happened in Asia. Photocopy. MIT.

Krugman, Paul. 1998b. Saving Asia: It's Time to Get Radical. *Fortune* 138 (7 September): 74-80.

Krugman, Paul. 1998c. Heresy Time. http://web.mit.edu/krugman/www/heresy.html. (28 September).

Krugman, Paul, and Julio Rotemberg. 1990. *Target Zones with Limited Reserves.* National Bureau of Economic Research Working Paper No. 3418 (August). Cambridge, MA: NBER.

Krugman, Paul, and Lance Taylor. 1978. Contractionary Effects of Devaluation. *Journal of International Economics* 8: 445-56.

Kuttner, Robert. 1998. When the Free Market Is Too Free. *Business Week* (12 October): 24.

LaPorta, Raphael, and Florenzio Lopez-de-Silanes. 1998. Creditor Rights. Photocopy. Harvard University.

Le Fort, Guillermo, and Carlos Budnevich. 1996. *Capital Account Regulation and Macroeconomic Policy: Two Latin American Experiences.* Levy Institute Working Paper No. 162. Annandale-on-Hudson, NY: Jerome Levy Economics Institute, Bard College.

Lee, Peter. 1998. Korea Stares into the Abyss. *Euromoney* (March): 32-37.

Litan, Robert. 1987. *What Should Banks Do?* Washington: Brookings Institution.

Litan, Robert et. al. 1998. Statement of the Shadow Financial Regulatory Committee on International Monetary Fund Assistance and International Crises, Statement No. 145, Shadow Financial Regulatory Committee. http://www.aei.org/shdw/shdw145.htm (4 May).

Macmillan, Rory. 1995. New Lease on Life for Bondholder Councils. *Financial Times* (15 August): 11.

Macmillan, Rory. 1997. Towards a Sovereign Debt Work-Out System. Photocopy.

Mann, Catherine L. 1998. The IMF, Moral Hazard, and Market-Oriented Solutions to International Financial Crises. Photocopy (September). Institute for International Economics.

McKinnon, Ronald, and Huw Pill. 1997. Credible Economic Liberalizations and Overborrowing. *American Economic Review Papers and Proceedings* 87: 189-93.

Meltzer, Alan. 1998. Asian Problems and the IMF. Testimony prepared for the Joint Economic Committee, US Congress (24 February). Washington.

Miller, Marcus, and Lei Zhang. 1997. *A Bankruptcy Procedure for Sovereign States.* Global Economic Institutions Working Paper No. 34 (August). London: Economic and Social Research Council.

Miller, Marcus, and Lei Zhang. 1998. *Sovereign Liquidity Crises: The Strategic Case for a Payments Standstill.* CEPR Discussion Paper No. 1820 (February). London: Centre for Economic Policy Research.

Minton-Beddoes, Zanny. 1998. The Perils of Prediction. *The Economist* (1 August): 61-62.

Mishkin, Frederic S. 1996. *Understanding Financial Crises: A Developing Country Perspective.* National Bureau of Economic Research Working Paper No. 5600. Cambridge, MA: NBER.

Neiss, Hubert. 1998. In Defense of the IMF's Emergency Role in East Asia. http://www.imf.org/external/np/vc/1998/100998.htm. (9 November).

Obstfeld, Maurice. 1986. Rational and Self-Fulfilling Balance-of-Payments Crises. *American Economic Review Papers and Proceedings* 76: 72-81.

Obstfeld, Maurice. 1994. Risk Taking, Global Diversification, and Growth. *American Economic Review* 84: 1310-29.

Obstfeld, Maurice. 1996. Models of Currency Crises with Self-fulfilling Features. *European Economic Review* 40: 1037-47.

Obstfeld, Maurice. 1997. Destabilizing Effects of Exchange Rate Escape Clauses. *Journal of International Economics* 43: 61-77.

Organization for Economic Cooperation and Development (OECD), Business Sector Advisory Group on Corporate Governance. 1998. *Corporate Governance: Improving Competitiveness and Access to Capital in Global Markets.* Paris: OECD.

Ozkan, F. Gulcin, and Alan Sutherland. 1998. A Currency Crisis Model with an Optimizing Policymaker. *Journal of International Economics* 44: 339-64.

Park, Daekeun, and Changyong Rhee. 1998. Currency Crisis in Korea: Could It Have Been Avoided? Photocopy. Hanyang University and Seoul National University.

Park, Yung Chul. 1998. Financial Crisis and Macroeconomic Adjustments in Korea, 1997-98. Photocopy. Korea University and Korea Institute of Finance.

Pinon-Farah, Marco A. 1996. *Private Bond Restructurings: Lessons for the Case of Sovereign Debtors.* IMF Working Paper WP/96/11. Washington: International Monetary Fund.

Polak, Jacques J. 1998. The Articles of Agreement of the IMF and the Liberalization of Capital Movements. Photocopy. Per Jacobsen Foundation.

Radelet, Steven, and Jeffrey Sachs. 1998a. *The Onset of the East Asian Financial Crisis.* NBER Working Paper No. 6680 (August). Cambridge, MA: NBER.

Radelet, Steven, and Jeffrey Sachs. 1998b. The East Asian Financial Crisis: Diagnosis, Remedies, Prospects. *Brookings Papers on Economic Activity* 1: 1-74.

Raffer, Kunibert. 1990. Applying Chapter 9 Insolvency to International Debts: An Economically Efficient Solution with a Human Face. *World Development* 18: 301-11.

Reisen, Helmut. 1998. *Domestic Causes of Currency Crises: Policy Lessons for Crisis Avoidance.* OECD Development Centre Technical Paper No. 136 (June). Paris: OECD.

Reuters. 1998. Russia, Western Banks to Form Creditors Club (24 August). http://biz.yahoo.com/finance/980824/russia_ban_1.html.

Rodrik, Dani. 1998. Who Needs Capital Account Liberalization? In *Should the IMF Pursue Capital Account Convertibility?* ed. by Peter B. Kenen. Essays in International Finance No. 207 (January). Princeton, NJ: International Finance Section, Department of Economics, Princeton University.

Roe, Mark J. 1987. The Voting Prohibition in Bond Workouts. *Yale Law Journal* 97: 232-80.

Rubin, Robert E. 1998. Strengthening the Architecture of the International Financial System. *Treasury News* (14 April).

Sachs, Jeffrey. 1994a. IMF, Reform Thyself. *Wall Street Journal* (21 July): A14.

Sachs, Jeffrey. 1994b. Do We Need an International Lender of Last Resort? Photocopy. Harvard University.

Sachs, Jeffrey. 1998a. Fixing the IMF Remedy. *The Banker* 148 (February): 16-18.

Sachs, Jeffrey. 1998b. The IMF and the Asian Flu. *The American Prospect* 37 (April/May): 16-21.

Sachs, Jeffrey. 1998c. Global Capitalism: Making It Work. *The Economist* (12-18 September): 23-26.

Sachs, Jeffrey. 1998d. Creditor Panics: Causes and Remedies. Photocopy. Harvard University.

Sachs, Jeffrey, and Daekeun Park. 1987. *Capital Controls and the Timing of Exchange Rate Regime Collapse.* NBER Working Paper No. 2250 (May). Cambridge, MA: NBER.

Sachs, Jeffrey, and Steven Radelet. 1998. Next Stop: Brazil. *New York Times* (14 October): A25.

Sachs, Jeffrey, Aaron Tornell, and Andres Velasco. 1996a. Financial Crises in Emerging Markets: The Lessons from 1995. *Brookings Papers on Economic Activity* 1: 147-215.

Sachs, Jeffrey, Aaron Tornell, and Andres Velasco. 1996b. The Mexican Peso Crisis: Sudden Death or Death Foretold? *Journal of International Economics* 41: 265-83.

Schwartz, Anna J. 1995. G-7 Countries at Halifax Summit Repeat the Mexican Myth. Communiqué of the Shadow Open Market Committee (10-11 September).

Schwartz, Anna J. 1998. *Time to Terminate the ESF and the IMF.* CATO Institute Foreign Policy Briefing No. 48 (26 August). Washington: CATO Institute.

Shin, Inseok, and Joon-Ho Hahm. 1998. The Korean Crisis C Causes and Resolution Photocopy (July). Korea Development Institute.

Shultz, George, William E. Simon, and Walter B. Wriston. 1998. Who Needs the IMF? *Wall Street Journal* (3 February): A22.

Soros, George. 1997. Avoiding a Breakdown: Asia's Crisis Demands a Rethink of International Regulation. *Financial Times* (31 December): 12.

Soros, George. 1998. *The Crisis of Global Capitalism*. New York: Public Affairs Press.

Soto, Claudio. 1997. Controles a los Movimientos de Capital: Evaluación Empírica del Caso Chileno. Photocopy. Central Bank of Chile.

Stein, Sol. 1989. *A Feast for Lawyers*. New York: M. Evans.

Taylor, Roger. 1998. Conference Fails to Agree Global Code for Business Standards. *Financial Times* (13 July): 4.

Tobin, James. 1978. A Proposal for International Monetary Reform. *Eastern Economic Journal* 4: 153-59.

Tornell, Aaron. 1998. Common Fundamentals in the Tequila and Asian Crises. Photocopy. Harvard University.

Tsang, Donald. 1998. Bonds Can Free Asia's Economy. *Wall Street Journal* (22 July): A14.

Valdes-Prieto, Salvador. 1998. Capital Controls in Chile Were a Failure. *Wall Street Journal* (11 December): A15.

Valdes-Prieto, Salvador, and Marcelo Soto. 1997. The Effectiveness of Capital Controls: Theory and Evidence from Chile. Photocopy. Universidad Catholica de Chile.

Volcker, Paul A. 1995. The Quest for Exchange Rate Stability: Realistic or Quixotic? The Stamp 50th Anniversary Lecture, the Senate House, University of London (29 November).

von Hagen, Juergen, and Ian Harden. 1994. National Budget Processes and Fiscal Performance. *European Economy, Reports, and Studies*.

Wade, Robert, and Frank Veneroso. 1998. The Asian Crisis: The High Debt Model Versus the Wall Street-Treasury-IMF Complex. Photocopy. Russell Sage Foundation.

Williamson, John. 1995. *What Role for Currency Boards?* POLICY ANALYSIS IN INTERNATIONAL ECONOMICS No. 40. Washington: Institute for International Economics.

Williamson, John. 1998. A New Facility for the IMF? In *Capital Account Regimes and the Developing Countries*, ed. by G. K. Helleiner. New York: St. Martin's Press.

Willman, Arpo. 1988. The Collapse of the Fixed Exchange Rate Regime with Sticky Wages and Imperfect Substitutability between Domestic and Foreign Bonds. *European Economic Review* 32: 1817-38.

Wolf, Martin. 1998. The Last Resort. *Financial Times* (23 September): 22.

World Bank. 1993. *The East Asian Miracle*. Washington: World Bank.

World Bank. 1998. *Global Economic Prospects 1998-1999: Beyond Financial Crisis*. Washington: World Bank.

Wyplosz, Charles. 1986. Capital Controls and Balance of Payments Crises. *Journal of International Money and Finance* 5: 167-97.

Wyplosz, Charles. 1998a. International Financial Instability. Prepared for the UNDP Conference on Global Public Goods (June). Photocopy (22 June). United Nations.

Wyplosz, Charles. 1998b. Globalizing Financial Markets and Financial Crises. Paper presented to the Conference on Coping with Financial Crises in Developing and Transition Countries, Forum on Debt and Development, Amsterdam (16-17 March).

Wyplosz, Charles. 1998c. International Capital Market Failures: Sources, Costs, and Solutions. Photocopy (April). University of Geneva.

Yeager, Leland B. 1998. How to Avoid International Financial Crises. *Cato Journal* 17: 257-65.

Yellen, Janet. 1998. Lessons from the Asian Crisis. Presentation to the Council on Foreign Relations, Washington (15 April).

Index

accounting and auditing standards, 21, 45

branches of foreign, 34-35, 46-48, 101

capital-adequacy standards, 43-45, 48-49, 63-64, 101

deposit insurance, 40, 43, 101

economic effects of crises, 39

foreign capital in, 12, 41-42, 48-49, 61, 70-71, 161t, 162, 170

fragility, 38-41, 81-82

government guarantees, 20-21, 42, 43, 138-40, 160, 170

importance in emerging markets, 37-38, 42, 160-61, 168, 170

as industrial policy instruments, 139, 160-61

information environment, 40, 65-66, 81-82

Japanese, 152n, 162, 169

limits on short-term borrowing, 48-49, 63-64, 161n

loan restructuring, 70-73

in mature financial systems, 38n

measures to increase stability, 12

narrow banking, 45-46, 102

problems as causes of currency crises, 20-21, 157-58

regional development, 101n

risk-management practices, 11, 43, 44

role in Asian crisis, 138-40, 157-58, 159, 162, 164-66, 169-70

short-term lending, 63

standby credit lines for governments, 64-65

subordinated debt, 44n, 101

See also central banks; regulation

Bank of Thailand, 157-58

Barings PLC, 26

Basle Capital Accord, 12, 24, 25, 34, 63-64

Market Risk Amendment, 24

reviews of, 11, 48

Basle Committee on Banking Supervision, 23, 24-25, 26, 32, 48

Core Principles, 24-25, 24n, 43n, 131

Benston, George, 44

Bergsten, C. Fred, 128

BIBF. See Bangkok International Banking Facility

BIS. See Bank for International Settlements

bonds

committees of holders, 75, 76-77

credit ratings, 166

differences between corporate and sovereign, 76

proposed clauses to aid restructuring, 15, 16, 65-66, 67-70, 71

proposed international insurance agency, 79, 80, 86-87, 125-26

See also debt restructuring

Brady bonds, 72, 156

Brazil, 56, 57, 99, 106, 156

Bundesbank, 94

Calomiris, Charles, 101-2, 127

Calvo, Guillermo, 168

Camdessus, Michel, 1, 143

Canada, reform proposals, 9, 92, 125

capital account, regulation of, 115-17

capital flows

controls, 50n, 55-58, 137, 161n

currency crises and, 41-42, 56, 164-66

exchange rate policy and, 105, 107-8, 162-64

foreign direct investment, 117

in foreign exchange market, 88-90

growth of international, 2-3, 20-21, 137, 168

IMF role in liberalization, 115-16

liberalization, 41-42, 116, 117-18, 164-66

securities markets, 117-18

taxes on short-term foreign inflows, 12, 17, 49-56, 64, 90, 119

volatility, 12, 88

See also foreign investors

central banks

independent, 57

information disclosure, 83

proposed global, 93-95, 127

role in banking system, 40

Chase Manhattan Bank, 151n

Chile

banking regulation, 52, 53-54

capital controls, 50n

short-term external debt, 52f

taxes on short-term capital inflows, 50, 51-54, 55, 64

China, 144t

Clinton, Bill, IMF reform proposals, 99-101

Cooper, Richard, 93

corporate disclosure standards, 10

corporate governance standards, 22, 23, 30, 35

Corporation of Foreign Bondholders, 76, 77

interest rates, 111, 111*f*
short-term debt, 145, 148*t*, 158*t*
inflation
  in Asia, 144*t*
  exchange rate pegs and, 106-7
information
  asymmetries in financial markets, 3,
    40, 80-82
  difficulties in gathering, 82-84, 168-69
  improving disclosure of financial data,
    10, 80-84, 129, 130-31
  increased role of technology, 65-66
  leading indicators of crises, 84-86
  in securities markets, 82
  Special Data Dissemination Standard
    (SDDS), 23, 27-28, 35, 83, 83*n*
  transparency of IMF, 113-15, 129, 130
insolvency procedures. *See* bankruptcy
Institute of International Finance, 76
Inter-American Development Bank (IDB),
  101*n*
interest rates
  in Asian countries, 110-12, 111*f*, 139,
    157
  effects on exchange rates, 111-12
  IMF advice on, 110-12
  links between domestic and foreign,
    137, 162-63
  rises as triggers of crises, 41, 48, 135-
    36, 139
  in United States, 156, 162-63
Interim Committee of finance ministers,
  9, 124-25
International Accounting Standards
  Committee (IASC), 22, 26, 33, 35
international bankruptcy court, proposal
  for, 15, 90-93, 126
International Bar Association, Committee
  J, 22, 29, 33, 35
international bond insurance agency,
  proposal for, 79, 80, 86-87, 125-26
International Corporate Governance
  Network (ICGN), 22
International Federation of Accountants,
  22
international financial system
  assumptions about, 2-4
  information asymmetries, 3, 40, 80-82
  information and transactions costs, 3-4
  instability, 3
  interdependence with domestic
    financial markets, 20-21
  liberalization, 2-3
  offshore centers, 89, 89*n*

technological innovations, 2, 65-66
  See also capital flows; reform proposals
International Monetary Fund (IMF)
  Articles of Agreement, 118-19
  bondholders committees and, 77-78
  capital-inflow taxes and, 55
  credit lines, 99
  crisis management, 19, 61, 98, 102
  criticism of actions in Asian crisis, 14,
    19-20, 56, 97, 103-4, 109-10, 111, 112,
    116
  debt contract provisions and, 69-70,
    113, 120
  encouraging adherence to international
    standards, 11, 12, 17, 22, 23-24, 32-
    33, 34
  exchange rate advice, 103-6, 109
  external program reviews, 115
  financial information disclosure, 83
  future role, 16-17, 119-20
  General Data Dissemination System
    (GDDS), 27
  increasing transparency, 113-15, 129,
    130
  international financial system reforms
    proposed by, 128-29
  international standards proposals, 22
  involvement in domestic policies, 19-
    20, 120
  lending capacity, 99-100
  lending into arrears, 15, 16, 17, 71-74,
    113
  limited administrative capacity, 11, 21
  limits on power of, 98-99
  Mexican crisis and, 14, 59
  monetary and fiscal policies and,
    109-12
  proposed international insurance
    agency and, 86, 87
  proposed jurisdiction over capital
    account, 115-16, 118-19
  role in debt restructuring, 113
  role in restructuring negotiations, 17
  role in standards development, 11, 23
  South Korean crisis and, 60, 109, 110,
    152
  Special Data Dissemination Standard
    (SDDS), 23, 27-28, 35, 83, 83*n*
  Supplemental Reserve Facility (SRF),
    100*n*
  Ukraine program, 68
  US funding, 156
  See also reform proposals

debt contract provisions, 15, 16, 65-66, 67-70, 113, 120, 129, 132
foreign bank depositors, 42, 70-71
moral hazard, 59
proposals, 127-28
recommendations for, 62-71

Radelet, Steven, 78
Raffer, Kunibert, 92, 126
reform proposals
author's recommendations, 4-5, 6, 9-18
British, 9, 124
Canadian, 9, 92, 125
contradictions among, 1-2
creditors' committees, 16, 17, 74-78, 93
crisis management, 14-16
crisis prediction, 13-14, 84-86
crisis prevention, 10-13, 42-44, 102
debt restructuring, 15-16
elimination criteria, 79-80
exchange rate target zones, 128
French, 9, 124-25
German, 9
global currency and central bank, 93-95, 127
global regulatory agency, 9, 93, 124, 126
Group of 7, 16, 67, 69, 73, 99, 100, 101, 129-30
Group of 10, 16, 67, 69, 72
Group of 22, 4, 16, 67, 69, 130-32
IMF proposals, 128-29
impracticality, 9
improving disclosure of financial data, 10, 80-84, 129, 130-31
international bankruptcy court, 15, 90-93, 126
international bond insurance agency, 79, 80, 86-87, 125-26
obstacles, 69
political feasibility, 80
taxes on short-term foreign borrowing, 12, 17, 49-55, 64, 90, 119
Tobin tax, 79-80, 88-90
United States, 99-101, 125
See also private sector, bailing in; standards
reform proposals, for International Monetary Fund, 2, 120-21
abolition, 97-98
author's recommendations, 5, 16-18
Calomiris proposal, 101-2, 127
Edwards proposal to break up, 102-3, 128

French, 9, 124-25
lending into arrears, 15, 16, 17, 71-74, 113
limiting role to lender of last resort, 126
US proposals, 99-101, 125
regional development banks, 101n
regulation
of financial markets, 10, 23, 25-27, 33
proposals for world regulators, 9, 93, 124, 126
weak enforcement in emerging markets, 31-32
regulation and supervision, banking
enforcement problems, 32, 40-41
international standards, 23, 24-25, 33
investment restrictions, 45
political constraints, 44-45
strengthening, 10, 11-12, 21, 32, 42-44, 63-64, 101-2, 117, 131
in United States, 34-35
weaknesses in emerging markets, 40-41, 159, 168-69
See also Basle Capital Accord
restructuring. See debt restructuring
Rhodes, Bill, 75
Roe, Mark, 69
Russia
banks, 92n
crisis of August 1998, 14, 59, 60, 62n, 70n, 75, 153, 156

Sachs, Jeffrey, 78
safety net, financial
deposit insurance, 40, 43, 101
government guarantees for banks, 20-21, 42, 43, 138-40, 160, 170
international bond insurance agency proposal, 79, 80, 86-87, 125-26
need for, 3, 40
Sammi Steel, 151
savings rates, in Asia, 143
SDDS. See Special Data Dissemination Standard
securities markets
in Asia, 144t, 149f, 150-51, 166
in emerging markets, 38, 117-18
foreign investors, 64, 117-18
information flows, 82
institutional and legal environment, 37
regulation, 10, 23, 25-27, 33
technology, 38
Singapore
credit growth, 163t

United Kingdom
  bonds issued in, 15, 69, 76
  reform proposals, 9, 124
United Nations Commission on
    International Trade Law
    (UNCITRAL), 23
United States
  bankruptcy code, 15, 30, 92
  bonds issued in, 15, 77
  fiscal policy, 57
  IMF funding, 156
  IMF reform proposals, 99-101, 125
  interest rates, 156, 162-63

Mexican crisis and, 59
regulation of foreign bank branches,
    34-35
South Korean crisis and, 60
US Federal Reserve Board, 114-15, 156,
    162-63
US Treasury, 12

Valdes, Rodrigo, 53
Valdes-Prieto, Salvador, 53
Veneroso, Frank, 112

Wade, Robert, 112

Other Publications from the
Institute for International Economics

POLICY ANALYSES IN INTERNATIONAL ECONOMICS Series

Latin American Adjustment: How Much Has Happened?
John Williamson, editor/*April 1990*

ISBN paper 0-88132-125-7 470 pp.

The Future of World Trade in Textiles and Apparel
William R. Cline/*1987, 2d ed. June 1990*

ISBN paper 0-88132-110-9 432 pp.

**Completing the Uruguay Round: A Results-Oriented Approach
to the GATT Trade Negotiations**
Jeffrey J. Schott, editor/*September 1990*

ISBN paper 0-88132-130-3 252 pp.

Economic Sanctions Reconsidered (in two volumes)
Economic Sanctions Reconsidered: Supplemental Case Histories
Gary Clyde Hufbauer, Jeffrey J. Schott, and
Kimberly Ann Elliott/*1985, 2d ed. December 1990*

ISBN cloth 0-88132-115-X 928 pp.
ISBN paper 0-88132-105-2 928 pp.

Economic Sanctions Reconsidered: History and Current Policy
Gary Clyde Hufbauer, Jeffrey J. Schott, and Kimberly Ann Elliott/*December 1990*

ISBN cloth 0-88132-140-0 288 pp.
ISBN paper 0-88132-136-2 288 pp.

Pacific Basin Developing Countries: Prospects for the Future
Marcus Noland/*January 1991*

ISBN cloth 0-88132-141-9 254 pp.
(out of print) ISBN paper 0-88132-081-1 254 pp.

Currency Convertibility in Eastern Europe
John Williamson, editor/*October 1991*

ISBN paper 0-88132-128-1 480 pp.

International Adjustment and Financing: The Lessons of 1985-1991
C. Fred Bergsten, editor/*January 1992*

ISBN paper 0-88132-112-5 358 pp.

North American Free Trade: Issues and Recommendations
Gary Clyde Hufbauer and Jeffrey J. Schott/*April 1992*

ISBN paper 0-88132-120-6 392 pp.

Narrowing the U.S. Current Account Deficit
Allen J. Lenz/*June 1992*
(out of print) ISBN paper 0-88132-103-6 640 pp.

The Economics of Global Warming
William R. Cline/*June 1992*   ISBN paper 0-88132-132-X 416 pp.

U.S. Taxation of International Income: Blueprint for Reform
Gary Clyde Hufbauer, assisted by Joanna M. van Rooij/*October 1992*

ISBN cloth 0-88132-178-8 300 pp.
ISBN paper 0-88132-134-6 300 pp.

Who's Bashing Whom? Trade Conflict in High-Technology Industries
Laura D'Andrea Tyson/*November 1992*

ISBN paper 0-88132-106-0 352 pp.

Korea in the World Economy
Il SaKong/*January 1993*   ISBN paper 0-88132-183-4 328 pp.

Pacific Dynamism and the International Economic System
C. Fred Bergsten and Marcus Noland, editors/*May 1993*

ISBN paper 0-88132-196-6 424 pp.

Economic Consequences of Soviet Disintegration
John Williamson, editor/*May 1993*

ISBN paper 0-88132-190-7 660 pp.

Reconcilable Differences? United States-Japan Economic Conflict
C. Fred Bergsten and Marcus Noland/*June 1993*

ISBN paper 0-88132-129-X 296 pp.

Does Foreign Exchange Intervention Work?
Kathryn M. Dominguez and Jeffrey A. Frankel/*September 1993*
ISBN paper 0-88132-104-4   192 pp.

Sizing Up U.S. Export Disincentives
J. David Richardson/*September 1993*
ISBN paper 0-88132-107-9   204 pp.

NAFTA: An Assessment
Gary Clyde Hufbauer and Jeffrey J. Schott/*rev. ed. October 1993*
ISBN paper 0-88132-199-0   216 pp.

Adjusting to Volatile Energy Prices
Philip K. Verleger, Jr./*November 1993*
ISBN paper 0-88132-069-2   298 pp.

The Political Economy of Policy Reform
John Williamson, editor/*January 1994*
ISBN paper 0-88132-195-8   624 pp.

Measuring the Costs of Protection in the United States
Gary Clyde Hufbauer and Kimberly Ann Elliott/*January 1994*
ISBN paper 0-88132-108-7   144 pp.

The Dynamics of Korean Economic Development
Cho Soon/*March 1994*
ISBN paper 0-88132-162-1   240 pp.

Reviving the European Union
C. Randall Henning, Eduard Hochreiter and Gary Clyde Hufbauer,
editors/*April 1994*
ISBN paper 0-88132-208-3   192 pp.

China in the World Economy
Nicholas R. Lardy/*April 1994*
ISBN paper 0-88132-200-8   176 pp.

Greening the GATT: Trade, Environment, and the Future
Daniel C. Esty/*July 1994*
ISBN paper 0-88132-205-9   344 pp.

Western Hemisphere Economic Integration
Gary Clyde Hufbauer and Jeffrey J. Schott/*July 1994*
ISBN paper 0-88132-159-1   304 pp.

Currencies and Politics in the United States, Germany, and Japan
C. Randall Henning/*September 1994*
ISBN paper 0-88132-127-3   432 pp.

Estimating Equilibrium Exchange Rates
John Williamson, editor/*September 1994*
ISBN paper 0-88132-076-5   320 pp.

Managing the World Economy: Fifty Years After Bretton Woods
Peter B. Kenen, editor/*September 1994*
ISBN paper 0-88132-212-1   448 pp.

Reciprocity and Retaliation in U.S. Trade Policy
Thomas O. Bayard and Kimberly Ann Elliott/*September 1994*
ISBN paper 0-88132-084-6   528 pp.

The Uruguay Round: An Assessment
Jeffrey J. Schott, assisted by Johanna W. Buurman/*November 1994*
ISBN paper 0-88132-206-7   240 pp.

Measuring the Costs of Protection in Japan
Yoko Sazanami, Shujiro Urata, and Hiroki Kawai/*January 1995*
ISBN paper 0-88132-211-3   96 pp.

Foreign Direct Investment in the United States, Third Edition
Edward M. Graham and Paul R. Krugman/*January 1995*
ISBN paper 0-88132-204-0   232 pp.

The Political Economy of Korea-United States Cooperation
C. Fred Bergsten and Il SaKong, editors/*February 1995*
ISBN paper 0-88132-213-X   128 pp.

Trade and Income Distribution
William R. Cline/*November 1997*
ISBN paper 0-88132-216-4   328 pp.

Global Competition Policy
Edward M. Graham and J. David Richardson/*December 1997*
ISBN paper 0-88132-166-4   616 pp.

Unfinished Business: Telecommunications after the Uruguay Round
Gary Clyde Hufbauer and Erika Wada/*December 1997*
ISBN paper 0-88132-257-1   268 pp.

Financial Services Liberalization in the WTO
Wendy Dobson and Pierre Jacquet /*June 1998*
ISBN paper 0-88132-254-7   376 pp.

Restoring Japan's Economic Growth
Adam S. Posen /*September 1998*
ISBN paper 0-88132-262-8   212 pp.

Measuring the Costs of Protection in China
Zhang Shuguang, Zhang Yansheng, and Wan Zhongxin/*November 1998*
ISBN paper 0-88132-247-4   96 pp.

Foreign Direct Investment and Development: The New Policy Agenda
for Developing Countries and Economies in Transition
Theodore H. Moran/ *December 1998*   216 pp.
ISBN paper 0-88132-258-X

Behind the Open Door: Foreign Enterprises in the Chinese Marketplace
Daniel H. Rosen/*January 1999*
ISBN paper 0-88132-263-6   344 pp.

Toward A New International Financial Architecture: A Practical Post-Asia Agenda
Barry Eichengreen/*February 1999*
ISBN paper 0-88132-270-9   216 pp.

SPECIAL REPORTS

1   **Promoting World Recovery: A Statement on Global Economic Strategy**
     by Twenty-six Economists from Fourteen Countries/*December 1982*
     (out of print)   ISBN paper 0-88132-013-7   45 pp.
2   **Prospects for Adjustment in Argentina, Brazil, and Mexico:**
     Responding to the Debt Crisis (out of print)
     John Williamson, editor/*June 1983*
     ISBN paper 0-88132-016-1   71 pp.
3   **Inflation and Indexation: Argentina, Brazil, and Israel**
     John Williamson, editor/*March 1985*
     ISBN paper 0-88132-037-4   191 pp.
4   **Global Economic Imbalances**
     C. Fred Bergsten, editor/*March 1986*
     ISBN cloth 0-88132-038-2   126 pp.
     ISBN paper 0-88132-042-0   126 pp.
5   **African Debt and Financing**
     Carol Lancaster and John Williamson, editors/*May 1986*
     (out of print)   ISBN paper 0-88132-044-7   229 pp.
6   **Resolving the Global Economic Crisis: After Wall Street**
     Thirty-three Economists from Thirteen Countries/*December 1987*
     ISBN paper 0-88132-070-6   30 pp.
7   **World Economic Problems**
     Kimberly Ann Elliott and John Williamson, editors/*April 1988*
     ISBN paper 0-88132-055-2   298 pp.
     Reforming World Agricultural Trade
     Twenty-nine Professionals from Seventeen Countries/*1988*
     ISBN paper 0-88132-088-9   42 pp.
8   **Economic Relations Between the United States and Korea:**
     Conflict or Cooperation?
     Thomas O. Bayard and Soo-Gil Young, editors/*January 1989*
     ISBN paper 0-88132-068-4   192 pp.

WORKS IN PROGRESS

**Explaining Congressional Votes on Recent Trade Bills:
From NAFTA to Fast Track**
Robert E. Baldwin and Christopher S. Magee
The US - Japan Economic Relationship
C. Fred Bergsten, Marcus Noland, and Takatoshi Ito
China's Entry to the World Economy
Richard N. Cooper
Economic Sanctions After the Cold War
Kimberly Ann Elliott, Gary C. Hufbauer and Jeffrey J. Schott
Trade and Labor Standards
Kimberly Ann Elliott and Richard Freeman
Leading Indicators of Financial Crises in the Emerging Economies
Morris Goldstein and Carmen Reinhart
The Exchange Stabilization Fund
C. Randall Henning
Prospects for Western Hemisphere Free Trade
Gary Clyde Hufbauer and Jeffrey J. Schott
The Future of US Foreign Aid
Carol Lancaster
The Economics of Korean Unification
Marcus Noland
International Lender of Last Resort
Catherine L. Mann
A Primer on US External Balance
Catherine L. Mann
Globalization, the NAIRU, and Monetary Policy
Adam S. Posen

DISTRIBUTORS OUTSIDE THE UNITED STATES

**Australia, New Zealand, and
Papua New Guinea**
D.A. INFORMATION SERVICES
648 Whitehorse Road
Mitcham, Victoria 3132, Australia
(tel: 61-3-9210-7777;
fax: 61-3-9210-7788)
email: service@dadirect.com.au
http://www.dadirect.com.au

Caribbean
SYSTEMATICS STUDIES LIMITED
St. Augustine Shopping Centre
Eastern Main Road, St. Augustine
Trinidad and Tobago, West Indies
(tel: 868-645-8466;
fax: 868-645-8467)
email: tobe@trinidad.net

**People's Republic of China (including
Hong Kong) and Taiwan**
(sales representatives)
Tom Cassidy
Cassidy & Associates
470 W. 24th Street
New York, NY 10011
(tel: 212-727-8943;
fax: 212-727-9539)

**India, Bangladesh, Nepal, and
Sri Lanka**
VIVA BOOKS PVT.
Mr. Vinod Vasishtha
4325/3, Ansari Rd.
Daryaganj, New Delhi-110002, India
(tel: 91-11-327-9280;
fax: 91-11-326-7224)
email: vinod.viva@gndel
http://globalnet.ems.vsnl.net.in

Mexico and the Caribbean
(non-Anglophone islands only)
L.D. Clepper, Jr., sales representative
Publishers Marketing & Research Associates
79-01 35th Avenue #5D
P.O. Box 720489
Jackson Heights, NY 11372
(tel/fax: 718-803-3465)
email: clepper@pipeline.com

Puerto Rico (School/College/Academic
markets)
David R. Rivera, sales representative
Publishers Marketing & Research Associates
c/o Premium Educational Group
MSC 609 #89 Ave. De Diego, Suite 105
San Juan, PR 00927-5381
(tel: 787-764-3532;
fax: 787-764-4774)
email:drrivera@coqui.net

South America
Julio E. Ernod
Publishers Marketing & Research Associates,
c/o HARBRA
Rua Joaquim Tavora, 629
04015-001 Sao Pãulo, Brasil
(tel: 55-11-571-1122;
fax: 55-11-575-6876)
email: emod@harbra.com.br

Canada
RENOUF BOOKSTORE
5369 Canotek Road, Unit 1,
Ottawa, Ontario K1J 9J3, Canada
(tel: 613-745-2665;
fax: 613-745-7660)
http://www.renoufbooks.com/

Central America
Jose Rios, sales representative
Publishers Marketing & Research Associates
Publicaciones Educativas
Apartado Postal 370-A
Ciudad Guatemala, Guatemala, C.A.
(tel/fax: 502-443-0472)

**Western and Eastern Europe , Russia,
Turkey, Israel, and Iran**
The Eurospan Group
3 Henrietta Street, Covent Garden
London, England
(tel: 011-44-171-240-0856;
fax: 011-44-171-379-0609)
email: orders@eurospan.co.uk
http://www.eurospan.co.uk

Japan and the Republic of Korea
UNITED PUBLISHERS SERVICES, LTD.
Kenkyu-Sha Building
9, Kanda Surugadai 2-Chome
Chiyoda-Ku, Tokyo 101, Japan
(tel: 81-3-3291-4541;
fax: 81-3-3292-8610)
email: saito@ups.co.jp

Northern Africa and the Middle East (Egypt,
Algeria, Bahrain, Palestine, Jordan, Kuwait,
Lebanon, Libya, Morocco, Oman, Qatar, Saudi
Arabia, Syria, Tunisia, Yemen, and United
Arab Emirates)
The Middle East Observer
41 Sherif Street
Cairo, Egypt
(tel: 202-392-6919;
fax: 202-393-9732

South Africa
Pat Bennink
Dryad Books
PO Box 11684
Vorna Valley 1686
South Africa
(tel: +27 11 805 6019;
fax: +27 11 805 3746)
email: dryad@hixnet.co.za

**Visit our website at:
http://www.iie.com**

**E-mail orders to:
orders@iie.com**